THE ARTISTRY OF ANGER

Gender and American Culture

The
Artistry
of
ANGER

Black and White
Women's Literature in
America, 1820–1860

Linda M. Grasso

The University of North Carolina Press

Chapel Hill and London

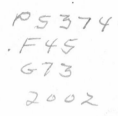
© 2002 The University of North Carolina Press
All rights reserved

Designed by April Leidig-Higgins
Set in Monotype Centaur by Keystone Typesetting, Inc.
Manufactured in the United States of America

The paper in this book meets the guidelines for permanence and durability of the
Committee on Production Guidelines for Book Longevity of the Council on Library
Resources.

Portions of Chapter 6 appeared previously, in somewhat different form, in "Anger in the
House: Fanny Fern's *Ruth Hall* and the Redrawing of Emotional Boundaries in Mid-
Nineteenth-Century America," *Studies in the American Renaissance* (1995): 251–61.

Library of Congress Cataloging-in-Publication Data
Grasso, Linda M.
    The artistry of anger : black and white women's literature in America, 1820–1860 /
Linda M. Grasso.
        p. cm. — (Gender and American culture)
    Includes bibliographical references and index.
    ISBN 0-8078-2682-0 (cloth : alk. paper) — ISBN 0-8078-5348-8 (pbk. : alk. paper)
    1. American fiction—Women authors—History and criticism. 2. Feminism and
literature—United States—History—19th century. 3. Women and literature—United
States—History—19th century. 4. American fiction—African American authors—History
and criticism. 5. American fiction—19th century—History and criticism. 6. Feminist
fiction, American—History and criticism. 7. African American women in literature.
8. Social problems in literature. 9. White women in literature. 10. Anger in literature.
I. Title. II. Gender & American culture.
PS374.F45 G73   2002
813'.3099287—dc21   2001040614

Cloth   06 05 04 03 02   5 4 3 2 1
Paper   06 05 04 03 02   5 4 3 2 1

To my teachers

Bonnie Anderson, Mari Jo Buhle, Kenneth Bruffee,
Thadious Davis, David Hirsch, Robert Lee,
Doris Meyer, Linda Miller, Katherine A. Monteiro,
Steven Murray, Lillian Schlissel, Michael Southwell

and to my students

at Brown University, Columbus State University,
and the City University of New York (Brooklyn
College and York College)

CONTENTS

ACKNOWLEDGMENTS

Over the years, I often wished that what many nineteenth-century women claimed had happened to them would happen to me: that a deity would write the book for me. Although this never occurred, I am grateful to the many individuals, communities, and institutions who extended intellectual energy, emotional sustenance, and financial resources during the many years I worked on this book. The generosity of these gifts was indeed godlike to the struggling scholar who "scribbled on," hoping that her manuscript would eventually enter the "port of Independence."

At Brown University, where this book assumed its first life as a doctoral dissertation, I was mentored by three extraordinary scholars: Thadious Davis, Mari Jo Buhle, and David Hirsh. Each guided me through the dissertation-writing process with patience, wisdom, and humor. I am particularly grateful to Thadious Davis for her steadfast belief in the project since its inception; to Mari Jo Buhle for teaching me how to understand nineteenth-century women on their own terms; and to David Hirsh for encouraging me to take intellectual risks. I regret that David is not here to see how I have continued to heed his counsel.

Many scholars and friends helped me to refine my ideas about nineteenth-century women writers and anger as this project evolved. Bonnie Anderson, Gail Bederman, Frederick DeNaples, Ann Du Cille, Nora Eisenberg, Ruth Feldstein, Cheryl Fish, Elizabeth Francis, Jane Gerhard, Katie Hogan, Eliza Laffin, Carol Mason, Melani McCalister, Bob McMichael, Kate Monteiro,

Louise Newman, Suzanne Oboler, Miriam Reumann, Dan Ross, Lyde Cullen Sizer, Michael Southwell, Sam Stoloff, and Carlyle Thompson all read drafts of chapters and provided helpful criticism and encouraging reassurance. I am indebted to Bonnie Anderson, Nora Eisenberg, Frederick DeNaples, Katie Hogan, Michael Rieser, Dan Ross, and Michael Southwell for helping me to become a better writer.

I also thank the anonymous readers for Cornell University Press and University of North Carolina Press for their critical appraisals and practical suggestions. I am especially grateful to Nora Eisenberg, Katie Hogan, Louise Newman, Suzanne Oboler, and Michael Southwell for their help at particularly crucial stages. In more ways than I could possibly acknowledge, Louise Newman provided incisive criticism as well as sound advice throughout this project's life.

I also wish to acknowledge the unflagging support of my editors at University of North Carolina Press, Barbara Hanrahan and Sian M. Hunter. Their trust in my ability and abiding enthusiasm for the work kept me hopeful and focused. Michael Southwell—colleague, mentor, and friend—played a crucial role in the project's final stage. Not only did he buoy my confidence when I needed it most; he also devoted countless hours to a meticulous and thoughtful reading of the entire manuscript. Editor *extraordinaire*, Michael provided invaluable suggestions and much-needed perspective. I offer him my deepest appreciation and gratitude for helping me to complete the project.

This book has benefited from rich intellectual exchanges with many friends and colleagues over the years: Pat Antoniello, Jose Aranda, Teresa Bill, Nan Boyd, Rose Ann Camacho, Oscar Campomanes, Krista Comer, Jim Cullen, Martha Cutter, Elizabeth Francis, Kevin Gaines, Todd Gernes, Matt Jacobson, Thorton Jordan, Dorothee Kocks, Jackie Konan, Bob Lee, Joan Lipton, Yuko Matsukawa, Joanne Melish, Linda Miller, George Monteiro, Kate Monteiro, Janice Okoomian, Barton St. Armand, Laura Santigian, and Penny M. Von Eschen.

The students I have had the privilege of teaching at Brown University, Columbus State University, Brooklyn College, and York College, City University of New York, have also contributed to this book: their appreciation of nineteenth-century American women writers, their eagerness to know more about them, and their wonderful insights about the women's lives and texts have given me much pleasure as well as stimulated my thinking. I thank them for their interest and intellectual fellowship.

Institutional support from Columbus State University, which granted me ·eleased time, and from the City University of New York, which enabled me to participate in its Faculty Publications Program and awarded me a PSC-CUNY Research Grant, made it possible to continue working on the book while also fulfilling other duties. I am grateful to my department chairs—Lee Friedman, Dan Ross, and Michael Southwell—for their belief in the project and their efforts to help me complete it. Librarians at both institutions greatly facilitated my work by getting me the books I needed. I especially want to thank Robert Litwin of Brooklyn College, and Hope Young and John Drobnicki of York College, for all their efforts on my behalf.

Loving friends and family members have sustained me over the many years that I have worked on this project. They also accepted, with patience and goodwill, that my dedication to this book prevented me from attending outings, parties, and family celebrations. I thank them for their understanding. Bonnie Anderson, Pat Antoniello, David Anton, Lorraine Anton, Elizabeth Illan, Bruce Birenberg, Nancy Violette, Maggie Birenberg, Danielle Birenberg, Mary Cash, Walter Goodman, Clem Goodman, Eamon Goodman, Kim Carmello, Otto Carmello, Julia DeLizza, Elizabeth Francis, Kevin Gaines, Virginia Grasso, Sal Grasso, Sal Grasso Jr., Norma Ewing, Jason Kantor, Joy Grasso Krebs, Michael Krebs, Julia Krebs, Ann Landsman, James Wagman, Adam Wagman, Tess Wagman, Ellen Le, Sanh Le, Bob Mc-Michael, Louise Newman, Elena Newman, John Prospero, Bill Rieser, Cathy Rieser, Dan Rieser, Bernadette Stillo, Amelia Jo Rieser, Margaret Rieser, Missy Meyers, Donna Rubens, Paul Rubens, Mira Ruth Rubens, Peter Landy, Hanah Landy, Maya Landy, Laura Zeisler, Chris Mason, Nicole Zeisler Mason, and Zachary Zeisler Mason have all brought love and warmth into my study.

Most of all, I wish to thank my dearest and closest friend, Michael Rieser, who has lived with this book almost as long as he has lived with me. Both companion and guide, Michael has traveled with me on this journey, bestowing material and emotional nurture at every turn. His love inspires me to do my best work.

PART ONE

The Anger Paradigm

Theories and Contexts

ONE

Anger as Analysis and Aesthetic
in American Women's Literature

[T]he emotion which accompanies the first steps toward liberation is, for most women, anger. . . . Through the exercise of your anger . . . you gain strength. . . . [A]nger finds its ultimate meaning as an experience shared with other women. All striving to understand their collective situation, women in a group can help each other through the first, painful phase of outward-directed anger. . . . Controlled, directed, but nonetheless passionate, anger moves from the personal to the political and becomes a force for shaping our new destiny.
—Susi Kaplow, "Getting Angry" (1971)

Women responding to racism means women responding to anger; the anger of exclusion, of unquestioned privilege, of racial distortions, of silence, ill-use, stereotyping, defensiveness, misnaming, betrayal, and co-optation. . . . Every woman has a well-stocked arsenal of anger potentially useful against those oppressions, personal and institutional, which brought that anger into being. Focused with precision it can become a powerful source of energy serving progress and change.
—Audre Lorde, "The Uses of Anger: Women Responding to Racism" (1981)

To women envisioning a new America in the 1970s, anger was a vital political tool. It enabled new perspectives, new understandings of oppressive conditions that had previously remained unquestioned. In essays, speeches, manifestos, and direct actions, feminist revolutionaries liberated anger from pejorative connotations by disassociating it from fear, destruction, and masculinity, and reassociating it with courage, growth, and sisterhood. They recognized anger's relationship to individual and collective political consciousness; they theorized its potential to become "a powerful source of energy serving progress and change"; they relished its transformative capacities. Anger demanded attention; it propelled insight, artistry, action; it exposed knowledge that had been buried, speech that had been silenced. Anger was a link to previous selves, suppressed histories, revolutionary coalitions. "I couldn't believe—still can't—how angry I could become, from deep down and way back, something like a five-thousand-year-buried anger," Robin Morgan declared in the introduction to *Sisterhood Is Powerful*, one of the earliest textual "actions" of the women's liberation movement. "Every Black woman in America lives her life somewhere along a wide curve of ancient and unexpressed angers," Audre Lorde observed. Only when women were able to feel anger, and then recognize, accept, and direct it at the real enemy—a patriarchal system that "launches rockets, spends over sixty thousand dollars a second on missiles and other agents of war and death, slaughters children in cities, stockpiles nerve gas and chemical bombs, [and] sodomizes our daughters and our earth"—could cross-racial female coalition occur.[1]

Thirty years later, it is incumbent upon the beneficiaries of the feminist movement to once again make women's anger at gender and racial injustice central. The fundamental premise of this book is that anger can be an organizing principle of American women's literary history when it is employed as a mode of inquiry. By identifying the sources of women's anger and analyzing how their anger assumes literary expression, anger can be used as a paradigm for understanding the ways in which women, at different historical moments, have responded to myriad forms of oppression through the literary imagination. With anger as an analytical fulcrum, it becomes possible to chart a history of women's literature that acknowledges inventive complexity and traverses racial boundaries. *The Artistry of Anger* tests this proposition by examining women's literary anger in the antebellum period.

In the chapters that follow, I suggest a method of reading that illuminates an unrecognized tradition in American literature, a specifically gendered tradition of literary discontent that is shaped by two equally powerful forces:

women's anger at exclusion from the failed promises of democratic America, and their inability to express that anger overtly. I explore the evolution of this tradition in the years before the Civil War by analyzing texts written by four major nineteenth-century women writers: Lydia Maria Child, Maria W. Stewart, Fanny Fern, and Harriet Wilson. Because their texts are declarations of personal and national discontent, I read them as political documents embedded in particular historical moments. As such, they are superb examples of the artistry of angry expression. Transforming their anger through the literary imagination, these writers bequeath their vision of an alternative America to both their contemporaries and subsequent generations.

By focusing on Lydia Maria Child's *Hobomok*, Maria W. Stewart's speeches and meditations, Fanny Fern's *Ruth Hall*, and Harriet Wilson's *Our Nig*, it is not my intention to establish a canon of representative writers and texts, nor to imply that the narrative I present precludes other formulations. On the contrary, my aim is to contribute to a more textured, empathetic understanding of American women's literary history by proposing a new organizing framework. By reconstructing what it meant for these nineteenth-century women writers to express anger in their literature, I hope to demonstrate the usefulness of the anger paradigm not only for this historical period, but for others as well.

Two concepts guide my interpretation of women's literary lives and texts and are the foundation of my reading practice: anger as a mode of analysis, and anger as the basis of an aesthetic. These concepts enable an interpretative strategy that analyzes how women's achievements, failures, frustrations, and desires are literally translated into artistic creation. They are also flexible enough to allow a mapping of similarities as well as differences between writers of different generations, ideological persuasions, religious affiliations, and racial groups.

Using anger as a mode of analysis and the basis of an aesthetic requires utilizing the following perspectives. First, definitions of anger, expressions of anger, and interpretations of anger must be situated in specific historical, ideological, and social contexts. Delineating these contexts enables an understanding of both the possibilities and limitations that affect women's literary imaginings. Second, recognizing that women invent and practice an artistry of anger to express anger in their literature is imperative. Because gendered ideologies have historically precluded anger from women's emotional repertoire, women create an art form to express publicly the angered discontent that is culturally prohibited. Third, the issue of power relations is central, not only within the internal worlds of texts, but also within the larger historical arena. Analyzing who has power over whom, how the power functions, and whose purposes it serves, as well as the ways in which women writers resist or embrace existing economic, cultural, class, and racial power relations, is essential. Finally, the supposition that women's literary anger is "a multifaceted response to the lived realities of the historical moment" is a given.[2] Because there is a relationship between feelings and the material world in which feelings are experienced, women's literary expressions of anger can not be regarded as singular, individual, and psychological. Rather, they must be analyzed as part of a larger, ongoing historical phenomenon. Women's literary anger is collective, political.

Subjecting texts and contexts to the following questions is equally crucial. What ideologies govern the definition, interpretation, and expression of anger in the culture? How are these ideologies created, disseminated, accepted, or rejected? In what ways are the social, economic, and material conditions of women's lives anger-producing? In what ways is that anger dramatized and expressed in their literature? What metaphors do women writers employ? What genres do they choose to write in? Do the authors create characters who see themselves as victims of injustice? How is the injustice characterized? How do the characters respond to it? What role does angered discontent play in the text? In the author's life? In the author's community?

The wealth of interdisciplinary feminist scholarship produced within the last thirty years makes it possible to locate women's anger and its expression in their literary texts. Psychological theories, historians' analyses of women's culture and politics, and literary critics' approaches to imaginative literature have taught us how to find women's anger, recognize its common manifestations, and ascertain its emotional, social, and economic causes. Moreover, the "folk theory of anger" elucidated by linguists Zoltan Kovecses and George Lakoff helps us to see that the lexicon of anger women writers employ is easily recognizable because it is a western cultural phenomenon that can be traced back to antiquity.

Kovecses and Lakoff formulated the "folk theory of anger" after they considered what conventional idioms such as "He was foaming at the mouth"; "You're beginning to get to me"; "You make my blood boil"; "He is just letting off steam"; "When I told him, he blew up," all had in common. They conclude that there is "a coherent conceptual organization underlying all these expressions, and that much of it is metaphorical and metonymical in nature." Their central insight is that what people perceive to be the physiological effects of anger, such as "increased body heat, increased internal pressure (blood pressure, muscular pressure), agitation, and interference with accurate perception," are also what people use to name, describe, and express the emotion itself. As I will show throughout this book, women writers often use two of the most common anger metaphors—anger as heat, and anger as a dangerous animal that needs to be held in check—in their literary texts.[3]

The anger paradigm asserts that in the same way there are telltale physical signs of anger—facial expressions, clenched fists, eruptions of violence—so, too, are there textual signs of anger—gestures and expressions that are specifically gendered. Feminist literary critics have identified white women writers' creation of doubled characters, crying protagonists, diminished men, and heroines' retreats into madness as coded signals of anger.[4] In this book, I suggest that illness, acts of sacrifice, supplicating tones, captivity motifs, death, hunger, and emaciated bodies are also often telltale signs—the textual gestures if you will—of women's forbidden angry expression. Recognizing how these gestures function in ideological contexts in which women are relegated to separate, unequal spheres in the public imagination provides insight into how women respond to oppression and exclusion, their own and that of the others with whom they identify—the enslaved, the powerless, and the economically disenfranchised.

The Artistry of Anger builds upon thirty years of feminist literary scholarship. The issue of anger is central to an understanding of women's literature, feminist critics have argued, because the writers' relationship to it and its expression determines the artistic devices they employ as well as the kinds of stories they tell.[5] Women's repressed anger, they have consistently noted, has had significant effects on their literary imaginings. The insight, for example, that English novelists needed to repress their rage led Sandra M. Gilbert and Susan Gubar to theorize that white nineteenth-century women writers split their protagonists into two, creating a "madwoman in the attic."[6] Carolyn Heilbrun sees the "record of anger" in May Sarton's 1973 *Journal of a Solitude* as a watershed in women's autobiography, because it is a public telling of what has always been forbidden to women. In Heilbrun's analysis, the prohibition against anger is integrally related to the articulation of voice in women's narratives. Because they are "[f]orbidden anger, women could find no voice in which publicly to complain; they took refuge in depression or madness."[7] At the same time, however, as Patricia Meyer Spacks notes in one of the field's earliest studies, women have historically used their anger to create art. In her words, "anger must have been a source of creative energy for . . . women writers; anger provided the impetus, the subject, and the inventiveness of their work. . . . The fact remains that many women have written marvelously out of anger."[8]

Feminist literary critics and scholars also wrote "marvelously out of anger." Like the political movement that engendered it, feminist literary criticism was born of anger and infused with the insights it made possible. Pioneering studies such as Kate Millet's *Sexual Politics*, Mary Ellman's *Thinking about Women*, and Judith Fetterley's *The Resisting Reader* were propelled by the writers' anger at exclusion from the masculinist world of artistic endeavor, the insidious male bias of literary criticism, and the devaluation of white women's lives, experiences, and creativity. Spurred by the clarity that anger made possible, these critics relentlessly exposed the ways in which perceptions about sexual difference affected how white women writers, as well as their texts, were regarded. They deplored the gendered separation of literature, the "working rule" that "there must always be two literatures like two public toilets, one for Men and one for Women," and excoriated the "phallic criticism" this separation engendered. "Books by women are treated as though they themselves were women, and criticism embarks, at its happiest, upon an intellectual measuring of busts and hips."[9] They analyzed the "sexual politics" of male dominance that pervaded male texts, demonstrated how "literary descriptions of sexual activity itself" revealed misogynistic notions of smug male superiority, and documented patriarchy's historical trajectory.[10] They discerned what happened when women were taught to read male-authored books that devalued their gender and experiences: "[T]he female reader is co-opted into participation in an experience from which she is explicitly excluded; she is asked to identify with a selfhood that defines itself in opposition to her; she is required to identify against herself." Heeding Adrienne Rich's call for "[r]e-vision—the act of looking back, of seeing with fresh eyes, of entering an old text from a new critical direction," feminist literary critics devised new ways of reading texts and writing literary history. "[T]he first act of the feminist critic," Judith Fetterley proclaimed, "must be to become a resisting rather than an assenting reader and, by this refusal to assent, to begin the process of exorcising the male mind that has been implanted in us."[11]

Refusing "to assent" to the "double jeopardy" of being both black and female, black feminist scholars were also conducting exorcisms. Asserting their presence in a world in which "all the women are white [and] all the blacks are men," they angrily dispelled the notion that both they and their literary forebears were nonexistent. "Merely to use the term 'Black women's studies' is an act charged with political significance," Gloria T. Hull and Barbara Smith asserted in the introduction to a path-breaking anthology devoted to that field. "At the very least, the combining of these words to name a discipline means taking the stance that Black women exist—and exist positively—a stance that is in direct opposition to most of what passes for culture and thought on the North American continent."[12] Black feminist critics published studies which "refus[ed] to pay homage to the 'system's' distortions of black women," and demanded respect for the "black women who are real-life models for images in literature."[13] They expressed outrage at the "white female chauvinism" practiced by white feminist colleagues in the movement and in the academy. The black women's equivalent of *Sisterhood Is Powerful*, *The Black Woman: An Anthology*, also published in 1970, "grew out of impatience," its editor Toni Cade Bambara reported, "an impatience with the fact that in the whole bibliography of feminist literature, literature immediately and directly relevant to us wouldn't fill a page."[14] Outraged impatience also motivated the excoriation of white feminist scholars and artists who produced work that routinely excluded black women and failed to acknowledge their humanity and womanhood. "[W]hite women who called themselves feminists," Alice Walker concluded in a 1979 essay published in *Ms*, were "as incapable as white and black men of comprehending blackness and feminism in the same body, not to mention within the same imagination."[15]

As Walker's remark suggests, black feminist critics, like their white colleagues, also directed their ire at male colleagues who produced exclusionary versions of literary history. Black women writers were "frequently excised" from African American literary history written by male scholars, they argued, and if their work was addressed, it was treated with condescension and contempt.[16] In example after example, scholars such as Barbara Smith, Deborah McDowell, and Mary Helen Washington documented the ways in which male scholars characterized black women's literature as shallow, domestic, and apolitical.[17] "Women's writing is considered singular and anomalous, not universal and representative, and for some mysterious reason, writing about black women is not considered as racially significant as writing about black men." The African American literary tradition, they theorized, was based on the exclusion of black women writers and their texts. "Tradition . . . [is a] word that has so often been used to exclude or misrepresent women," Mary Helen Washington astutely observed in the introduction to an anthology of black women's literature that included nineteenth-century as well as twentieth-century women's texts that male scholars typically devalued or ignored. The power that male scholars had to make aesthetic judgments and write literary history based on sexist assumptions, Washington argued, "account[ed] for women's absence from our written records."

> It is always something of a shock to see black women, sharing equally (and sometimes more than equally) in the labor and strife of black people, expunged from the text when that history becomes shaped into what we call tradition. Why is the fugitive slave, the fiery orator, the political

activist, the abolitionist always represented as a black *man*? How does the heroic voice and the heroic image of the black woman get suppressed in a culture that depended on her heroism for its survival? What we have to recognize is that the creation of the fiction of tradition is a matter of power, not justice, and that that power has always been in the hands of men—mostly white but some black. Women are the disinherited. Our "ritual journeys," our "articulate voices," our "symbolic spaces" are rarely the same as men's. Those differences and the assumption that those differences make women inherently inferior plus the appropriation by men of the power to define tradition account for women's absence from our written records.[18]

Exclusion, absence, misrepresentation, disinheritance. For both black and white feminist literary scholars in the 1970s and 1980s, these words were revolutionary concepts. Like their nineteenth-century predecessors, twentieth-century feminist intellectual activists used their outraged anger to expose, explain, condemn, and reimagine a more just American literary landscape. Although the twentieth-century intellectual movement was riven by racism like its nineteenth-century predecessor, both white and black women scholars were driven by the same angry impulses. Yes, black women, unlike white women, directed their anger at multiple targets, including white feminists who ironically oppressed black women in the same ways men oppressed them. Nevertheless, what black and white feminist critics shared was anger at their own and their subjects' exclusion, misrepresentation, and disinheritance. Their quest for academic and literary justice, by no means a collective, racially harmonious endeavor, united black and white women in the monumental task of rewriting literary history from a feminist perspective.

The Artistry of Anger continues the project these scholars initiated by recovering women's anger as a subject, and proposing that its use as a mode of inquiry has the potential to transform the writing of American women's literary history. Several fundamental principles, culled from the work of feminist activists, psychologists, sociologists, and philosophers, undergird my formulation of the anger paradigm and guide my investigation of women's literary and life anger in this book. Most central is the idea that anger can be a life affirming, self-protecting emotional response to unjust violation of self and community.[19] Thus, in the context of this study, expressions of anger are integrally related to issues of power and justice. Because anger can be regarded as "an emotion specifically engineered to protect us against physical threats to our survival," it safeguards by defending against attack; because anger can be regarded as "an emotion of defiance," it challenges the attacker's power by asserting an equal claim to desire; and because anger can be regarded as an emotion that forces confrontation, it has the potential to disrupt existing power relations.[20]

There is no better example of this latter phenomenon than the havoc that feminist discourse and spectacle wreaks. Women who publicly express anger about gender injustice are threatening, psychotherapist Harriet Lerner notes, because they challenge gender arrangements and emotional responses that naturalize unequal power relations. If women feel guilt, depression, and self-doubt, existing power relations remain unchanged because these responses, the result of anger turned inward, keep women in a state of paralysis, unmoving in their subordinate place. In these instances, if women do take action, it is usually self-destructive. But when women recognize and direct their anger at its real sources, "they may change and challenge the lives of us all."[21] As Lerner and others suggest, the conflict anger inevitably causes can lead to rebellion, change, and even, perhaps, a revolutionary restructuring of social arrangements. Revolution occurs when "the anger that is affliction" is "transmut[ed]" "into the anger that is determination to bring about change," Barbara Deming asserts. While anger "that is affliction" is fearful and murderous, anger that is "determination to bring about change" is courageous and life-affirming.[22]

Deming's distinction between a corrosive anger that seeks destruction and a generative, resourceful anger that "concentrates all one's energies" on the struggle to achieve social justice is a pivotal formulation that is essential to the anger paradigm. I recognize that anger without knowledge of cause and disciplined focus can result in debilitating fear, conflict, and disunion that can be lethal to the individual and community. At the same time, however, Audre Lorde and other feminist theorists convince me that anger named, understood, and directed at the root cause of grievances fosters growth, alliance, and a radical reconception of self, world, and political agency. "[A]nger between peers births change, not destruction," Lorde declares in an essay that explores the perilous subject of anger between women of color and white women in the women's movement. "[T]he discomfort and sense of loss it often causes is not fatal, but a sign of growth."[23]

Other students of anger share Lorde's conviction that anger can be a positive, creative source of personal and political insight. The "power of anger and rage" can be "potentially constructive—even creative" although it also contains the "notorious capacity for destructiveness, violence, and evil," argues clinical psychologist Stephen A. Diamond in a study that posits that consciously integrating anger into our lives and psyches will alleviate our culture's raging violence. When "[t]he volatile emotions of anger and rage" are "demonized," when they are "vilified, maligned, and rejected as purely pathological, negative impulses with no real redeeming qualities," then "most 'respectable' Americans habitually suppress, repress, or deny their anger" which "[sow[s] the evil seeds of psychopathology, hatred and violence." But when we recognize anger's capacity for both destruction and creativity and utilize it constructively, Diamond contends, "[a]nger—and rage, the most extreme form of anger—can be an enlivening, animating, transformative, creative, even spiritual force."[24] Philosopher J. Giles Milhaven concurs. He, too, believes a certain form of anger is "constructive" when it is directed toward achieving "betterment" and "liberation." "Purely constructive anger wants destruction only as a means. It wants to destroy obstacles or oppression purely as means to its constructive goal: a change for the better or greater freedom."[25]

The fact that anger is a form of communication that reveals important information about the obstacles oppressed people encounter is another critical component of the anger paradigm. "Signal[ing] the necessity for change," anger telegraphs a message that there is a problem, that the sanctity of self or community is in danger.[26] When individuals or groups are capable of decoding the message by locating, naming, and analyzing the source of the problem, they can use the "information and energy" that anger is "loaded with" to alter human relationships and oppressive power arrangements.[27] Thus anger not only communicates information to the individual about his or her feelings and what might be causing them; when it is expressed publicly, it also communicates information to the individual's or group's culture. Public expressions of anger inform the larger culture that the individual or group are human beings of consequence who are seeking attention, respect, and equal rights and privileges. They legitimate grievances that are supposed to remain unarticulated, suppressed. Equally significant, expressions of public anger provide insight into what individuals or groups value, want to protect, and hope to attain.[28]

Justice is certainly one of those values, and the expression of anger in its pursuit is analogous to courtroom drama. The angry person or group assumes the role of judge in a trial that subjects the behavior and actions of wrongdoers to public scrutiny. Because anger involves making judgments about what constitutes injustice, what vehicles of expression are appropriate, and what remedies are most effective, it is a moral emotion that plays an essential role in personal, social, and civic governance. "[A]nger is the emotional foundation of civil order in its *moral* form, the capacity for moral outrage by which society defends its mores and sacred values," sociologist Peter Lyman contends. If that civil order strives to be democratic, than the anger of oppressed people directed at the sources of injustice is a defiant assertion of their equal claim to define moral law and guarantee its enforcement. The expression of such anger, Elizabeth V. Spelman argues, is "an act of insubordination" because the angry person or group is "acting as if [they] have as much right to judge [the more powerful person or group] as [the more powerful person or group] has to judge [them]." Another way anger equalizes unequal relationships, J. Giles Milhaven observes, is when oppressed people's quest for justice includes a desire for vengeance. "Vindictive anger is good," Milhaven reasons, "because it is an elemental lunge of our self to be with others as their equal in power and will. Our wanting to make others suffer for making us suffer is our wanting to make ourselves equal to them in personal power and freedom. However blind be our rage and however brutal and inhuman be the act we in our rage strain to do, we are straining to be by that act, with the other person as equal persons."[29]

The connection between righteous anger and justice is embedded in western classical tradition. Aristotle, for example, defines anger as the "desire, accompanied by pain, for revenge of an obvious belittlement of oneself or one's dependents, the belittlement being uncalled for." The "prospect of revenge" is gratifying, he asserts, because "it is pleasant to think that one will achieve what one seeks" which is the opportunity to, at the very least, imagine avenging one's injury. St. Thomas Aquinas reiterates Aristotle's definition: "[A]n angry reaction arises only when one has endured some pain, and desires and hopes for revenge." As long as the desire for revenge is guided by reason and its object is "the correction of vice and the maintenance of justice," rather than the infliction of harm on the perpetuator for harm's sake only, it is "laudable," Aquinas contends.[30]

Two unstated assumptions underlie these premises: one, that the rational, righteously angry person is entitled to desire self-satisfaction, pleasure, and just treatment; and two, that the rational, righteously angry person possesses the power to make judgments about one's own and others' behavior. Both of these assumptions have, historically, not applied to women. Gendered ideologies that classify sacrifice and selflessness as female virtues disallow women's sense of entitlement. This phenomenon has led feminist psychologists to the realization that, for women, the expression of anger and the creation of an autonomous self are integrally linked. Before a woman can recognize her anger, they have argued, she has to recognize that she is entitled to a self. When women acknowledge that they are angry and use their anger effectively, which entails clarifying their own position, and then using that understanding to disrupt unequal power relationships, they achieve personal power and independence. Because anger demands change, it forces a confrontation not only with the person or situation with whom one is embattled, but also with the self. In Harriet Lerner's words, the "pain of anger" "preserves the very integrity of . . . self."[31]

The same ideologies that deem selflessness and sacrifice exclusively female virtues also contend that women are inferior to men in intellect, imagination, and physical ability. These notions of gender difference eradicate women's belief that they are powerful social actors capable of making important decisions. As a result, women have not had the same access to anger and its political uses as have men. Indeed, one of the central points feminist activists, psychologists, philosophers and sociologists emphasize is that the ability to feel and express anger in response to injustice requires respect and love for one's self and one's community. Anger is "a kind of love" for self, community, and even offender, J. Giles Milhaven argues, because it resists human maiming and insists upon establishing social justice. In order for an individual or group of people to acknowledge that they feel anger and trust that those feelings are justified, they must believe that the self and community are valuable, that they are worth defending. They must also believe that they have the right, ability, and power to judge.[32]

The historical suppression of white and black women's anger has been enacted through a proliferation of ideas that have at their center the notion that anger is the sole prerogative of white men in power. Carol Tavris notes that "a major role of anger is its policing function. . . . [W]ith its power of forcefulness and its threat of retaliation, [anger] helps to regulate our everyday social relations: in family disputes, neighborly quarrels, business disagreements, wherever the official law is too cumbersome, inappropriate, or unavailable (which is most of the time)."[33] Tavris's observation raises a central question: in a culture stratified by hierarchical power arrangements, whose anger is policing whom? Whose anger is regulating family disputes, neighborly quarrels, and business disagreements? The people who have the power to define anger and establish the rules for its social functioning and expression are the ones who police those who have lesser power and status. It is also they who use anger to intimidate, threaten, and silence the anger of those they perceive as challenging their hegemony.

Feminist scholarship elucidates this phenomenon. In one of the first analyses of the importance of anger in women's liberation struggles, Susi Kaplow argues that the repression of women's anger is oppressive, because denying a woman "the forthright expression of her healthy anger," denies her equality with men. While men can express anger verbally and physically without imperiling their gender roles or their integrity, taboos against the female expression of anger cause women to deny it, express it indirectly, or nurse it silently until it "burn[s] down to a bitter resentment or become[s] such a pressurized force that it [can] only come out in a rage so uncontrollable that the man (and the audience) can dismiss it as irrational." Amplifying Kaplow's analysis, Naomi Scheman and Teresa Bernardez also stress the significance of who has control over the definitions and interpretations of anger and its expression. When the powerful label the anger of those they wish to maintain their power over as irrational, infantile, and unjustified, they protect their privileged status. Trivializing and dismissing the anger of those in the less powerful class, race, or gender position undermines the latter's critique by insisting that their perceptions are invalid and unwarranted. "[O]ne of the major ways in which domination is kept in force," Teresa Bernardez argues, "[is] by convincing women that if they feel anger, bitterness, and resentment this is a sign of their inferiority, sickness, lack of virtue or lack of femininity, not the result of their unequal status." Elizabeth Spelman lists other "major ways" the powerful dissuade "subordinate groups" "from thinking about their situation": "denial of basic education; the erasure of facts about how they've been treated; the availability of drugs, alcohol, and other inducements to placidity or madness." In these instances, the suppression of anger is the suppression of public protest.[34]

When these tactics are successful, when ideologies of subordination, inferiority, and worthlessness are internalized, the anger that is denied expression manifests itself in other forms. Turned against the self and community, unnamed and unrecognized anger can result in depression, self-hate, and illness. Turned against others, anger without benefit of knowledge and appropriate target can exacerbate conflict and lead to violence. Attacking, blaming, whining, nagging, crying, and self-imposed silence may all be signs of an unidentified discontent that is being ineffectively addressed and expressed. Indirect and displaced expressions of anger are especially prevalent in unequal power relationships because in this context they are a form of protection against the threat of retaliation.[35]

Understanding the ways in which women have historically created a public discourse of anger when anger and womanhood are antithetical, enables an appreciation of how they have historically created the necessary conditions to effect social change. By developing a public vocabulary to express angered discontent in their literature, women have invented a language through which the history of their quest for justice can be known and shared.[36] When we identify what makes women angry, how they express that anger, and whether the constraints they encounter are still operative, we gain information about the cultures in which women live, their artistic practices, and the history of their gendered and racial oppression. The writing woman and the written text provide insight into how women at different historical moments have written themselves into agency and fantasized liberation and revenge. The writing woman and the written text also provide evidence—a public record—of the struggle to achieve equality and freedom, as well as inspiration for continued efforts in the twenty-first century.

In the following chapters I put these theories into practice by applying them to the antebellum period. Chapter 2 considers the implications of using the anger paradigm for the pre–Civil War era, including the ways in which it enables a new conceptualization of women's lives and literature, as well as how it provides a way out of semantic quagmires. Because the anger paradigm foregrounds women writers' responses to anger-producing situations in their lives and culture, it compels a reassessment of prevailing interpretative modes that stress the domestic nature of antebellum women's literature. Equally important, because the anger paradigm proposes examining the ways in which nineteenth-century women writers define, express, and dramatize anger, it liberates scholars' dependence on variable classifications such as sentimental, domestic, exploratory, or local color. The anger paradigm also makes possible a fluid and widely encompassing methodology for literary analysis, one that is applicable to a variety of genres. Attention to aesthetics is a central component of this methodology. Through a sophisticated invention of masking techniques, antebellum women writers practice an artistry of anger that enables them to express what their culture forbids.

Chapter 3 delineates the ideological meanings of anger and how those meanings affect black and white women's literary culture in pre–Civil War America. Integrally related to the white, middle-class nation-building project, gendered ideologies of anger make it possible for antebellum Americans to maintain two views of anger simultaneously. On the one hand, the righteous anger that preserves God's moral laws and enforces justice is gendered male. On the other hand, the ungoverned anger that threatens the fate of the republic is gendered female. At the same time that this ideology upholds race, gender, and class hierarchy, it also allows black and white women engaged in antiracist, antislavery, and gender liberation struggles to claim righteous anger as a moral woman's right, which they then use to create a public discourse of gendered outrage. In the antebellum period, abolitionism provides the single most important opportunity for such discourse. Yet, even for women involved in the movement, the expression of moral outrage is always in tension with gendered codes of middle-class respectability.

Chapters 4 through 7, which comprise the second half of the book, examine the ways in which Lydia Maria Child, Maria W. Stewart, Fanny Fern, and Harriet Wilson invent and practice an artistry of anger that is integrally related to the culture they are hoping their words will transform. "In the human soul, the steps between discontent and action are few and short indeed," the white pioneers of the woman's rights movement pronounced in evangelical tones. "You, who suppose the mass of women contented, know but little of the silenced indignation, the deep and settled disgust with which they contemplate our present social arrangements."[37] By articulating in print "the silenced indignation" of the mass of women in their communities, Child, Stewart, Fern, and Wilson contemplate social relations and move their audience to action. For these writers, expressing anger at exclusion in a culture that denies women the right to do so entails reinventing national community. Lydia Maria Child imagines a historical community in which white women's rightful privileges are restored; Maria W. Stewart imagines a spiritual community in which direct communion with God transcends men's laws; Fanny Fern imagines a secular community in which white women share equally in capitalist enterprise; Harriet Wilson imagines a gothic community in which the diseased inhabitants of the patriarchal house of slavery rob black women and children of their rights and life blood.

For Child, Stewart, Fern, and Wilson, moving their audience to action also necessitates appropriating imaginative spaces into which they can project their anger for public consideration in the marketplace. Historical myth-making, evangelical discourse, domesticity, and abolitionist rhetoric are the spaces into which Lydia Maria Child, Maria W. Stewart, Fanny Fern, and Harriet Wilson express their versions of enraged truths. Through the imagination, these writers build a republic in which the expression of women's anger transforms the meaning of emotional, cultural, and political freedom.

TWO

Using the Anger Paradigm

The Antebellum Period as Case Study

Of their peculiar light
I keep one ray
To clarify the Sight
To seek them by—
—Emily Dickinson (1362)

When feminist historians and literary critics began to reconstruct the history of American women and their literary activity, they found that the antebellum period contained "peculiar light" indeed. Irony and paradox were everywhere apparent. At the same time that an ideology of gender difference assigned women to the home and men to the marketplace, women used this ideology to justify civic involvement in America's nation-building project. At the same time that America proclaimed itself the exemplar of democracy, it institutionalized slavery and excluded women, "free" people of color, Native Americans, and people of Asian descent from equal rights and citizenship. At the same time that the culture insisted women rely on men for economic and emotional support, racial discrimination, the deaths of fathers, sons, brothers, and husbands, and frequent economic upheaval forced women to become wage earners, laboring in tedious, low-paying jobs. At the same time that Emily Dickinson invented a new poetic grammar behind the mask of mental instability in her father's household, scores of her contemporaries published novels about the trials and tribulations of poverty-stricken, orphaned female characters who yearned to attain the genteel living conditions Dickinson spurned. At the same time that European immigrants flocked to America to escape persecution and poverty, two American women intellectuals, Margaret Fuller and Harriet Jacobs, experienced freedom for the first time while in Europe. At the same time that cultural arbiters maintained that anger and its expression must be removed from the home in order to protect the stability of the newly developing nation, anger in the culture led to civil war.

The ironies and paradoxes at the heart of antebellum America make it an especially fruitful period for testing the anger paradigm. Concerned with the dynamic interplay between the anger-producing conditions of women's lives and the ways in which they make meaning of those conditions through the literary imagination, the anger paradigm provides a new lens through which the ironies and paradoxes of the period can be viewed and understood. Not only does the anger paradigm offer a new perspective on imprecise critical terms and classifications, including a reassessment of literary domesticity; it also encourages a new appraisal of women writers' artistic achievements and a richer understanding of the role of writing in antebellum women's lives.

Nineteenth-century women writers, Carolyn Karcher argues, "produced some of the century's most intellectually serious, politically radical, and artistically innovative prose." Yet the question of how to characterize, define, and evaluate this literature continues to vex us. Even though feminist critics agree that nineteenth-century women's literature has been devalued by a male-dominated literary establishment and deserves to be reassessed on its own terms, we do not share a common language when it comes to describing specific authors, genres, and styles. Indeed, as Joanne Dobson notes, the word sentimental, which is often used to describe this literature, "is perhaps the most overworked, imprecise, misapplied, emotionally loaded, inadequately understood term in American literary classification." A revisionist literary history without a mutually agreed upon vocabulary remains fragmented and idiosyncratic.[1]

The case of Harriet Beecher Stowe is an excellent example of this confusion. According to Nina Baym, who renames "sentimental" fiction "woman's fiction," Stowe is not one of its practitioners because she does not write stories about orphaned young girls who experience the "trials and triumphs" of having to "[win their] own way in the world." To Baym, Stowe is "apart from the other American women writing fiction in her day." To Mary Kelley, however, Stowe's experience as a nineteenth-century woman writer is emblematic of the difficulties other white women writers faced entering the public stage at a time when domestic ideology informed every aspect of women's lives. Like Baym, she gives "sentimental" fiction a new name by calling it "literary domesticity." Jane Tompkins, on the other hand, retains the label "sentimental" but redefines it. In her reassessment of *Uncle Tom's Cabin*, she refers to Stowe as a "sentimentalist," but to Tompkins, the "sentimental" novel is "a political enterprise, halfway between sermon and social theory, that both codifies and attempts to mold the values of its time." To Josephine Donovan, however, there is no connection between Stowe and sentimental fictionalists. In her study of late-nineteenth-century white women writers, she includes a chapter on Stowe in which she writes that Stowe "pioneered the women's tradition of local color realism." Because the sentimentalists created a formulaic and unimaginative genre, Donovan argues, their texts are unworthy of serious literary study.[2]

Using anger as a mode of analysis and the basis of an aesthetic helps to solve these evaluative and semantic quagmires. Instead of classifying and evaluating writers and their texts based on contested classifications such as sentimental, domestic, exploratory, or local color, I propose examining the ways in which nineteenth-century women writers define, express, and dramatize anger. Using this methodology enables the reconceptualization of domestic literature, the formulation of a new aesthetic, and the consideration of a variety of genres—historical novels, fictionalized autobiographies, slave narratives, short stories, speeches, meditations, and sensation stories—within the purview of one study.

When expressions of anger are made into an analytical category, new ways of conceptualizing women's literary activity in the nineteenth century become apparent. Indeed, in the same way questions of race, class, and conflict have prompted women's historians to rethink the paradigm of separate spheres, the question of angry expression compels a rethinking of the paradigm of literary domesticity.[3] This paradigm, most elaborately formulated by Nina Baym and Mary Kelley, posits that nineteenth-century women's literature is in every way—formally, thematically, and ideologically—concerned with the problems of women's domestic lives. Nina Baym, for example, laid the groundwork in 1978 by examining critically a large body of texts written in the nineteenth century by white women for white women from a feminist perspective. Not only did she call attention to dozens of writers and novels that the traditional canon had long neglected; she also created one of the field's most fundamental and enduring paradigms based on the structural and thematic qualities of the texts. Finding that the novels shared a remarkably similar plot consisting of an orphaned young girl, deprived of supports who is forced to make her way in the world, and then succeeds in marrying at the end, Baym theorized that these stories were "about the psychology of women"—that they were didactic tales of feminine "trials and triumph" that were "immensely pleasurable to a huge number of American women."[4]

Six years later, in a richly nuanced and historically complex biographical portrait of twelve of the same writers, Mary Kelley enriched our understanding of Baym's findings by studying not only the women's published novels, but also their unpublished private diaries and letters. Arguing that every aspect of these authors' lives—their expectations, imaginative visions, and careers as writers—was profoundly affected by "the perspective, the language, the metaphor, and the meaning of domesticity for women," Kelley contends that the writers were incapable of reconciling a private, domestic sense of self with that of a public "creator of culture." Thus, whereas Baym analyzed the plot of the published stories and concluded that the texts were not "beset by contradictions, defenses, or duplicities," Kelley, on the other hand, analyzed the plot of the lives and found nothing but "contradictions, defenses, and duplicities." By doing so, Kelley helped us to see that these writers did not lack imagination, but rather that the prevailing angle of their vision was circumscribed because "domesticity provided the matter and the metaphor for their lives."[5]

As critically important as these studies continue to be, one of the limiting consequences of the literary domesticity paradigm has been the tendency to obscure the *political* ways in which nineteenth-century women's texts participate in national conversations about gender, race, republicanism, education, religion, economics, and reform. Although scholars recognized the importance of the home as a political space from the start, the metaphorical implications of domestic iconography were not adequately addressed.[6] Within the last several years, however, scholars such as Jane Tompkins, Hazel Carby, Claudia Tate, Susan Harris, Gillian Brown, Lora Romero, and Elizabeth Young have addressed this issue, demonstrating how domestic metaphors encode women writers' political critiques. The anger paradigm continues this line of inquiry.

Analyzing expressions of nineteenth-century women writers' anger significantly challenges the notion that their literature is confined to domestic themes. Although many women writers camouflaged their ideas in domestic metaphors, they addressed issues as wide-ranging as republican nationalism, economic panics, gender and race relations, and educational reform. When anger is used as a mode of analysis and the basis of an aesthetic, nineteenth-century women's literature can be read as a complex response to slavery, industrialization, imperialism, war, and poverty. Excluded from institutionalized avenues of power, women writers use the literary realm to claim self, home, educational opportunity, racial equality, economic security, and imaginative autonomy in a nation that denies them their rights and privileges as citizens.

Making women's angry expression the focus of analysis also illuminates the ways in which gendered ideologies proclaiming women's maternal, loving, moral natures profoundly affected nineteenth-century women's literary imaginings. Changing economic conditions in the post–Revolutionary War years spurred the development of these belief systems. As the economy shifted from a self-contained, agricultural system of exchange to one based on competitive waged labor in an increasingly anonymous capitalist marketplace, women's domestic roles assumed a new emphasis. Associated with ethical, spiritual, and emotional matters in the domestic sphere, women were entrusted with the responsibility of inculcating tenets of republican virtue, such as piety, thrift, sobriety, honor, and self-control, in the family. Their newly acquired role as republican mothers became possible when the moral matters that had once been under the church's aegis were relegated to the private realm of the Christian family. "Woman is God's appointed agent of *morality*, the teacher and inspirer of those feelings and sentiments which are termed the virtues of humanity," Sarah J. Hale declared in *Woman's Record*, a biographical encyclopedia containing over two thousand entries. "[T]he progress of these virtues, and the permanent improvement of our race, depend on the manner in which her mission is treated by man." Through her greater spiritual influence, the republican wife and mother performed the moral work of the nation by sacrificing her own needs and desires in order to ensure the success of the grand republican experiment.[7]

For "free" African Americans, the notion that woman was the human conduit through which "the virtues of humanity" could be instituted in the American republic took on added meaning. Because of the imperatives of racial struggle, black women were expected to use their greater emotionality and virtue for the welfare of the black community, as well as for the nation. Black women's "virtuous, pious and industrious" influence, the proponents of moral emotionalism contended, had the power to change the "degraded condition of society."[8] As upstanding members of their communities, black women could refute racist stereotypes by becoming literal embodiments of decorum and gentility; as mothers to both their children and their community, they could transmit the intellectual and practical knowledge that future generations needed to continue the struggle for democratic rights and freedoms.

Invested with this kind of moral authority and virtuous feeling, antebellum women used what they believed was their innately greater moral emotionalism as a source of empowerment, transforming it into a politics and an art. In the texts I investigate in Part II of this book, I demonstrate how Lydia Maria Child, Maria W. Stewart, Fanny Fern, and Harriet Wilson respond to the gendered ideology of moral emotionalism in order to promote their political and artistic visions. While Maria W. Stewart embraces it and Fanny Fern revises it, Lydia Maria Child and Harriet Wilson disclaim it, but in different ways and for different reasons.

Lydia Maria Child's reservations about the ideology of moral emotionalism are conveyed implicitly in her first novel, *Hobomok*. The ideology limits aspiring white middle-class women's expressivity, she implies, because it does not allow them to express anger at men of their own race and class who refuse to admit them to the democratic homeland. In Maria W. Stewart's case, however, the ideology of moral emotionalism buttresses her authority as God's spokesperson because it sanctions the notion that women's greater spirituality makes them closer to God. In the secular world of *Ruth Hall*, Fanny Fern expands the boundaries of the ideology to include white women's right to express angered indignation at white men who deny them the right to compete in the capitalist marketplace. But from the point of view of Harriet Wilson, a woman who was not permitted to own her own body or labor, the politics of moral emotionalism preserves white women's power over blacks.

In *Our Nig*, Harriet Wilson reveals how white women have the capacity to manipulate moral emotionalism so that it advances the patriarchal culture's racist project. In Wilson's imaginative universe, when a young black woman is virtuous and emotional, a white mother whips and tortures her. Although the ideology of moral emotionalism enables the white mother's authority and status in the community and household, her actions confirm the ideology's racial exclusivism. In the novel, after James's death, when Frado has the audacity to "[present] herself unasked in the parlor" so that she, too, can receive consolation from a clergyman's prayers, her mistress "upbraid[s] her," causing the young woman to lose "all control of herself" and weep "aloud." This, Wilson notes, was "an act of disobedience."

Stung by unmerited rebuke, weak from sorrow and anxiety, the tears rolled down her dark face, soon followed by sobs, and then losing all control of herself, she wept aloud. This was an act of disobedience. Her mistress grasping her raw-hide, caused a longer flow of tears, and wounded a spirit that was craving healing mercies.

Racist white women, Wilson makes it clear, used the politics of moral emotionalism to sustain and reinforce their race and class privilege.[9]

"[T]he subjects of which [most female writers] write," John S. Hart pronounced in the preface to the 1857 edition of the nation-building anthology, *The Female Prose Writers of America*, "are chiefly of an emotional nature, carrying with them on every page the unmistakeable impress of personal sympathy, if not experience. Women, far more than men, write from the heart."[10] But writing from a heart that contained anger and bitterness, rather than love and sympathy, was a liability for nineteenth-century women. Although they used notions of their greater moral emotionalism to authorize their literary and political interventions, their power base was severely circumscribed because the range of emotions they could acceptably express was limited by cultural dictates. While feelings of joy, love, sympathy, and reverence were encouraged, even celebrated, because they were considered essential to women's domestic role as wife and mother, feelings of disapproval, discontent, vengeance, and hatred were regarded as the exclusive province of men. For women to express unwomanly feelings publicly would mean undermining the basis of their authority, for then they would be acting like men in the marketplace. Thus women were forced to operate from a power base that did not include the potential for angry expression and strident disapproval. Faced with this dilemma, they invented ways to express anger at exclusion from the democratic promises of America through an artistry of angry expression that is aesthetically sophisticated and politically significant. From behind the mask of moral emotionalism, they manipulated conventional ideologies of womanhood to write about personal discontent and public injustice, and in the process, presented their own versions of America.

In a nineteenth-century context, women's anger is the dangerous, daring, "other" side of domesticity, the side that helps us best understand how a historical tradition of women's literary discontent emerges and develops in the period. To aid this scholarly shift to domesticity's "other" side, I now examine briefly the lives and work of two major writers, Louisa May Alcott and Harriet Jacobs, as pivotal touchstones. Doing so elucidates what happens when the anger paradigm informs and supplants literary domesticity as a primary mode of interpretation. In the close readings of Alcott's and

Jacobs's lives and texts that follow, I explain why both are paradigmatic practitioners of the artistry of angry expression.

Raised in a civic-minded community by parents who cherished the notion that individuals guided by discipline, self-sacrifice, and honorable principles could create a virtuous republic, Louisa May Alcott grew up nurtured by democratic ideals. Indeed, as Sarah Elbert notes, her father regarded his own family as a testing ground for the creation of model citizens. "The child must be treated as a free, self-guiding, self-controlling being," Bronson Alcott believed. "He must be allowed to feel that he is under his own guidance and that all external guidance is an injustice which is done to his nature unless his own will is intelligently submissive to it. . . . He must be free that he may be truly virtuous, for without freedom there is no such thing as virtue."[11]

Bronson Alcott's reference to the model citizen as male is indicative of the central contradiction that plagued his daughter and her contemporaries. In a culture that gendered freedom and will as male prerogatives, women could not be ambitious and independent self-regulators. On the contrary, they were expected to accept cheerfully their subsidiary roles as self-sacrificing enablers of the masculine nation-building enterprise. Like Alcott's own mother who tried to convince herself to "do cheerfully with a hoping heart and willing hand what each day presents to be done" when she was continually faced with anger-producing situations, women internalized these prescriptions and attempted to ennoble their self-sacrificing role. In reality, women's unpaid physical, emotional, and domestic labor in the household, and enslaved women's unpaid physical, emotional, and domestic labor in fields and on plantations, made the self-reliant male nation-builder possible.[12]

Like many of her contemporaries, Louisa May Alcott used both private and public writing to make meaning of the anger that resulted from this contradiction—the anger she was not supposed to feel, let alone acknowledge experiencing. Ironically, it was the parents who conveyed the message that anger was detrimental to the sanctity of home and nation, who were the ones to establish the relationship between anger and writing that Alcott maintained throughout her life time. Because Alcott's parents believed literacy was fundamental to good character development, pens, paper, and books were regularly exchanged among family members; so, too, was the injunction that they be used for worthy purposes. On Louisa May Alcott's tenth birthday, her mother gave her a "pencil-case" because she "observed that [Louisa was] fond of writing, and [she] wish[ed] to encourage the habit." Having their children keep journals in which they recorded "their struggles and desires" also encouraged the habit. The journal writing was not just for the children's edification, however; the parents also used it to supervise the children's moral progress by reading and commenting on its contents. In this capacity, the journal became an important medium for mother/daughter intimacy. In letters, and sometimes in the pages of the journal itself, the mother and daughter carried on a written conversation about the daughter's faults and virtues. Thus the journal writing provided opportunities for self-reflection, parent/child intimacy, and reinforcement of proper values and behavior.[13]

By the time Louisa May Alcott was seventeen, she had not only internalized her parents' and her culture's gendered injunctions. She had also become reliant upon writing as a mode of self-examination, using it to explore the desires, frustrations, and conflicting feelings that would become the hallmark of her public writing. One entry in particular pointedly reveals what happened when Alcott attempted to both embrace and defy gendered expectations. She hoped to become "a truly good and useful woman," she wrote, one who was capable of "managing" her self-absorption, "quick tongue," ambitious desires, and mounting anger at being denied the opportunity to design her own fate. But the impossibility of actualizing this goal resulted in angered feelings of self-defeat, expressed as the desire to commit suicide.

> In looking over our journals, Father says, "Anna's is about other people, Louisa's about herself." That is true, for I don't *talk* about myself; yet must always think of the wilful, moody girl I try to manage, and in my journal I write of her to see how she gets on. . . . My quick tongue is always getting me into trouble, and my moodiness makes it hard to be cheerful when I think how poor we are, how much worry it is to live, and how many things I long to do I never can.
>
> So every day is a battle, and I'm so tired I don't want to live; only it's cowardly to die till you have done something.[14]

In the entry, the "battle" between assertion and repression, as well as the way in which Alcott splits herself into two—the "wilful, moody girl" and the anxious observer attempting to control her—anticipates the ways in which she defined, expressed, and dramatized anger in her public writing. The seventeen-year-old Louisa May Alcott recognized that repressing ambition, will, anger, and desire was essential to being a good republican daughter in both the familial and national household.

Years later, Alcott encoded this vision of the dwarfed republican daughter in *Little Women*, the autobiographical novel she wrote to make money and satisfy an enterprising publisher's desire for a profitable "girls' story."[15] In the

Camp Laurence chapter, Alcott's nationalist sentiments are explicitly rendered. When the "bright little band of [March] sisters, all looking their best" (123), meet the "English boys and girls" who are friends of their monied, well-traveled neighbor, Laurie, for a "jolly" afternoon of frolic (121), they discover that one English child is lame, the other is prissy and pedantic, and yet another is a liar and a cheat. The American children, by contrast, are healthy, unpretentious, honest, and fun-loving. And their tenacity, intelligence, and feisty spirit make them better competitors. Although "[t]he Englishers played well," Alcott's narrator concedes when describing the children's croquet game, "the Americans played better, and contested every inch of the ground as strongly as if the spirit of '76 inspired them" (124).

In construing American identity as superior to that of the former colonizers, Alcott invokes America's cherished myth about itself. Compared to the English who once held Americans in subjection, liberated Americans are the epitome of virtue, vigor, industriousness, and prosperity. Their rebellious quest for liberty transformed them into what J. Hector St. John de Crèvecoeur called a "a new race of men, whose labours and posterity will one day cause great changes in the world." Leaving behind the squalor, poverty, and inequitable class systems of Europe, "[t]he American is a new man, who acts upon new principles [and] must therefore entertain new ideas and form new opinions." [16]

In the Camp Laurence chapter, Alcott shows what happens when the new American is a white woman: her ability to "act upon new principles" is compromised by gendered prescriptions of proper female behavior. During the croquet game, when Jo realizes that Fred, one of the English boys, is cheating, she becomes enraged, telling him, "We don't cheat in America; but *you* can, if you choose" (125). But after he denies wrongdoing and retorts that "Yankees are a deal the most tricky," Jo "checked herself in time" before rudely responding. Deflecting her unexpressed rage into physical motion, "Jo stood a minute, hammering down a wicket with all her might" (125). In this angered gesture, the censored republican daughter symbolically claims her stake in American soil, but she is forced to do so mutely, squelching the righteous indignation that the "spirit of '76" celebrates. Employing the tactic her mother has recently taught her, she keeps her lips sealed and removes herself from the scene of provocation. Her sister Meg, the embodiment of female decorum, then commends her for keeping her temper under "dreadfully provoking" conditions (125). But Jo makes it clear that she resents having to get her "rage enough under to hold [her] tongue," because she still wants to "box [Fred's] ears" (126).

Although Jo's ingenuity enables her to win the game anyway, what this scene evinces is that when the new American is a white woman, she can not use the "spirit of '76" to protest injustice. When "temper" is defined as a fault republican daughters must conquer, they are prohibited from using angered indignation to combat the social practices that endanger the republic in which they are equally invested. Yet, in this same chapter, Alcott also reveals how republican daughters attempt to overcome the problem. They get revenge through the use of language, the one area in which they have leeway; for literacy, the ideology of republican motherhood contended, enabled women to be better conduits of virtue. When playing the game of Truth, Jo shames the English boy into admitting he did cheat during the croquet game. Significantly, however, she can do so only after Laurie sanctions her vindictive impulses. Because Laurie is male, advocating vengeance is not an issue. "Let's give it to him," he urges Jo when it is Fred's turn "to answer truly any questions put by the rest" (131). While republican brothers can utilize "the spirit of 76" with relish, republican daughters are required to restrain their righteous indignation and squelch their desire for revenge.

Here Louisa May Alcott renders yet another exquisite nineteenth-century irony. At the same time that emotion is gendered female and reason is gendered male, it is women's ability to contain dangerous emotionality through reason that becomes the symbolic representation of the nation's ability to control irrational impulses that endanger the exercise of virtue. Thus women's ability to control, if not suppress, dangerous angry feelings is the literal personification of the nation's ability to govern itself independently. Although the new republic cherishes the "spirit of '76" when it is manifested in men in justifiable circumstances, it also desires to create a postcolonial identity that emphasizes its ability to govern through reason as opposed to coercive force. By making women the symbolic representation of a rational, angerless republic, men could still feel, express, and utilize anger without imperiling their gender identity or the national democratic project.[17]

Dispossessed of rights and privileges, and constrained by gendered notions of emotional propriety in both the familial and national households, is it any wonder that nineteenth-century women writers use houses and their contents as symbolic representations of their longings and forbidden angers? Women writers' delineation of houses—their measurements, surfaces, and interiors, what they contain and what they do not—provides a key to their political vision as well as to their artistry of anger. Once again, Little Women is an excellent example. In this text, Alcott's anger at exclusion from the democratic promises of America, which results in her fantasy of a new class formation, is conveyed through the imagery of two houses, the March house and the Laurence house. Separated by a hedge, the two houses signify different classes. While the March house represents the class that genteel poor women inhabit, the Laurence house represents the class that genteel rich men inhabit. The interactions between members of the two houses signify Alcott's fantasy of how a merger between the two can produce a new class of educated, propertied citizens bound together by humility, patience, and love.

The merger is made possible when the occupants of each house discover the appeal of the other's. Jo wants what is in Laurie's house—his books, his opportunity to travel and go to college, his privileged ease, wealth, and material possessions. Conversely, Laurie wants what is in the March's house—mothering, warmth, excitement, virtuous principles, and loving community. When the two houses are united by love—love between Mr. Laurence and Beth; love among Jo, Laurie, and Amy; love between Meg and John Brooke—the unification results in a new class in which wealthy privilege, virtuous principles, and loving community are conjoined.

An essential part of Alcott's fantasy is the eradication of the lower class, and this, too, is figured through the imagery of houses. Unlike the interaction between the members of the March and Laurence houses, there is no such exchange between the members of the March house and the house that contains the unassimilated, poverty-stricken immigrants who threaten the health of the nation. On the contrary, the one-way contact between the March and Hummel houses results in deathly consequences, illustrating the dire need to rectify class inequity. And when Jo inherits Aunt March's house—symbolic of the upper class—and transforms it into a school for poverty-stricken boys, such a rectification becomes possible: the poverty-stricken are literally taken into the republican daughter's newly transformed house, a house that she owns and controls.

Houses are also freighted with meaning in Alcott's "blood and thunder tale," "Behind a Mask, or, A Woman's Power," which she published two years before *Little Women* in a sensationalist newspaper. From behind the mask of a pseudonym, Alcott's anger at exclusion and her fantasy of the white woman's rightful restitution takes on a different tenor and assumes a different emphasis. Whereas in *Little Women*, the "girl's story," she delineates her heroine's valiant struggle to suppress anger because it engenders chaotic destruction and threatens womanhood, in the sensationalist fiction, she creates shrewd and enterprising protagonists who use their anger to achieve vengeance, status, security, and power.

In "Behind a Mask," Jean Muir is enraged because of her dispossession from class privilege, economic solvency, and national prosperity. Her desire to secure "a blessed sense of safety" (181) so that she will not be "thrust out penniless into the world, which had not pity for poverty" (191), signifies her desire to secure the rights and privileges she has been denied.[18] Dispossession has transformed the formerly "happy, innocent, and tender" Jean Muir into a "gloomy woman" who was "brooding over some wrong, or loss, or disappointment which had darkened all her life" (106). The "wrong," "loss," and "disappointment" fuel her rage, which in turn enables her witchlike powers. "I *am* a witch," she tantalizingly admits to one of the men she has ensnared, "and one day my disguise will drop away and you will see me as I am, old, ugly, bad and lost. Beware of me in time. . . . [L]ove me at your peril" (183). Woman's greatest power, Jean Muir knows, is her ability to perform the gendered roles of erotic object, humble servant, and devoted caretaker while tricking those duped by her agile disguises into believing no performance is occurring. The quality of the acting determines the quality of the dispossessed woman's restitution. Entry into the masculine house of comfort and authority requires deception as well as power over script writing and performance.

Jean Muir, a bitter and hardened thirty-year-old divorced actress, enters the home of the wealthy Coventry family pretending to be a pious, docile, nineteen-year-old governess. Through a series of elaborate intrigues, the theatrical genius connives her way into the affections of all the men in the Coventry household, including the richest and most powerful Coventry patriarch, whom she marries. Acting her role to perfection, Jean Muir maintains the upper hand in each interaction she maneuvers. By the end of the tale, she succeeds in mocking the men who have foolishly fallen in love with her, exposing how harmful their idealized notions about women and love are to their own integrity, that of the sanctified nuclear family's, and, by implication, that of the national homeland's.

At her boldest and most defiant, Jean Muir even manages to burn a series of letters that contain written proof of her own duplicity. In this final victory, Alcott demonstrates how her vengeful heroine maintains ultimate control over the stories that are told about her; it is she who controls what is the truth about her own life, and how that truth may or may not be disseminated. When the Coventrys realize that the woman who has the power "to annihilate the whole family" (199) has just burned her incriminating letters, Jean Muir retorts, "Hands off, gentleman! You may degrade yourselves to the work of detectives, but I am not a prisoner yet. Poor Jean Muir you might harm, but Lady Coventry is beyond your reach" (201). Endowed with the title of Lady Coventry, Jean Muir practices her art protected by her husband's wealth and status. A brilliant story about deception, manipulation, economic deprivation, and the ludicrousness of genteel feminine roles, Alcott's text makes a powerful political statement about the act of writing itself.

Cloaking her rage in a gothic tale about an enterprising governess, Alcott delivers a biting critique of nineteenth-century gender relations and economic discrimination that speaks to white women, like herself, who inhabit the precarious middle class.

In "Behind a Mask," Alcott's anger at exclusion does not result in a vision of a new class system in which white republican daughters assume power and facilitate a new social order. On the contrary, when Alcott temporarily frees herself from the impress of her parents' and culture's gendered dictates, and her own internalization of these strictures, her anger at exclusion results in a fantasy of restitution that rewards no one but the woman herself. Alcott's use of the governess plot and the English setting reflects, of course, her familiarity with English fiction such as Charlotte Brontë's *Jane Eyre*, and widely popular sensationalist tales, published in both England and in the United States. Nevertheless, these devices also function as a sneering condemnation of America's gendered exclusionary practices. By having her heroine achieve her objectives in an aristocratic household in England, Alcott expresses her rage at her own country's unwillingness to allow women like herself equal power in the democratic project. Although American mythology glorifies the notion that all Americans are capable of advancing from servitude to prosperity, Alcott ironically implies that only in Europe is such mobility possible.

Years after Louisa May Alcott published "Behind a Mask," woman's rights activist Emily Collins recalled how the historic Seneca Falls convention in 1848 provided the language and understanding she and her contemporaries needed to make sense of the anger and discontent that riddled their lives. "[F]rom the earliest dawn of reason I pined for that freedom of thought and action that was then denied to all womankind," Collins asserted. "I revolted in spirit against the customs of society and the laws of the State that crushed my aspirations and debarred me from the pursuit of almost every object worthy of an intelligent, rational mind. But not until that meeting at Seneca Falls in 1848, of the pioneers in the cause, gave this feeling of unrest form and voice, did I take action."[19] Louisa May Alcott's "Behind a Mask" serves the same function in a literary context: it gives "form and voice" to the collective "feeling of unrest" that runs like an undercurrent throughout antebellum women's literature, but is never explicitly rendered. Although writers interpret and disguise the "unrest" differently, depending on their race and class subjectivity, the issue of exclusion is paramount for all of them. What distinguishes Alcott's "Behind a Mask" from its pre-war predecessors, is its delineation of the politics and poetics of a female gendered literary culture of masked discontent that began in earnest when American women experienced what Catherine Maria Sedgwick termed the "writing itch."[20]

Living behind a mask in a northern household, Harriet Jacobs, another paradigmatic practitioner of the artistry of anger, experienced the writing itch when she was confronted with racist lies that denied the truth of her own experiences. Incensed that the wife of a former president publicly proclaimed that slaves were not routinely sold away from their families, Jacobs wrote a response that became her first publication. Anger, coupled with her desire to be "useful" to the abolitionist cause, propelled her to write. "I felt so indignant," she confided to her friend and correspondent, Amy Post, "I determined to reply." Her desire to correct other egregious untruths, even though it entailed revealing publicly the "cruel wrongs" that shamed and embarrassed her, led her to the decision "to give a true and just account of [her] own life in Slavery."[21]

Unlike the republican daughter Louisa May Alcott, the fugitive ex-slave Harriet Jacobs did not inherit literacy as a birthright; she did not have influential connections to publishers; and she could not use writing to support herself and her family. On the contrary, Jacobs was painfully aware of her literary "deficiencies" caused by "the loss of early opportunities to improve [herself]" while she was enslaved, and the economic imperatives that disallowed her the time to rectify the "deficiencies" while living as a fugitive in the North.[22] Ironically, although she worked as a domestic in the home of Nathaniel Parker Willis, a well-connected writer and editor, she did not benefit from the close proximity to wealth, power, and opportunity. Because she feared Willis's condemnation and reprisal, she disguised her literary ambitions from her employers. "Mr. W[illis] is too proslavery," she informed Amy Post. "[H]e would tell me that it was very wrong and that I was trying to do harm or perhaps he was sorry for me to undertake it while I was in his family." In another letter to Post, she wrote, "Mrs W[illis] dont know from my lips that I am writing for a Book and has never seen a line of what I have written."[23]

Harriet Jacobs was forced to be a fugitive from writing as well as from slavery. Compared to Louisa May Alcott whose family and community nurtured her literary ambitions, Jacobs was isolated and unsupported in the confines of a white household and a patriarchal publishing industry. Although she received encouragement from white woman's rights activists and abolitionists such as Amy Post and Lydia Maria Child, her enabling network was radically circumscribed, and her domestic duties always took precedence over her literary activities. As a housekeeper and caretaker of three children, she had "but a little time to think or write." As a black woman exposing sexual abuse under slavery, she had to contend with publishers who demanded that her story be validated by "some one known to the public—to effect the sale of the Book."[24]

Yet, like Louisa May Alcott, Harriet Jacobs practiced an artistry of anger that expressed her rage at exclusion from the democratic promises of America. And like Louisa May Alcott, Harriet Jacobs yearned for a familial and national home that was untainted by bigotry, poverty, and disunion. In a sentiment strikingly like that of Jean Muir's, she confided to Amy Post, "I could do anything for the sake of a little shanty to call home and have my children to come around me."[25] The persistent theme of homelessness in nineteenth-century women's texts signifies their sense of exile from the national homeland and their anger at this betrayal.[26]

In *Incidents in the Life of a Slave Girl*, Jacobs demonstrates how both the familial and national houses are desecrated under a system in which African Americans are imprisoned in their own homelands. One chapter in particular, "Fear of Insurrection," illustrates perfectly Jacobs's primary concerns. In this chapter, Jacobs's pseudonymous autobiographical narrator, Linda Brent, describes what she and her community endured in the immediate aftermath of the Nat Turner insurrection.[27] Terrified that other blacks—both "free" and enslaved—were also armed and ready to revolt, whites searched the homes of blacks looking for weapons or other incriminating evidence. Jacobs's detailed description of how Linda Brent prepared for the soldiers betrays her rage at their incursion into her home, her literacy, and her tenuous privileged status. Because Brent knows the search will be performed by "country bullies and the poor whites," who will be particularly "annoyed" at "see[ing] colored people living in comfort and respectability," she attends to "arrangements" with "especial care" (63). She makes sure "every thing in [her] grandmother's house [is] as [neat] as possible"; she puts "white quilts on the beds" and "decorate[s] some of the rooms with flowers"; she calmly sits down by the window "to watch" and wait (63).

Linda Brent's "arrangements" are a parody of nineteenth-century housekeeping. When "the door [is] rudely pushed open" and the visitors tumble in "like a pack of hungry wolves" (64), we see Jacobs's rage at the ways in which black women are denied rights and power in what is supposed to be woman's domain. We also see her rage at a government that sanctions the tyranny of "innocent men, women, and children" who are beyond reproach (64). The invasion by "a motley crowd of soldiers," accompanied by "martial music" is an ironic inversion of national succor and protection (63). The house is infiltrated as if it were enemy territory; the security of its occupants depends upon "a white gentleman" who is a family friend (65).

In this chapter, Jacobs also expresses her rage at a slave system that creates a pecking order of illiterate, power-hungry white men "who exulted in . . . a chance to exercise a little brief authority, and show their subserviency to the slaveholders," while she and other upstanding members of her community are subject to their abuse (64). In the ultimate perversion of neighborly social relations, these men tyrannize, pillage, and kill. In the ultimate perversion of democratic freedom, the only place black people can find refuge after the "lawless rabble" (67) becomes intoxicated with its own brutality is in the town jail (66). Behind the mask of middle-class gentility, Jacobs excoriates a political system that deprives her and her enslaved sisters of the privileges white women take for granted.

In Jacobs's vision, the pillaged house is a metaphor for the black woman's body under slavery. Once inside her grandmother's house, the men "snatch at everything within their reach" (64); they destroy the one piece of writing Linda Brent has forgotten to hide; and they invade a pantry closet. In the same way the wolfish, brutal white men invade the home Brent's grandmother has worked so hard to establish and maintain, so, too, do wolfish, brutal white men invade black women's bodies, using them at their will. Thus the pillaged house is a metaphor for rape, and rape assumes both literal and symbolic significance. Although Linda Brent informs us that she successfully avoids being raped by Dr. Flint, symbolically she is continually raped by her country. Deprived of her body, home, and children, and forced to labor without recognition, respect, or compensation, Linda Brent is violated, ravished, outraged, by a nation that denies her freedom.

Hidden in the garret, raped in the home, imprisoned in the nation—this, according to Harriet Jacobs, is how black women under slavery experience American democracy. By exploding the notion that white men provide security and protection, Jacobs exposes the hypocrisy of a system of gender relations that valorizes white male hegemony. In *Incidents in the Life of a Slave Girl*, it is not white men who provide economic support, comfort, love, and care; it is a black woman, Linda Brent's grandmother. As Jacobs notes early in the narrative, "I was indebted to *her* for all my comforts, spiritual or temporal. It was *her* labor that supplied my scanty wardrobe" (11). It is the grandmother's house that provides shelter, not the national house. It is the grandmother's presence that protects and defends, not the laws of a democratic nation. When Dr. Flint physically abuses Linda under her grandmother's roof, the elder woman intervenes and orders him out: "Get out of my house!," she exclaimed. "Go home, and take care of your wife and children, and you will have enough to do without watching my family" (82). The grandmother's injunction to one white male abuser echoes her granddaughter's injunction to a nation composed of many: get racism and slavery out of the desecrated house before it collapses.

The pillaged home as metaphor for the pillaged black woman's body is the ultimate expression of Harriet Jacobs's enraged critique of American democracy. In *Incidents in the Life of a Slave Girl*, Jacobs demonstrates that black women are held captive by a slave system in their own homeland, and the perversion of democratic ideals leads to a perversion of motherhood. The mother nurturing her children in the tranquility of her parlor becomes an "imprisoned mother" (118), "the poor captive in [a] dungeon" (133) who is forcefully separated from her children in her own house, literally hidden in the garret. The enslaved mother is not only deprived of her most important function; her presence is literally obliterated.

Confinement in the garret symbolically represents confinement in the nation. As both woman and mother, Linda Brent is held hostage by a culture that deprives black women of choice, dignity, and power. When Linda is consigned to Dr. Flint's son's plantation, it is significant that Ellen, her daughter, cries herself to sleep beneath the slave holder's house, and it is there that she is almost killed, because it is also the sleeping quarters of a snake. Whether in the garret or under the house, caring for white children, or fleeing from slave captors, both mother and daughter are exiled from the home's most sanctified interiors. By the end of the narrative, Linda Brent's desire to secure a home of her own remains an elusive pursuit: "The dream of my life is not yet realized," Jacobs writes, "I do not sit with my children in a home of my own. I still long for a hearthstone of my own, however humble. I wish it for my children's sake far more than my own. But God so orders circumstances as to keep me with my friend Mrs. Bruce. Love, duty, gratitude also bind me to her side" (201). As William Andrews notes, the "[t]hree times repeated, 'my own' expresses Jacobs's still-frustrated, consuming desire for the possession and control of self and circumstance that evil men in the South and, the supreme irony, a 'sacred' woman in the North had as yet prevented her from achieving."[28]

In "Rape and the Inner Lives of Black Women in the Middle West: Preliminary Thoughts on the Culture of Dissemblance," Darlene Clark Hine proposes that "rape and the threat of rape influenced the development of a culture of dissemblance among Black women." She defines dissemblance as "the behavior and attitudes of Black women that created the appearance of openness and disclosure but actually shielded the truth of their inner lives and selves from their oppressors." She goes on to posit that "[o]nly with secrecy . . . could ordinary Black women accrue the psychic space and harness the resources needed to hold their own in the often one-sided and mismatched resistance struggle."[29] In *Incidents in the Life of a Slave Girl*, Harriet Jacobs is a prime architect of the culture of dissemblance, and she assumes a variety of masks in order to "accrue the psychic space and harness the resources" she needed to write about the rape of black women under slavery, and to express the rage that experiencing and writing about rape engendered.

"[T]he constant fear of rape," Annette Niemtzow contends, was for Linda Brent, "a central experience, that which defined her sense of self, that which distinguished her plight as a female slave from that of the male."[30] In the "Fear of Insurrection" chapter, Jacobs assumes the mask of an educated and virtuous elite witness in order to present her vision of rape as both experience and metaphor. She also articulates a view of writing not unlike that of Louisa May Alcott's in "Behind a Mask." The ability to control language in written form is a tremendous source of power for women who are deprived of a familial home and a national homeland. As Jacobs suggests, however, for a woman who is enslaved, the power has even more subversive implications. Linda Brent's literacy allows her to assert superiority over illiterate, intoxicated whites who are supposed to be the "administrators of justice" (66); it also allows her to claim the upper hand in power struggles with enraged white men. When the captain demands that Linda "bring [him] all [her] letters," and asks who writes to her, she responds by informing him that white people are her correspondents and that the letters are nonexistent (65). "Some request me to burn them after they are read, and some I destroy without reading" (66). In this retort, Linda Brent goes beyond making herself the captain's equal. Because she is the one who determines what to do with her correspondence, it is she who controls her own literacy as well as that of others. If we interpret the delineation of the contest between the illiterate rabble rousers and the verbally astute Brent and her grandmother as a parody of southern white / slave relations, as William Andrews suggests, is this not yet another mask behind which Harriet Jacobs deploys her rage?[31]

Louisa May Alcott's and Harriet Jacobs's work dramatically suggests that one of the central aesthetic features of the artistry of anger is the way in which writing women, both white and black, invent masking techniques in order to critique cultural norms and practices in socially acceptable configurations. Given that masking operates as a form of protection for women and other disenfranchised groups in unequal power relationships, it is not surprising that it is central to their artistry.[32] Masking encourages risk-taking; it creates a shield against incursion and retaliation; it enables imaginative and intellectual free play; and it provides the opportunity to safeguard one's own, as well as one's community's, secrets, motives, and dignity.

By concealing self and information, the masked writer achieves power over her readers; by masking her message in subterfuge, elusion, irony, and shifting personas, she obscures the impropriety of her critique while conveying it simultaneously. Considering that in the antebellum period, gendered ideologies posited that women's innately superior sincerity assured virtuous social relations in an environment increasingly infiltrated by duplicitous male tricksters, we can see how transgressive it was for writing women to assume this role for themselves and their protagonists. As Karen Halttunen notes, "In the sentimental view, the natural sincerity of woman granted her a special responsibility for counteracting the pervasive deceit of the larger society lying outside the realm of private experience. Because she was involuntarily transparent, she served as a natural foil to the villainous confidence man, who was dangerous insofar as he contrived to be emotionally opaque."[33] Masking techniques allowed women writers, as well as the protagonists they created, to be "emotionally opaque" and sometimes even downright villainous.

Feminist scholarship has long recognized that nineteenth-century women writers engaged in duplicity, disguise, and manipulation, and that these practices shaped their literary lives and culture. "For women writers in the nineteenth century, duplicity was the one royal road to artistic triumph," Alicia Ostriker asserts in her study of American women poets. "As a consequence, the greatest women writers are usually the most profoundly and excitingly duplicitous."[34] Emily Dickinson has been singled out as an especially gifted masker who assumed a variety of disguises in both her life and her poetry.[35] Scholars who study popular white women writers also address the prevalence of women's masked ambitions, desires, and conflicts. Helen Papashvily, Ann Douglas, and Mary Kelley all discern a hidden subtext in both the literature and culture of the women writers they variously term sentimentalists and literary domestics. To Papashvily, the literary practice of sentimentality cloaks "unbearable truth[s]"; to Douglas, it is a cheap veneer that disguises women's anti-intellectual proclivities and materialist desires; to Mary Kelley, it illuminates women's anguished inability to reconcile their public and private lives.[36] From yet another perspective, Susan Harris posits that the traditional endings of women's domestic novels disguise their radical middles. Studies by Nell Painter and Carla Peterson help us see that the domestic novelists' African American peers also participated in a culture of dissemblance, and utilized masking techniques to great effect. They both discuss the sophisticated ways in which "free" black women in the urban northeast, such as Sojourner Truth, masked and manipulated their self-images in order to attain authority in the public sphere.[37]

Scholars who study other genres and cultural contexts also confirm the foundational role of masking in women's literary lives and texts. In her study of evangelical women's culture in late-eighteenth- and early-nineteenth-century America, Susan Juster concludes that because women were "[d]enied the outlet of a legitimate and respected public voice in the institutional life of the church, [their] efforts to express themselves were forced to take on a veiled, underhanded aspect that came to be described in evangelical writing as 'dissimulation.' The tendency to dissemble, to substitute appearance for reality, false impressions for true observations, was the logical outgrowth of a cultural system that removed all agency from its women members." In her work on women's historical writing, Nina Baym notes that one way white women gained agency in the nation-building project was by writing about history in a variety of forms and genres, including historical narratives, patriotic poetry, textbooks, novels, drama, biography, journalism, and travel books. In these different guises, women articulated "their party politics."[38]

Each of the writers I consider in Part II of this book enriches our understanding of the way masking relates to women's literary and life anger. All of them use a pseudonym or narrative persona to mask their gendered vulnerability as political arbiters in the literary marketplace. Lydia Maria Child publishes *Hobomok* anonymously under the consciously nationalist designation, "an American"; within the text, she uses a male narrator to tell her story. Maria W. Stewart assumes the authority to speak and write in public by wearing the mask of a patriarchal God. Fanny Fern publishes *Ruth Hall* behind the mask of her cherished pseudonym, and her autobiographical protagonist does the same. Harriet Wilson publishes her scathing critique of race relations under the provocative pseudonym "Our Nig," and within the text, her narrator speaks from behind a variety of masks—destitute mother, diffident author, domestic fictionalist, abused victim, social critic, and enraged male abolitionist.

Between the lines and behind their masks, Lydia Maria Child, Maria W. Stewart, Fanny Fern, and Harriet Wilson propose an alternative vision of America as homeland, criticize economic, gender, and race relations, and express anger about the woman writer's unequal status. Their masked political critiques are profound acts of transgression, resistance, and inventiveness in a culture that does not allow women a full range of expression.

For nineteenth-century women authors, writing behind a mask is intellectually and emotionally gratifying. Students of anger have noted that for disenfranchised people, the ability to recognize and express anger at oppressors requires self-worth and the belief that they have the right to judge the behavior of powerful others.[39] When nineteenth-century women writers confront their anger at the broken promises of democratic America and transform it into cultural critique, they value their own opinion and assert their right to make judgments about national issues. In the imaginative space of the literary text, they establish their own standards of conduct and subject their oppressors to them. The text becomes a courtroom in which oppressors are put on trial, and the writer, as both jury and judge, pronounces judgment. The reader is left to decide whether the judgment is fair and warranted.

Ultimately, this book suggests that women who confront anger in their lives and in their literature practice a kind of *political* activism that is not often recognized as such. When Harriet Lerner's formulation that "the pain of anger preserves the very integrity of self" is applied to nineteenth-century women's texts, we can see that the century-long struggle over the right to claim a voice, a home, educational opportunities, racial equality, economic security, and imaginative autonomy that these texts encode is most fundamentally a century-long struggle over the right to claim a presence in the national homeland, and the power to alter cultural practices and institutions. "[T]he pain of anger" these texts express "preserves the very integrity" of women's literary history. With this conceptual framework in place, it becomes possible to read nineteenth-century women's texts as both "signals [of] the necessity for change," and artistic documents of that effort.[40] Before we do so, however, it is imperative to consider the ideological and emotional contexts in which Lydia Maria Child, Maria W. Stewart, Fanny Fern, and Harriet Wilson express anger and imagine America.

THREE

Suppressing Treasonous Anger

Nation-Building and Gendered Ideologies of Anger in Antebellum America

It is important that children, even when babes, should never be spectators of anger, or any evil passion. They come to us from heaven, with their little souls full of innocence and peace; and, as far as possible, a mother's influence should not interfere with the influence of angels.

The first and most important thing, in order to effect this is, that the mother should keep her own spirit in tranquility and purity; for it is beyond all doubt that the state of a mother affects her child.

—Lydia Maria Child, *The Mother's Book* (1831)

Early in her career, Lydia Maria Child recognized that she had to exert a great deal of effort to disguise and control her anger. "If people knew half the extent of my vehement, and impetuous temperament," she informed her sister, "they would give me credit for governing myself as well as I do." That Child, one of the angriest women writers in the nineteenth century, denounced anger as an "evil passion" in *The Mother's Book*, the domestic manual for "American mothers" that she published in 1831, bespeaks an irony that profoundly affected antebellum women writers' personal, political, and literary lives. When women such as Child heeded the "call" to become authors, they participated in the creation of an ideology that deemed the suppression of women's anger central to middle-class identity, and it was this identity that was crucial to national self-definition.[1]

Middle-class identity was the pivot upon which postrevolutionary nation-builders defined America as a sovereign entity that was fundamentally different from, and superior to, the European power that had recently held it in subjection. To be middle-class meant to be mobile, to be unfixed in fated hierarchies; to be middle-class meant cherishing democracy and excoriating the abuses of aristocracy; to be middle-class meant that the "only acknowledged distinction" between people was "that which is denoted by superiority of mind and manners." "Superiority of mind and manners" was an egalitarian pursuit because attainment was dependent upon the cultivation of intellect and behavior, not on wealth, race, ethnicity, or family status. Anyone who governed himself or herself according to right principles was a virtuous citizen playing an important role in making the new nation the homeland of freedom.[2]

A white male-dominated republic inhabited by angerless women served important political functions. When women were the literal embodiment of self-governance in the home, the nation could retain its unruly masculine character and exult in the righteous anger that spurred its creation. When the fate of the virtuous republic depended upon women's behavior, their ability to censor angry feelings became a civic duty. This ideology not only ensured the silence of discontented groups of women; it also reserved anger and its expression for the use of those in power, creating an emotional pecking order based on gender, race, and class.

In the intensely Christian culture of the antebellum period, righteous anger was considered a Godlike power, the ultimate patriarchal prerogative. Divinely inspired leaders attempting to actualize God's prophetic plan appropriated anger for their own uses, masterfully manipulating its associations with justice, destruction, and transformation. The rhetoric of righteous anger infused revolutionary, evangelical, and abolitionist discourse; it underlay the nation's identity and sense of inspired purpose. But in an era in which women were supposedly the custodians of peace, love, and family harmony, and their "writings . . . more like the dew than the lightning," the rhetoric of righteous anger assumed a decidedly male cast.[3] In order to use righteous anger to advance their vision of the nation, and their struggle for gender and racial equality within it, women had to combat men's claim to absolute emotional power and authority.

Abolitionism was the primary arena in which this battle occurred. Implicit in Angelina Grimké's argument that women had the right to intervene in slavery debates because they were moral beings, is the notion that women also have an equal right to respond to injustice with righteous anger. "All moral beings have essentially the same rights and duties, whether they be male or female. . . . The denial of our duty to act, is a bold denial of our right to act; and if we have no right to act, then may we well be termed 'the white slaves of the North'—for, like our brethren in bonds, we must seal our lips in silence and despair." By insisting that "the women of the nominally free states" unseal their closed lips and engage in resistant action, Grimké asserts that moral responsibility transcends gender difference. Arguing that women have an equal right to determine the nation's institutions, practices, and moral character, Grimké construes women's righteous anger as a patriotic duty. "Are we aliens because we are women?" she acerbically inquires. "Are we bereft of citizenship because we are the mothers, wives and daughters of a mighty people? Have women no country—no interest staked in public weal—no liabilities in common peril—no partnership in a nation's guilt and shame?"[4]

The "oppositional discourse" that black and white antislavery women created provided an essential opening for women to articulate and express anger against gendered and racial injustice as the century progressed.[5] Yet, one of the significant dilemmas antislavery women faced was how to distinguish their expression of anger from that of the people who virulently opposed them: the clergymen who feared women's threat to their ecclesiastical and cultural power; the enraged mobs that attacked them and burned down their lecture halls; the journalists and cultural arbiters who were outraged by their intrusion into masculine terrain. Because the anger of the latter individuals and groups helped to maintain racism, slavery, and women's political silence, it served oppressive functions and advanced a flawed republic.

The anger of abolitionist women, however, resulted from justifiable moral outrage and its purpose was to rectify national corruption. Their anger was righteous; the anger of their adversaries was tyrannical. Claiming the moral high ground required three strategies: assuming an "angelic" stance in the midst of "the spirit of slavery's wrath"; writing in genteel, female-gendered styles to emphasize middle-class respectability; and figuring themselves as instruments of divine justice, human enforcers of God's righteousness. Sarah

Grimké's description of an antislavery woman's moral superiority in the midst of a "tempest of passion" perfectly illustrates abolitionist women's determination to differentiate their righteous anger from that of their opponents. "She arose amid the yells and shouts of the infuriated mob, the crash of windows and the hurling of stones. She looked to me like an angelic being descended amid the tempest of passion in all the dignity of conscious superiority." Unlike the ungoverned anger of the "infuriated mob," which wreaks havoc and defies Christian morality, the anger of "angelic beings" is sanctioned by God.[6]

The righteous anger that black and white abolitionist women shared spurred the creation of an interracial discourse in which American hypocrisy and gender injustice were relentlessly critiqued. Yet the racial anger black and white women felt for each other spurred the creation of a different kind of "oppositional discourse." Subjected to racial and gender tyranny by those who were supposed to be innately virtuous, tender, and maternal, black women directed their anger at white women who refused to acknowledge their humanity and womanhood. Cloaked in the genteel lines of a neoclassical poem, Sarah Louisa Forten's insistence that white, antislavery women regard black women as "sisters," whose shared humanity as members of God's family make them deserving of "A sister's privilege, in a sister's name," is an expression of black women's anger at white women's racist beliefs and practices. Rooted firmly in the male-gendered discourse of rage that abolitionism authorized, Harriet Jacobs's and Harriet Wilson's depictions of white mistresses as bestial perversions of womanhood are an expression of black women's enraged contempt at white women's collusion in the slave system.[7]

As Jacobs's and Wilson's texts suggest, enslaved black women harbored enormous anger at the individuals who deprived them of selfhood, family, rights, dignity, and health. Although their vulnerable position made it dangerous to express the anger directly, fear of retaliation did not prevent some black women from overtly and covertly lashing back at abusive masters and mistresses. Aware of black women's physical and expressive power, white women attempted to suppress black women's anger in the same way white men attempted to suppress their own: they used the threat and infliction of emotional and physical violence to maintain their ability to dominate. The recollection of one slave's descendant uncannily echoes in language and deed what Harriet Wilson's autobiographical protagonist, Frado, experiences when her mistress repeatedly stuffs her mouth with wood and threatens to kill her if she exposes her infamous behavior. The slave's granddaughter recalls that when her grandmother informed her mistress that it was "young marster'" who was "messin with [her] down there," the mistress threatened violent maiming if she revealed the truth publicly. "Old mistress run to her and crammed these socks in her mouth and say, 'Don't you ever tell nobody. If you do, I'll skin you alive.' "[8]

This chilling anecdote reveals how some white women were equally enraged at black women. Because racial privilege granted white women power over black women, one way some of them exerted that power was by displacing the rage they felt at men of their own race and class onto the women they perceived as threats to their social, sexual, and emotional well-being. Condemning the impertinence and violent temper of their enslaved female servants, racial privilege enabled white women to enforce emotional control over their perceived inferiors in the same way gendered ideology enforced emotional control over them. "Minerva is smart, honest, neat, & truthful, but has a violent temper & [is] often impertinent," one southern matron complained to her correspondent.[9]

Casting black women as licentious jezebels who were enticing their husbands, sons, and brothers into profligate behavior, white women found an easy target for the rage their feelings of powerlessness and injustice engendered. The "disgust" that Mary Boykin Chestnut privately expressed in her diary is a prime example of the "short-sighted fury about miscegenation" that Joan E. Cashin posits was "typical of white Southern women." "In slavery, we live surrounded by prostitutes. . . . God forgive us, but ours is a monstrous system, a wrong and an iniquity. Like the patriarchs of old, our men live in one house with their concubines; and the mulattoes one sees in every family partly resemble the white children. Any lady is ready to tell you who is the father of all the mulatto children in everybody's household but her own. . . . My disgust sometimes is boiling over."[10]

White women's "disgust" frequently "boiled over" into emotional and physical violence against the black women who served them. The testimony of ex-slave women is full of accounts of white women's brutality. In Harriet Jacobs's *Incidents*, for example, there is no gendered distinction between the abusive behavior of the aptly named master and mistress, Mr. and Mrs. Flint. When Linda Brent's mistress was "in her angry moods, no terms were too vile for her to bestow upon me," Jacobs writes (32). Enraged by jealousy, dishonor, and betrayal, Mrs. Flint stalks Linda while she is sleeping, "bending over [her]," testing to see how she responds to sexually suggestive whisperings (32). As Deborah Garfield notes, this behavior replicates Mr. Flint's attempts at rape.[11]

Displaced anger at black women also motivated the "fiendish" behavior of the white woman who ordered the flogging of three black women who bore white men's children, two of whom were her own husband's offspring. Relating the details of this all too common "disgusting stor[y]" in a letter to a friend, Fanny Kemble writes:

> It was not a month since any of them had been delivered, when Mrs. King came to the hospital, had them all three severely flogged, a process which she personally superintended, and then sent them to Five Pound—the swamp Botany Bay of the plantation . . . —with farther orders to the drivers to flog them every day for a week.
>
> Now, E, if I make you sick with these disgusting stories, I can not help it; they are the life itself here. Hitherto I have thought these details intolerable enough, but this apparition of a female fiend in the middle of this hell I confess adds an element of cruelty which seems to me to surpass all the rest. Jealousy is not an uncommon quality in the feminine temperament; and just conceive the fate of these unfortunate women between the passions of their masters and mistresses, each alike armed with power to oppress and torture them.[12]

In addition to racial privilege, a woman's middle-class status also permitted her to feel anger at the inferiors she believed were supposed to serve her without question or complaint. Writing to her sister, one southern matron bitterly complained about "the trouble . . . in housekeeping." Because "the servants have the highest finish of any that the Devil has imported lately," her temper has been "a good deal tryed." Another harried southern wife expresses the same sentiments. Writing in her journal, she rails against "the trial of having servants" whose behavior does not conform to her expectations.

> Sometimes when I think that I shall probably be subject to the trial of having servants about me as long as I live, I feel a kind of desperation that is difficult to overcome & I am ready to cry with the poet, 'O for a lodge in some vast wilderness.' It is *impossible* to inspire them with any gratitude— although I have been extremely kind to both Mary & her baby—a kindness to which I am sure she has never been accustomed for she bore a dreadful character. She manifests no interest either in me, or the children, & tries my patience sorely.[13]

Once again, white women displace their anger at the constraints of their gender-prescribed lives, full of domestic drudgery and selfless caretaking, onto those over whom they have power. The diarist whose patience is sorely tried by her disinterested, ungrateful servants is also the wife who resents her husband's lack of appreciation and respect for her plight. "I do not wish to *complain* of any hardship or trial, but I so long for a *little sympathy* sometimes.

My poor husband has so many demands on his time & patience in the performance of his responsibilities as man of all work, that I try to say as little as possible about my own trials of nerve & strength." At the same time that the sufferer valiantly attempts to suppress her discontent, she also recognizes that "[i]t is *impossible* for [her] to accomplish all that is necessary to be done without such weariness & suffering as at times to make life almost a burden." Taught that she should be patient, gentle, and humble "under the trials & vexations to which [she has] been subjected," she condemns herself for not "bearing [her] cross as [she] should."

> O! if I could only feel that I was becoming more patient, more gentle & humble under the trials & vexations to which I have been subjected, it would go far towards reconciling me with the lot assigned by me to Providence. Often, when thoroughly worn out by the incessant strain of mind & body to keep things in order the injustice of things expected of me, or charges brought against me, of neglect & indifference. I give way to impatience & this hasty retort which shows that I am not *bearing* my cross as I should.[14]

Projecting her rage onto servants helps her to bear the cross of the gendered "lot" she has been assigned by providence.

Paradoxically, however, at the same time that the privileges of race and class afforded white women the opportunity to displace their anger onto less powerful others, race and class status also limited their access to the emotion itself. In the antebellum period, the suppression of women's anger was essential to the white, middle-class, nation-building project. If America's future citizens were to be properly socialized, anger had to be driven from the mother's heart. "It is important that children, even when babes, should never be spectators of anger, or any evil passion," Lydia Maria Child instructs women "on whose intelligence and discretion the safety and prosperity of our republic so much depend." Children "come to us from heaven, with their little souls full of innocence and peace; and, as far as possible, a mother's influence should not interfere with the influence of angels." It is especially incumbent on mothers to "keep [their] own spirit in tranquillity and purity; for it is beyond all doubt that the state of a mother affects her child."[15]

Child's linkage of a mother's psychic state to the "safety and prosperity" of the republic indicates how seemingly private, domestic affairs reverberate with public meanings in the first decades of the nineteenth century. Because Child is writing when women's domestic roles assumed a new political emphasis, she believes a woman's personal "state" is integrally related to the condition of the republican state. Such ideas, Linda Kerber explains, are first formulated in the aftermath of the Revolution when women's political role in the new republic becomes the subject of public discourse.

> Long before the famous New York Women's Rights convention in 1848, American women had begun to explore the implications of the republican revolution for their lives. Searching for a political context in which private female virtues might comfortably coexist with the civic virtue that was widely regarded as the cement of the Republic, they found what they were seeking in the notion of what might be called "Republican Motherhood." The Republican Mother integrated political values into her domestic life. Dedicated as she was to the nurture of public-spirited male citizens, she guaranteed the steady infusion of virtue into the Republic.[16]

Eliminating women's anger in the household made that "steady infusion" possible. As the repository of virtue and its primary channel, a republican mother was required to model appropriate behavior at all times. "The first rule, and the most important of all," according to Child, "is, that a mother govern her own feelings, and keep her heart and conscience pure" (4).[17]

Because women were considered the custodians of civic virtue and Christian values, it was their behavior that would ultimately determine the fate of the republican experiment. This idea was embraced by nation-building whites as well as "free blacks," even though the two groups interpreted the meaning of the experiment differently. Gendered ideologies proclaiming women's innately greater virtue and morality permeated racial boundaries. "Woman was created to be the 'helpmeet,' and not the idol nor slave of man," a columnist in the *Colored American* pronounced, "and in everything truly virtuous and noble, she is furnished by our bountiful Creator, with all the intellectual, moral, and physical requisites for her important place." As mothers, wives, sisters, and daughters, women had a crucial role to play "in the perfecting of human character and the elevation of human customs and usages." Their participation was urgently needed: "If ever *any class of any community, in any age or country*, was called upon to act definitively . . . colored females are called upon to do so." By practicing womanly "virtues," colored females had the capacity to "influence, mightily, . . . future posterity."[18]

Lydia Maria Child's contemporary, Catherine Beecher, best expressed the way in which antebellum Americans infused gendered ideas with nationalist meanings in her influential *Treatise on Domestic Economy for the Use of Young Ladies at Home and at School* (1841).

> The success of democratic institutions, as is conceded by all, depends upon the intellectual and moral character of the mass of the people. If

they are intelligent and virtuous, democracy is a blessing; but if they are ignorant and wicked, it is only a curse, and as much more dreadful than any other form of civil government, as a thousand tyrants are more to be dreaded than one. It is equally conceded, that the formation of the moral and intellectual character of the young is committed mainly to the female hand. The mother writes the character of the future man; the sister bends the fibers that hereafter are the forest tree; the wife sways the heart, whose energies may turn for good or for evil the destinies of a nation.[19]

Because women were entrusted with "the exalted privilege of extending over the world [the] blessed influences" of their superior characters, whether they suppressed their anger had decidedly political consequences. When the success of the American Republic depended upon women's "gentleness, patience, and love," for them to indulge in an "evil passion" like anger was to commit treason.[20]

In *The Mother's Book*, Lydia Maria Child affirms and reshapes prevailing male ideologies of anger. Her contention, for example, that children become angry only when they are taught to feel and experience the emotion echoes a view propounded by the Roman stoic philosopher, Seneca: "[W]e ought to take pains neither to develop in [children] anger nor to blunt their native spirit."[21] Child, however, adds a gendered element to this perspective by making anger management the sole responsibility of mothers. Yet her assertion that anger in the household was destructive to republicanism is typical of her generation.

Nation-building antebellum Americans feared anger because they believed it could potentially interfere with rational self-governance. If not carefully controlled, its impetuous indulgence was equivalent to aristocratic excess, and it was "the aristocratic principle" that was "send[ing] its poison from under a mask[,]" preventing republicanism from flourishing. Equally troubling was anger's capacity to impose partisan claims. "[E]ach one must act in freedom, according to his own perceptions of right and wrong, advisable or unadvisable—being, first of all things, careful that he is not guided by selfishness," Lydia Maria Child proclaimed in a letter to a friend three years after publishing *The Mother's Book*.[22]

The selfishness of ungoverned anger imperiled the republican ideal of collective responsibility; it also had the ability to create chaos in both the private and public homeland. To guard against its evils, antebellum Americans launched "a campaign against anger in the Victorian family," Carol Zisowitz Stearns and Peter N. Stearns note in their comprehensive study, *Anger: The Struggle for Emotional Control in America's History*. This phenomenon, they believe, is a result of the new ideology of domesticity that glorified the family as a sacred refuge from the industrial marketplace.[23] What Stearns and Stearns do not consider, however, is how this phenomenon draws from western classical sources and is related to the white, middle-class nation-building project.

Antebellum Americans understood the meaning of anger from two distinct mediums: the Bible and classical Greek and Roman philosophy. While these sources provide different answers to the question of whether anger is morally justified, and if so, under what circumstances, one idea resonates through them all. Human anger is a tremendously powerful, complex "passion" that is capable of causing pain, havoc, and destruction. Only when *men* control it through the exercise of reason, can anger enforce and protect the sanctity of God's moral laws and uphold a just social community.

This fundamental concept is conveyed in the Old Testament as well as in Aristotle's and St. Thomas Aquinas's philosophical treatises. In the Old Testament, for example, after hearing the "great cry of the people and of their wives against their brethren" who were selling their children "into bondage" for profit, Nehemiah becomes "very angry." Yet, before "rebuk[ing] the nobles, and the rulers," he "consulted with [himself]." Guided by reason, Nehemiah's anger achieves the restoration of moral order. "Restore, I pray you, to them, even this day, their lands, their vineyards, their oliveyards, and their houses, also the hundreth *part* of the money, and of the corn, the wine, and the oil, that ye exact of them. Then, said they, We will restore *them*, and will require nothing of them; so will we do as thou sayest."[24]

The reasonable exercise of anger is also central to Aristotle. Anger, Aristotle posits, is the "desire, accompanied by pain, for revenge for an obvious belittlement of oneself or of one's dependents, the belittlement being uncalled for." The desire for revenge, however, must be moderated by a reasonable "mean." "With regard to anger . . . there is an excess, a deficiency, and a mean. . . . [L]et us call the mean good temper; of the persons at the extremes let the one who exceeds be called irascible, and his vice irascibility, and the man who falls short an unirascible sort of person, and the deficiency unirascibility." The Aristotelian St. Thomas Aquinas reiterates this view. If avenging an injury is guided by reason, it is a "praiseworthy" endeavor. But when the avenging is "against the order of reason," it is "vicious" and unethical. Punishment must be administered to one who deserves it, meted out in accordance with the crime and "the legitimate process of law," for the purpose of correcting fault and maintaining justice.[25]

In the antebellum period, Americans' obsession with self-governance, combined with their rigidly fixed notions of gender difference, resulted in the creation of a distinctly new *gendered* ideology of anger, which aided the white, middle-class nation-building project. By gendering the positive aspects of anger as male and making the management of its negative capacities a female responsibility, Lydia Maria Child and her contemporaries devised a way to preserve the positive meanings of anger articulated by Aristotle and St. Thomas Aquinas, and implied in various ways in the Bible, while concurrently condemning its evils. Policed by women in the home, anger that threatened the nation-building project was at best eradicated, at second best, bounded and controlled. Articulated by men in sermons, speeches, and political treatises, as well as in Congress and in the marketplace, anger that assisted nation-building was expressed with Biblical and philosophical sanction.

An ideology of anger premised on gendered separation advanced progressive and oppressive causes simultaneously. On the one hand, the positive male-gendered associations of anger and justice enabled abolitionists, women, laborers, and moral reformers to use God's and their own anger to agitate for social change. On the other hand, however, the gendered separation created a mask behind which the anger of powerful white men and their female collaborators promoted capitalism, imposed religious and cultural hegemony, and spearheaded imperialistic maneuvers in the service of the white, middle-class nation-building project.

The gendered ideology of anger also sustained and intensified white men's emotional privilege. As Carol Zisowitz Stearns and Peter N. Stearns note, although writers of domestic manuals believed that anger was dangerous and disruptive and should be assiduously avoided, they acknowledged that white men were capable of feeling anger, especially in the competitive workplace. At the same time that popular literature decried any sign of anger in white women, it also dispensed advice about how white men should channel their anger into useful action. As industrialization advanced, Stearns and Stearns posit, "Victorian culture developed a new ambiguity where anger was concerned. The basic message was simple, though its ramifications were potentially complex: anger was a bad emotion at home, but it was a vital emotion in the world of work and politics. Women should remain anger free, in keeping with their domestic roles, but men were set the challenging task of curbing the anger within the family while utilizing its potential to spur actions necessary to competition or social justice."[26]

It is yet another nineteenth-century irony, however, that at the same time the gendered ideology of anger maintained white patriarchal power, it could also be advantageous to women because it provided class privilege. Adhering to the emotional laws that the gendered ideology of anger codified was an important determinant of middle-class status, especially when that status was imperiled by the sudden loss of a father's, brother's, or husband's income and property. "Keep perfect control of your disposition," a white southern mother advised her marriageable-aged daughter after the death of her property-holding husband left her without financial resources. "[N]ever suffer yourself to become so fretted as to speak without thinking and weighing every word, and you will be very apt not to act imprudently."[27]

Enacting the tenets of middle-class propriety that the gendered ideology of anger required assured female practitioners tangible rewards. "Keeping perfect control of their disposition" guaranteed women respect, leisure, educational opportunities, and sometimes reliance on "hired" hands and servants to keep them from the most arduous drudgery of household and agricultural labor. "Keeping perfect control" also meant that they could feel emotionally, socially, and culturally superior to those who did not. Charlotte Forten Grimké's description of an omnibus "crowded to suffocation with odorous Irish and their screaming babies" reveals a decided distaste for a group of people she perceives as lacking civility, self-control, and cleanliness. The teenaged Susan Warner's reaction to the behavior of "the girls who come to help [her aunt] in harvest time" is yet another example. "One thing annoys me much," she recorded in her journal. "The girls who come to help her in harvest time will call Aunt Fanny by her Christian name, and will come into the front room and sit down as if they were equals. This worries me and makes me angry, though Aunty says it is foolish."[28]

In the latter instance, the privileged white daughter, descendant of "Mayflower" settlers and child of a wealthy lawyer, feels entitled to anger because it is directed at those who she believes are socially inferior. It is significant, however, that her disgruntled feelings, like those of Charlotte Forten Grimké's, are acknowledged in intimate private spaces—written in a journal and confided in conversation. A few years later, when the Warner family's "affairs were on a steady progress down hill," Susan's "annoyance, worry, and anger" about class impropriety intensified; only this time the impropriety was the result of her father's catastrophic financial reverses (176). The young woman who was used to "waiter and coachman and cook," "dainty silks and laces," and "new bonnets with every turn of the season," was forced to rely on "the skill of [her] own hands," "calicoes fashioned by [her] own fingers," and "what headgear [she] could get" after her father lost his fortune (176). In the imaginative universe of her best-selling novel, *The Wide, Wide World*, Warner transforms her rage at the loss of class status into an ethic of heroic self-renunciation and religious piety, thereby adhering to a middle-class code of emotional restraint. Conforming to this code was the mask behind which she railed against her expulsion from the world of leisure, power, and privilege that her former class status had conferred.[29]

As the previous examples demonstrate, the gendered ideology of anger reinforced race and class stratification. White men and women who were, or aspired to be, middle-class defined their emotional behavior in contrast to that of the people they believed were uncivilized or undemocratic—"free" blacks and slaves, Indian "savages," and the "influx of untutored foreigners,"[30] especially the Irish "with all their Celtic infirmities . . . their half savage ways—[and] their blunders."[31] They maintained that unlike working-class people, people of color, and "untutored foreigners," they adhered to standards of propriety and restraint that ennobled their character and made them fit for leadership.

The claim to moral and emotional superiority provided a way for whites and elite blacks to forge a middle-class identity; it also allowed whites to displace the emotions they were prohibited from expressing onto the people they excluded.[32] Ample evidence of this phenomenon exists in the fiction of white, middle-class women. When an "untutored" lower-class character, or a character of color, articulates the anger a genteel, white protagonist is prohibited from uttering, it is evident that the author is using her "othered" character as a safe ventriloquist.[33] White, middle-class women writers use such characters to vocalize their angered discontent without jeopardizing the privileges of their own class status.

To "free" African Americans involved in their own nation-building enterprises, adhering to the conventions of propriety and emotional restraint that were fundamental to the gendered ideology of anger was more than a determinant of middle-class status; it signified freedom. In a racialized context in which black women were associated with illicit sexuality, and black men were deprived of their manly function as protectors and providers, self-governance meant that black men and women could actively resist slavery's legacy of emasculation and rape. Exhibiting "good moral character" enabled members of the "free" black community to demonstrate that they were upstanding citizens who in no way resembled debased racist stereotypes. Behaving in accordance with middle-class precepts bolstered self-respect and procured community status. Membership in many African American women's benevolent associations was contingent upon the public exercise of strict moral standards. As Anne M. Boylan notes, although these groups took "a less hierarchical approach to benevolence than white women's organizations, . . . class standing [was] a precondition for joining." In order to achieve "class standing," a woman had to uphold chastity and virtue by not engaging in "immoral conduct," which included illicit sexual behavior and public displays of inebriation.[34]

Like whites, cultural arbiters in the "free" black community construed women's emotional behavior as a key marker of middle-class status. The pronouncements of Samuel Cornish, a Presbyterian minister and editor of the black newspaper *Freedom's Journal*, regarding the gendered significance of anger control, resemble those found in Lydia Maria Child's *The Mother's Book*, and other conduct books written by white, middle-class authors addressing white, middle-class readers. There is one major difference however. Whereas the white writers exhort that women should not *feel* anger, let alone express it, Cornish acknowledges that women do, indeed, experience the emotion.

> It is particularly necessary for girls to acquire command of their temper. . . . A man, in a furious passion, is terrible to his enemies; but a woman, in a passion, is disgusting to her friends; she loses all that respect due to her sex; she has not masculine strength and courage to enforce any other kind of respect. . . . The happiness and influence of women, both as wives and mothers, and indeed, in every relation so much depends on the temper, that it ought to be most carefully cultivated.[35]

Cornish's unstated implication is that under the right circumstances, carefully controlled anger expressed in an appropriate manner is acceptable. It is the anger that threatens respectability, self-control, and masculine hegemony that is at issue.

The challenge black women faced was how "to acquire command of their temper" and still be paragons of virtue and respectability when they encountered gender and racial injustice. "[Miss Church] wishes me to cultivate a Christian spirit in thinking of my enemies; I know it is right, and will endeavor to do so, but it does seem very difficult," the seventeen-year-old Charlotte Forten Grimké confided to her diary. In another entry she fretted, "how can I hope to be worthy of [God's] love while I still cherish the feeling towards my enemies, this unforgiving spirit? This is a question which I ask myself often. Other things in comparison with this seem easy to overcome. But hatred of oppression seems to me so blended with hatred of the oppressor I cannot separate them."[36]

According to a letter published in the *Liberator*, some women had more success forgiving the oppressor than did Charlotte Forten Grimké. The letter-writer, Zillah, tells the story of an enslaved woman who, after gaining her freedom, goes back to help her former mistress when she is in need.

Although the former mistress had "forgot her gentle nature" when she beat the enslaved woman for caring for her child instead of performing her domestic duties, Zillah relates how "woman-like, weeping that a lady should be so reduced, [the ex-slave woman] obeyed the call." In these two instances, "cultivating a Christian spirit" means the same thing the harried southern matron believed it did. Women must assiduously repress the anger that results from feelings of frustration and injustice, and in its stead practice the Christian art of forbearance, which necessitates patient acceptance of vexation and spirit-breaking trials.[37]

Since "ladies" were supposed to be more gentle, patient, and forgiving, forbearance was a specifically gendered virtue that took on even more meaning in the context of racial struggle. Responding to one's "enemies" with forgiveness was fundamental to the ethic, a rule that women, more than men, were expected to obey. When antislavery activist and author Sarah L. Forten, Charlotte Forten Grimké's aunt, informs Angelina Grimké that even some of "our professed friends . . . have not yet rid themselves" of "prejudice . . . toward the descendants of Africa," she valiantly attempts to practice Christian forbearance.

> I recollect the words of one of the best and least prejudiced men in the Abolition ranks. Ah said he, 'I can recall the time when in walking with a Colored brother, the darker the night, the better Abolitionist was I.' He does not say so now, but my friend, how much of this leaven still lingers in the hearts of our white brethren and sisters is oftentimes made manifest to us—but when we recollect what great sacrifices to public sentiment they are called upon to make, we cannot wholly blame them.[38]

Forten's letter reveals how an ethic of selfless renunciation protects a "free" black woman's psychic sanctity at the same time that it censors her emotional freedom. The effect of white people's prejudice has "often embittered [her] feelings," Forten writes, because black people are "innocent victims" who are excluded and despised based on "the color of the skin, as much as from the degradation of Slavery." "I must also own," she asserts, "that *it* has often engendered feelings of discontent and mortification in my breast when I saw that many were preferred before me, who by education-birth-or worldly circumstances were no better than myself—thier [*sic*] sole claim to notice depending on the superior advantage of being *White*—but I am striving to live above such heart burnings and will learn to 'bear and forbear' believing that a spirit of forbearance under such evils is all that we as a people can well exert." Enacting the Christian art of forbearance is the ultimate manifestation of black people's self-control. It requires repressing the anger that causes the "heart burnings" and transforming it into forgiveness, thereby assuring one's moral and emotional superiority over the oppressors.[39]

To "free" African Americans who believed it was their duty to work tirelessly to end slavery and uplift the race, selflessness was an especially significant virtue. Charlotte Forten Grimké's tortured attempt to actualize this ethic is a repeated refrain throughout her journal entries. "I have been examining myself tonight,—trying to fathom my own thoughts and feelings; and I find, alas! Too much, too much of *selfishness!*" Upon reading a book about "a poor peasant girl," Grimké enthusiastically praises the heroine because she possessed the "heroic, self-sacrificing spirit" that she yearned to acquire.

> Studied Latin this evening and again looked over "Madeline" by Julia Kavanagh, a tale founded on fact. The character of the heroine, a poor peasant girl of Auvergus, is *very* noble. Her pure, heroic, self-sacrificing spirit affected me much. Strengthened my own aspirations for something high and holy.—My earnest longings to do *something* for the good of others. I know that I am very selfish. Always the thought of *self-culture* presents itself *first*. With that, I think I can accomplish something more noble, more enduring, I will try not to forget that, while striving to improve myself, I may at least *commence* to work for others.[40]

In the "free" black community, "do[ing] something for the good of others" assumed specifically gendered meanings. To best serve the race, black women had to refine their minds and manners and be model citizens, not only within their own communities, but in the white world as well. A model citizen, especially a female model citizen, sacrificed her own desires for the good of the community. She also governed her anger with military precision, hiding it behind a mask of Christian forbearance. Sarah L. Forten's remarks about racist humiliation are a poignant example of how one middle-class black woman heroically attempted to repress her anger in order to serve the needs of the larger antislavery and antiracist struggle.

In her letter to Angelina Grimké, Sarah L. Forten's comments are so painfully measured and controlled, that the conflict between expression and repression is palpable. Her impulse to express anger collides with her desire to maintain decorum and preserve her privacy. Although she discloses having "embittered feelings" and "feelings of discontent," as soon as she gets close to examining those feelings, or elaborating on their cause, she stops herself and retreats into the rhetoric of forbearance. Forten's withdrawal may be as much self-protection as it is a response to gendered injunctions about self-control.

Nevertheless, one implication is irrefutable. Her shift to a rhetoric of forbearance at the very moment that she begins to focus on her rage, indicates that she is withholding and masking volatile emotions, perhaps even from herself.

For elite black women such as the Grimkés, activism in the antiracist and antislavery freedom struggle, in conjunction with class status, both enabled and circumscribed their access to angered expression. On the one hand, "when [they] beheld the oppressor lurking on the border of [their] own peaceful home[s]," feeling and expressing righteous indignation was appropriate. Throughout Charlotte Forten Grimké's diary, for example, there are numerous exclamations of rage against American hypocrisy, expressed in the militant tones of male-gendered abolitionist rhetoric. "Went out with Aunt M.[argaretta] and visited Miss J.[ames] and Mrs. C.[hew,] also went to Independence Hall. The old bell with its famous inscription, the mottoes, the relics, the pictures of the heroes of the Revolution—the *Saviours* of their country—what a mockery they all seemed, *here* where there breathes not a free man, black or white." Condemning the mockery of American democracy was permissible, even encouraged. Yet, on the other hand, because gendered notions of middle-class respectability, which counteracted racist stereotypes, required that elite black women conduct themselves with Christlike forbearance, they subsumed anger at their own experiences of racial and gender injustice into the collective anger of the race.[41]

This phenomenon is strikingly apparent in Charlotte Forten Grimké's journals. "I know not why it is that when I think and feel the most, I say the least. I suppose it is in my nature, not to express by word or action [how] much I really feel," the relentlessly self-reflective diarist writes in one entry.[42] What the journals make clear is that Grimké thought and felt the most, and said the least, about two equally painful topics: her excruciatingly humiliating experiences of racism, and the frustration she endured attempting to enact middle-class codes of gendered selflessness when, in reality, she harbored an intense desire to nurture, unfettered, her intellect and ambitions.

An entry that describes an episode of public humiliation is emblematic of the first of Grimké's two articulate silences, both of which result from her repression of explosive anger.

I have suffered much today,—my friends Mrs. P. and her daughters were refused admission to the Museum, after having tickets given them, solely on account of their complexion. Insulting language was used to them.— Of course they felt and exhibited deep, bitter indignation; but of what avail was it? none, but to excite the ridicule of those contemptible creatures, miserable doughfaces who do not deserve the name of men. I will not attempt to write more.—No words can express my feelings, but these cruel wrongs cannot be much longer endured. A day of retribution must come. God grant that it may come very soon![43]

More often than not, when Grimké relates racist episodes in which she identifies with the sufferer, or is the sufferer herself, rage paralyzes expression and she pleads for God's intervention. On the other hand, when she records anger at national hypocrisy, rage liberates effusive indignation. On one fourth of July, for example, she writes, "The celebration this day! What a mockery it is! My soul sickens of it. Am glad to see that the people are much less demonstrative in their mock patriotism than of old." Like her aunt, Grimké subsumes anger at her own racist humiliation and the denial of class privileges into the collective anger of the black community.[44]

The second articulate silence in Grimké's journals results from rage at gender confinement. Raised in a prestigious and public-spirited community of intellectuals and abolitionists, Grimké yearns to be the epitome of a self-sacrificing heroic moral agent. Over and over again throughout the dairy she condemns her "selfish" impulses and ennobles selfless duty. "I will pray that God in his goodness will make me noble enough to find my highest happiness in doing my duty." At the same time, however, the young woman with the "restless nature . . . constantly crav[ing] excitement, action," who is "seized with the very spirit of adventure," and who harbors a desire for public recognition, is enraged by the constraints that respectable middle-class womanhood in the "free" black community impose on her. "Constantly I ask myself Cowley's question 'what shall I do to be forever known?' This is ambition, I know. It is selfish, it is wrong. But, oh! How very hard it is to do and feel what is right." Grimké's repeated laments of "how hard it is to do and feel what is right" are the mask behind which she hides her rage at being forced to deny her own desires.[45]

Nowhere is Grimké's "selfish" longing more poignantly illustrated than in an entry in which she exults in the "elevated position" that assuming a male-gendered stance makes possible.

Have been very busy to-day.—On my return from school did some sewing, and made some gingerbread.—Afterwards adopted "Bloomer" costume and ascended the highest cherry tree, which being the first feat of the kind ever performed by me, I deem worthy of note.—Obtained some fine fruit, and felt for the first time "monarch of all I surveyed," and then descended from my elevated position. In the evening spent some time very delightfully with Miss Shepard looking over her beautiful books and many elegant curiosities.[46]

This evocative passage records Grimké making an imaginative shift from female-gendered stultification to male-gendered freedom. Before she changes clothes and climbs a tree, she "did some sewing and made some gingerbread." Sewing and baking are female chores performed in domestic enclosures that take women away from intellectual pursuits. As Grimké noted in an entry just a few weeks before, "I must confess I am beginning to be heartily tired" of sewing. "I think it would be different if I had some one to read to me while I sew." Like countless other women of her era, Grimké resents spending time performing repetitive, nonintellectual domestic drudgery instead of cultivating her mind. "The best women, the brightest women, the noblest women, are the very ones to whom house-keeping is the most irksome," Gail Hamilton declared in the postwar years. "A noble discontent, not a peevish complaining, but a universal and spontaneous protest, is a woman's safeguard against the deterioration which such a life threatens, and her proof of capacity, and her note of preparation for a higher."[47]

The most dramatic rendering of this "noble discontent" is an entry the sixty-two-year-old Lydia Maria Child made in her diary in which she painstakingly records her domestic and intellectual activities during the Civil War. In addition to writing over two hundred letters and six articles, correcting page proofs, and reading "to [herself] 7 volumes" and "6 pamphlets and 21 volumes" aloud, she "made 25 needlebooks for Freedwomen," knit socks, suspenders, baby shirts, and an "affghan [along with] the fringe," mended draws and stockings, made a spectacle case, door mat, woolen cape, corsets, and shirts, cooked over six hundred dinners, and "Swept and dusted sitting-room & kitchen 350 times." The majority of the housekeeping items are for the comfort and use of others—injured soldiers in the hospital, freedwomen, friends, and her husband. "Cut and made 1 Sac for myself" stands out in bold relief. The meticulous rendering of each activity, including the number of times each task was performed, is an articulate expression of Child's resentment. Moreover, as Gerda Lerner observes, "the way in which [the list] is constructed—intellectual activities above, domestic activities below, and the dramatic discrepancy in the quality of the two sets of activities—makes its own comment."[48]

The "comment" Child's journal entry makes is one Charlotte Forten Grimké understood in spirit, if not in actuality. In the journal entry cited above, domesticity and self-attainment are diametrically opposed. When she leaves sewing, baking, house, and constricting female clothing, she enters a masculine world of adventure, power, and self-fulfillment. Once there, she excels in physical feats of bravado that engender self-esteem; she secures the "fine fruit" of power which makes her feel like a "monarch of all [she] surveyed." That evening, she spends "some time very delightfully" "looking over [her friend's] beautiful books and many elegant curiosities." More than anything else, the entry captures Grimké secretly reveling in the forbidden pleasure of self-indulgence.

The tension between Grimké's desire to enact the ideals of respectable, middle-class womanhood and her equally pressing desire to "explor[e] dangerous places" and feel "a wild intoxicating delight," coupled with her rage at racial exclusion and injustice, explain her incessant self-condemnation and belittlement of her writing. She characterizes herself as "without the gifts of Nature, wit, beauty and talent; without the accomplishments which nearly every one of my age, whom I know, possesses" and pronounces that she is "not even *intelligent*" and blames herself for her failings. "[I]t is entirely owing to [her] own want of energy, perseverance and application" that she has not improved her abilities. In addition to excoriating herself for character flaws, she continually denigrates her writing. Because she believes her work is unworthy of publication, she is astonished when respectable journals accept it. These judgments contrast starkly to the entry in which she applauds her ability to "[ascend] the highest cherry tree." While the ascent is a metaphorical rendering of Grimké's entrance into the male-gendered terrain of adventure, power, and self-esteem, the self-deprecation is a metaphorical rendering of her confinement in a racist country in which gendered codes of middle-class respectability afford her dignity, at the same time that they effect her descent from a white, male world of pleasure and power.[49]

For women like Charlotte Forten Grimké, the abolitionist movement provided the single most important challenge to oppressive gendered ideologies of anger. Within the movement, however, notions of gender difference, coupled with strict standards of middle-class propriety, impacted on the ways in which its most vocal participants made meaning of, and expressed, anger. Publicly, a woman such as Sojourner Truth used acerbic wit and humor because she constructed herself as an "exotic primitive" who was not bound by middle-class rules. Sister activist and lecturer Frances Ellen Watkins Harper worked within middle-class boundaries, alternating between the genteel rhetoric of middle-class cultural codes and the thunderous tones of male-gendered abolitionist rhetoric. Harriet Jacobs did the same. She presents a fusion of both discourses in her portrait of Aunt Martha, Linda Brent's beloved grandmother, as well as in Linda Brent's narrative persona. Aunt Martha espouses middle-class codes of propriety at the same time that she uses her "unruly tongue" and deceptive wiles to protect her family's and her community's rights and dignity. Linda Brent employs male-gendered abolitionist rhetoric when she speaks fiercely against racial injustice, but retreats into genteel subterfuge when she presents herself as an agent of her own sexual transgression.[50]

When black women, such as Harriet Jacobs, added to abolitionist discourse the specific concerns of women under slavery, they introduced the figure of the "outraged mother" to American culture. Unlike the heroic male slave who single-handedly struggles to achieve literacy and freedom, the heroic female slave, Joanne Braxton theorizes, is an "outraged mother [who] travels alone through the darkness to impart a sense of identity and 'belongingness' to her child. She sacrifices and improvises to create the vehicles necessary for the survival of flesh and spirit. Implied in all her actions and fueling her heroic ones is abuse of her people and her person."[51]

By inflecting abolitionist discourse with a female-gendered perspective, antislavery female activists made women's indignation at gender and racial injustice a respectable part of that discourse. It is this phenomenon that Harriet Beecher Stowe fruitfully exploits in *Uncle Tom's Cabin*. The narrator, as well as the characters, Mrs. Bird and Cassy, express the moral indignation that interracial, woman-centered abolitionist discourse made possible. This expression, however, is always in tension with gendered codes of middle-class respectability. Although women succeed in claiming righteous anger as a female right by the outbreak of the Civil War, in the public imagination, and even in the consciousness of some activist women, it remained a "manly" right and a masculine expressive mode.

For antebellum Americans, middle-class identity and nation-building were inextricably linked. In order to distinguish their political and cultural traditions from those of Europeans, postcolonial Americans created a mythology that celebrated independence, democracy, and rational self-governance. The new gendered ideology of anger that emerged in the period was an essential component of that mythology. Righteous anger was associated with men and reason; tyrannical anger was associated with women and irrationality. Male-gendered anger preserved the republic; female-gendered anger imperiled it.

This ideology created a complex set of contradictory forces, all of which ironically aided a variety of nation-building projects. At the same time that the gendered ideology of anger sustained patriarchal power, it also afforded women who practiced its tenets cultural influence and class status. At the same time that the gendered ideology of anger created an emotional pecking order based on gender, race, and class, it enabled differentially disenfranchised groups of people such as white women and African American men and women the opportunity to utilize righteous anger to agitate for gender and racial justice.

Equally significant, the gendered ideology of anger reinforced the notion of immutable gender difference, which in turn facilitated nation-building impulses. While men used righteous anger to preserve the country's unique characteristics and restore its moral integrity, women protected their families, their communities, and the new republic from anger's destructive evils. In order to perform this patriotic duty, however, women had to forfeit their psychic freedom: white women were supposed to eliminate anger from their emotional lives; black women were supposed to forgive their oppressors and submerge their personal anger into the collective anger of the race. These expectations exacted an emotional toll on white and black women, and greatly affected their literary imaginings.

Prescriptions against the expression of anger made it difficult, if not impossible, for many white women to acknowledge that their feelings of disappointment were in actuality their feelings of anger. Instructed that domesticity was their highest calling, their sole reason for being, more often than not, revolutionary white daughters were disappointed when they encountered its constrictions. "In education, in marriage, in religion, in everything, disappointment is the lot of woman," Lucy Stone, one such daughter, declared. "From the first years to which my memory stretches, I have been a disappointed woman. When, with my brothers, I reached forth after the sources of knowledge, I was reproved with 'It isn't fit for you; it doesn't belong to women.' . . . I was disappointed when I came to seek a profession worthy an immortal being—every employment was closed to me, except those of the teacher, the seamstress, and the housekeeper."[52]

Segregated in the most menial, backbreaking domestic professions, "free" black women were also "disappointed" by the lack of professional opportunities that were available. "How long shall the fair daughters of Africa be compelled to bury their minds and talents beneath a load of iron pots and kettles?" Maria Stewart demanded. Excluded from the category of womanhood, black women were also "disappointed" by their "fairer sisters" who dehumanized them and exploited their labor in order to protect their own class and race privilege. "[W]hy are not our forms as delicate, and out constitutions as slender, as yours?" Stewart rhetorically queried her "fairer sisters." And for enslaved black women, "disappointment" was a birthright.

Denied the right to own their own bodies, to reap the rewards of their labor, to love whom they chose, to mother their own children, to cultivate their talents, and to live in liberty, their "disappointment" was that human beings possessed more evil than good and were continually defying God's moral laws.[53]

Anger emerges from such disappointment, when one's desires are obstructed. Expectations create hope; when they are thwarted, feelings of frustration, deprivation, and betrayal lead to anger.[54] In antebellum America, women's expectations were shaped by a rhetoric of democracy and freedom, the responsibilities of ennobled republican motherhood, and the imperatives of nation-building projects. There was an enormous breach, however, between what the culture promised women and what they actually experienced. Indeed, perpetual disjunction characterized antebellum women's lives: disjunction between the rhetoric of female superiority and the reality of economic and legal disenfranchisement; disjunction between the rhetoric of separate spheres and the reality of inequality; disjunction between the rhetoric of freedom and the reality of oppression; disjunction between the rhetoric of a united national community and the reality of exclusion.

Whether enslaved or "free," living in squalor, wealth, or anywhere in between, antebellum women had a great deal to be angry about in the sanctified borders of the American Republic. Excluded from the Edenic promise of democratic America, they were denied inclusion in its community and decision-making bodies and betrayed by its broken promises. All women came of age in a country that glorified an ethos of personal, economic, and artistic self-reliance but denied them the right to be personally, economically, and artistically self-reliant. Black women were enslaved in a country that was founded on the principles of freedom; and they were treated as sexual objects and inhuman breeders in an era in which white women's chastity and maternity were revered. The "daughters of a despised race," who were not enslaved legally, were subject to racist laws and practices in the supposedly "free" North. After lecturing for "nearly four years," visiting "every New England State, . . . New York, Canada and Ohio," Pennsylvania "is about the meanest of all, as far as the treatment of colored people is concerned," Frances Ellen Watkins Harper reported in the *Liberator*. "I have been insulted in several railroad cars." The white daughters of a revolutionary generation, in whom the "heroic element was strong," and who were "as ready as any [men] to pledge [their lives], fortune[s], and sacred honor" to uphold democratic principles, found they could do so in one way only: through circumscribed familial roles.[55]

Some women responded to these disjunctions by internalizing the prohibition against angered expression and denying that they were angry. Others acknowledged their anger but assiduously attempted to hide its presence. These reactions fostered the development of a female emotional culture that was characterized by repression, secrecy, and women's psychic sundering. The exchange between the hot-tempered daughter, Jo March, and her equally hot-tempered mother, Marmee, in Louisa May Alcott's *Little Women* is a classic example of how this culture was transmitted in countless white, middle-class households. Marmee's disclosure that she has "been trying to cure" her anger "for forty years" betrays the longevity and potency of her volcanic feelings (79). Although she has not been able to eradicate the debilitating disease of discontent, she has learned how to keep it under control. Suppression is the medication. Behind the veneer of psychic wholeness, Marmee vigilantly guards a masked interior life in which anger seethes.

For Marmee, as well as many other antebellum women, the ideology and practice of male superiority in the national community, as well as in white and black culture, engendered incessant anger-inducing situations. Notions of gender difference transcended race and class boundaries. Even though the material conditions that shaped "free" black women's lives blurred the line between home and world and made their relationship to political activism less problematical than it was for white women, black women, like their white contemporaries, were constrained by an ideology of gender relations that was conceived of in hierarchical terms. Debates about the propriety, extent, and definition of women's roles in political affairs outside the home filled the pages of black newspapers as well as white. In the black community, conflict especially arose around the question of what role women should play in state and national conventions—the primary arenas in which leadership agendas, styles, and strategies were formulated—and whether activities such as petitioning strained the boundaries of appropriate feminine behavior. Like their white counterparts, black women were sometimes excluded from male-dominated organizations entirely, and when they were included, they were expected to assume a supportive, behind-the-scenes, "helpmate" role, usually by fundraising in sexually segregated committees.

Black men who supported women's rights did not reject an ideology of separate spheres. "Even the most liberal black men," James Oliver Horton notes, "saw the woman's natural place as in the home." Black women were expected to defer to male authority intellectually, emotionally, and politically. This deference was, of course, complicated by the fact that slavery deprived black men from assuming what was considered to be their rightful privileges as men. The urgency of united opposition against racist ideas and practices compelled all but a few black women to silence anger at their own men. Black women's anger at black men is an articulate absence in their public literature.[56]

In a culture structured in male dominance, black and white women were excluded from national governance, as well as from positions of authority in churches and reform organizations. Their imaginations were straitjacketed by economic necessity and the notion of acceptably feminine topics and genres. Their literature was devalued. They were denied educational and economic opportunities. Domestic duties afforded them little solitude or time to think. They had no control over earnings and property. Physical labor and incessant child-bearing robbed them of health. Yet women were told they should not be angry about the structural inequalities that determined their life choices, and that if they were, they were imperiling the new nation's stability.

Women's anger at their exclusion from the democratic promises of freedom, independence, and equality profoundly shapes their literary culture in the antebellum period. So does the prohibition against its open expression. Gendered ideologies of anger impact on the tone, themes, and forms that women's literary imaginings assume, regardless of what factors motivate women to pick up a pen. Whether women writers deny their anger by extolling the advantages of their circumscribed status as conduits of virtue in the newly formed republic, or express it behind a mask in textual gestures and metaphors, they are all responding to a culture that excludes them from the inalienable rights of democratic citizenship, including the right to protest in anger the injustice of their exclusion.

There is no better barometer of cultural attitudes toward the collective expression of white women's discontent than the contemptuous response of hostile critics to the advent of the woman's rights movement at mid-century. Characterizing activists as a "few disaffected embittered women" who held conventions "for the purpose of giving vent to petty personal spleen and domestic discontent," or as an "infuriated gang" of "poor creatures who take part in the silly rant of 'brawling women,' " the movement's detractors were engaging in a potent delegitimizing tactic.[57] The implication was not only that "embittered women" were a deviant anomaly, but also that their "domestic discontent" had no validity. On the contrary, it was "petty," "personal," not worthy of public consideration. As Jean Baker Miller observes, this strategy of delegitimization is often used by dominant groups to enforce, maintain, and obscure unequal power relations. Because the subordinate's articulation of discontent threatens the dominant's hegemony, the dominant attempts to silence the subordinate's anger by denying its existence; the dominant insists that the subordinate's angered protest is incomprehensible, abnormal, unwarranted.[58] Whether imaged as exceptions to the norm, or as lower-class "brawlers" who lacked decorum and self-control, woman's rights activists were vilified because their presence, as well as their rhetoric, dared to challenge the sanctified notion that women were loving, gentle, self-sacrificing mothers, daughters, and wives for whom anger was an alien emotion.[59]

The response of one woman's rights activist, Elizabeth Oakes Smith, to the charge that women involved in the cause were "disaffected" and "embittered" reveals the difficulties that even woman's rights women faced when they began to express anger about gendered injustices in public. Speaking at the 1852 woman's rights convention, Oakes Smith argued that the "wrongs" women "have come here to talk over" were the result of public injustices, not private failings. "No woman has come here to talk over private griefs, and detail the small coin of personal anecdote," she assured her audience, but rather "the wrongs [of] unjust legislation; the wrongs [of] corrupt public opinion; the wrongs which false social aspects have fastened upon us."

By adopting this line of reasoning, Oakes Smith shifts the terms of debate from the notion that women's "bitterness"—in this case a synonym for corrosive anger—is a sign of defective character, to the notion that women have every right to experience such feelings. Because "[a]ll who take their stand against institutions, are in some sense embittered," women, like men, are affected by "the conviction of wrong." They, like "the men of '76," speak not as individuals, but rather "as the embodied race." Yet, at the same time that Oakes Smith justifies women's right to acknowledge and articulate bitterness, she, like many others of her generation, expresses ambivalence about whether it is a socially acceptable feeling. "Bitterness is the child of wrong," she proclaims. "[I]f any one of our number has become embittered (which, God forbid!), it is because social wrong has so penetrated to the inner life that we are crucified thereby, and taste the gall and vinegar with the Divine Master."[60]

For antebellum women writers to "taste the gall and vinegar with the Divine Master" in public required the invention of an art form. In the following chapters, I explore the complexities and political meanings of this art form, the artistry of anger that Lydia Maria Child, Maria W. Stewart, Fanny Fern, and Harriet Wilson invent and practice in their literary texts. "[W]oman's discontent increases in exact proportion to her development," the editors of the *History of Woman Suffrage* observed after nearly forty years of public activism.[61] Each of the authors and texts I consider advances women's development by delineating their discontent. Exclusion from the democratic promises of republicanism is their subject as well as the hallmark of their experiences as women in antebellum America. Their age, race, community, and class status determine how they define exclusion, imagine its contours, render its ramifications, and propose its elimination.

PART TWO

Anger in the House and in the Text

Four Case Studies

FOUR

Anger, Exile, and Restitution in Lydia Maria Child's *Hobomok*

I remember you once saide that Shakspeare would have beene the same great poet if he had been nurtured in a Puritan wildernesse. But indeed it is harde for incense to rise in a colde, heavy atmosphere, or for the buds of fancie to put forth, where the heartes of men are as hard and sterile as their unploughed soile.

—Mary Conant, writing to her English grandfather, in *Hobomok* (1824)

Over twenty years after Lydia Maria Child made her debut as a pioneer in the emerging field of American letters, the prestigious literary critic Rufus Griswold asked her for information about her career because he intended to include an entry on her in his nation-building anthology *Prose Writers of America*. In her reply, Child characterized "the first thing [she] ever attempted to write for print"—her historical novel *Hobomok* published in 1824—as "[h]asty, imperfect, and crude."[1] When angry expression is the aesthetic by which *Hobomok* is evaluated, however, these terms do not apply. On the contrary, Child achieves an artistry of anger both literary and political in her first novel: literary in that the author, even though a neophyte, succeeds in masking her anger at the failed promises of American democracy by using ironic reversals, clever disguises, and complex characterizations; political in that she urges women writers and female readers to claim a country and a self. And this, in nineteenth-century terms, is a radical act indeed.

Lydia Maria Child's anger at a male-dominated culture that excluded her from intellectual, emotional, and sexual freedom propelled artistic creation as well as political critique. In *Hobomok*, she transforms that anger into a vision of history and gender relations that questions male-authored national mythologies, Puritanism's emotional austerity, and the stunting of women's potential. She does so by infusing captivity motifs with new meanings and creating a fantasy of gender reversals that ultimately allows her protagonist to reclaim the rightful privileges of a white, republican daughter in a democratic Eden.

Lydia Maria Child's first novel is a classic example of the ways in which some antebellum women writers expressed anger through displacement. Because they internalized their culture's prescriptions against the expression of female anger, they feared directly confronting the causes of anger-producing situations. As a result, women writers took advantage of the emotional pecking-order that ideologies of anger created, and displaced their anger onto those they perceived as different and less powerful. In *Hobomok*, Lydia Maria Child displaces the anger she feels at men of her own race and class onto a man of color, Hobomok, the titular Indian character. At the same time, however, she also uses Hobomok to imagine a new kind of sexual partner, an emotionally responsive man who respects women's culture and values. In Child's complex fantasy, the man of color is a target for displaced anger as well as a weapon of revenge. For what can be more satisfyingly vengeful than to imply that a supposedly "uncivilized savage" is more sexually desirable than a man of her own race and class?

Writing fiction enabled the twenty-two-year-old Lydia Maria Child to mask her anger under the cover of a historical tale. Set in seventeenth-century Salem, *Hobomok* claims to be a "New England novel" that takes the United States' "early history" (3) as its primary theme.[2] Within this framework, however, the story of the maturation and marriages of Mary Conant takes precedence. A young woman with a "native elegance of mind" and "a native fervor of imagination," Mary loves the wrong kind of man: an Episcopalian (35). Aided by her stern "unyielding" father's disapproval, Mary's lover—Charles Brown—is banished from the settlement by the authoritarian Puritan elders because of his religious sacrilege. When the news reaches Mary that Brown has died at sea, in "[a] bewilderment of despair that almost amounted to insanity" (120), she acknowledges her "deep and bitter re-proaches against her father" (121) and agrees to marry Hobomok, the de-voted Indian man who adores her. Mary's "desperate resentment towards [her father]" motivates her rebellion against him and the culture which holds her in captivity (122). Deciding "to exchange the social band, stern and dark as it was, for the company of savages," Mary spurns her father's world, pronounces it imprisoning, and chooses to join that of his rivals (122).

After a brief interlude however, we learn that Charles Brown is not dead after all but had been held in captivity—"a prisoner on the coast of Africa" (145). Thus he, like his estranged lover Mary, experiences incarceration first hand. In the same way Mary is held in captivity by the values and practices of white, Puritan men, so, too, Charles Brown is held in captivity by the very people white Americans enslave. When Hobomok learns of Brown's miracu-lous return, he chooses to "forever [pass] away from New England," relin-quishing claims on both his beloved wife and their young son so that Mary can be free to marry the man of her choice (141). Hobomok's profound act of self-sacrifice makes it possible for Mary to reenter the dominant white culture which once held her in captivity. Because her father regrets his previous tyrannical behavior, he lovingly accepts Mary, her new husband, and Mary's son from her union with Hobomok.

In Child's ironic reversal of captivity motifs, the most unlikely people are tyrants, and the most privileged, their prisoners. Charles Brown, a white man, is held captive by Africans; Mary Conant, a white woman, is held captive by male-dominated Puritan culture. Captivity breeds anger and resentment; it generates rebellion. In Hobomok, Child renders Mary's rebellion from white male captivity personally empowering and politically significant: not only does it enable her reintegration into white culture; it also fosters the creation of a system of social relations that values sensitivity and tolerance.[3]

Mary's new relationship with her father symbolically encodes this phe-nomenon. While Mary is held captive, Mr. Conant is cold and domineering; after her escape, he is affectionate and forbearing. Once the Puritan father recognizes the full impact of his "transgression" against his daughter, he changes from an "unyielding" dogmatist to a loving and compassionate parent. Child uses a spatial metaphor to signify how Mr. Conant's transfor-mation affects Mary's status in the white community. After she marries Charles Brown, she no longer lives on the outskirts of civilization, in a wigwam with an untutored "savage." On the contrary, her "new house was . . . erected near Mr. Conant's" (149). Because Mary's intermittent relationship with an Indian man allowed her to find a liberatory space in which she could forge an identity separate from the one patriarchal culture imposed on her, she is able to assume a rightful place next to her father's in a home of her own making.

In *Hobomok*, Lydia Maria Child's focus on identity, rebellion from white patriarchal captivity, and community formation rectifies white women's exclusion from America's history, culture, and politics. She accomplishes this feat by creating a series of openings where none previously existed. By writing a historical novel that recreates a Puritan past, she makes space for a female-centered vision of nation-building. By depicting an imaginative young white woman who craves intellectual stimulation, she advocates space for female education. By exposing the harmful effects of dogmatic Calvinism, she insists on space for feminine styles of emotional expression. And by rewriting American history, she claims space for female imaginative autonomy.

Child's preoccupation with space as both concept and metaphor reveals her profound anger at the constrictions white, middle-class women like her endured in early nineteenth-century America. There was precious little space for precocious, intellectually ambitious young women to define themselves outside of domestic roles, let alone receive the rigorous education that was part of their brothers' birthright.[4] Experiencing these constraints firsthand, Child explored her feelings of exile and exclusion by writing a historical tale. Doing so, she resolved the problem of how an intellectual young woman like herself could achieve emotional and economic independence, create something meaningful, and command respect in the larger community. Claiming authorship as "an American," Lydia Maria Child includes herself in the republic by writing a historical novel that aids the white, middle-class nation-building project.

Biographical details illuminate the genesis of the anger, ambivalence, and desire that infuse Lydia Maria Child's first novel. The death of her mother at the impressionable age of twelve aroused feelings of anger, abandonment, and sorrow. In addition, the rapid succession of other losses which left her alone with a grieving and inattentive father compounded her sense of alienation.[5] Her grandmother died, a sister married, and her favorite older brother left home to attend Harvard College. Child's self-imposed silence about these adolescent traumas is the most revealing evidence of their devastating effect. At the age of forty-five, Child confided to a close friend that her "childhood and youth" were "[c]old, shaded and uncongenial," and that "[w]henever reminiscences of them rise up before me, I turn my back on them as quickly as possible." According to the editors of her letters, "[s]he never hints at the nature of her unhappiness."[6] In the same letter, however,

Child vaguely suggests one source of that "unhappiness": a profound sense of alienation and placelessness. When she was "quite a little girl," she writes, she remembers fantasizing "that gypsies had changed me from some other cradle and put me in a place where I did not belong."[7]

This remembered imaginative reverie suggests another reason why Child was attracted to spatial themes and metaphors. It is significant that the young Child imagines a nomadic, alien group of people—the gypsies—responsible for "putting [her] in a place where [she] did not belong." Outcasts themselves, they force the innocent, young child to become like them: an outcast in her own home and culture who must rely on her own resources for survival. This childhood fantasy reveals much about Child's ambivalence toward people she sees as "others." On the one hand, the cunning, darkly exotic gypsies cause her dislocation. On the other hand, however, the gypsies are adventuresome, mobile, and creative. Because they play fanciful tricks with her destiny, they possess a tantalizing power.[8]

The same ambivalence characterizes Child's representation of Hobomok. On the one hand, she pays tribute to the noble Indian's gentle and self-sacrificing "reverence" by naming the text in his honor. On the other hand, however, he becomes the novel's—and Child's—sacrificial victim. By imagining Hobomok in the archetypical feminine position—selfless, loving, and willing to sacrifice personal desires for the good of others—the twenty-two-year-old Child displaces her own gendered sense of powerlessness onto a man of color. Thus, like the gypsies in her childhood fantasy, Hobomok becomes a way for Child to displace the real source of her profound anger and pain: the deprivation of a meaningful place in her family, culture, and history.

Child's father was responsible for some of that sense of deprivation. After his wife's death, he decided to send his young daughter to live with her newly married older sister in another state. Raised on Old Testament Biblical stories that repeatedly told the tale of banishment and exile, as well as a Puritan-authored version of history that understood European emigration to the new world using the same concepts, the young Child interpreted her experiences of leave-takings, deaths, and dislocation by applying Biblical themes to her own life.[9] She felt as if she was being exiled from her parental home, banished by an unloving father to the wilderness of an alien state, a surrogate family, and an unknown destiny.

During this time, Child's relationship with her erudite, book-loving older brother provided emotional sustenance and intellectual camaraderie. Yet, at the same time this relationship fulfilled Child's desire for companionship, it also subconsciously intensified her feelings of anger. Her brother enjoyed the privileges her culture prevented her from acquiring. Regarding him as confidant and friend, Child freely expressed opinions about religion, books, and her budding ambitions. After she secured her first teaching position at the age of nineteen, for example, she breathlessly announced: "I can't talk about books, nor anything else, until I tell you the good news; that I leave Norridgewock, and take a school in Gardiner, as soon as the travelling is tolerable. . . . I hope, my dear brother, that you feel as happy as I do. Not that I have formed any high-flown expectations. All I expect is, that, if I am industrious and prudent I shall be *independent*."[10] Child later acknowledged that her powerful, well-connected brother's support encouraged her to believe that she was capable of economic and intellectual risk-taking.[11]

Child's fierce determination to achieve autonomy and actualize her literary ambitions is evidenced in her decision to adopt both a religion and name of her own choosing. Indeed, it is significant that Child gave herself a new name during the same period that she first became a published writer.[12] She later claimed that she "added the name of Maria" because "some associations of childhood [made] the name Lydia unpleasant to me."[13] The name Maria resonates with symbolic meaning. Mary, the Biblical mother of Jesus Christ, conceived a child without the aid of a father.[14] To rename oneself is to relinquish a past in which one did not have the authority to name oneself. Moreover, self-naming is a powerful act of confidence, hope, and reclamation; it signifies a belief in new beginnings, new possibilities, and new angles of vision. Most significantly, especially in Lydia Maria Child's case, the act of renaming demonstrates the will and desire to create. For if God's ultimate act of artistry is the creation and naming of the world and its inhabitants, the individual's is the creation and naming of the self.

The yearning desire to create that led Child to fashion a new identity also led her to authorship. Although more than twenty years after *Hobomok* was published she reported to Rufus Griswold that she did not know what "impelled [her to write the book]; [that she] had never dreamed of such a thing as turning author," her early letters betray a fervent desire for independence and accomplishment, a keen longing for intellectual engagement, and the realization that she had to work hard to "govern" her "vehement and impetuous temperament."[15] Given that writing, as opposed to the only other genteel female employment of the time—teaching young children—was an ideal way for a woman such as Lydia Maria Child to channel her intellectual exuberance and anger, it is not surprising that as soon as she found a congenial space to create—her beloved brother's home—she wrote *Hobomok*, her first book.[16]

Even more revealing are the steps Child took to ensure the successful launching of her literary career. At a time when authors were required to finance both the printing and distribution of their books, Child managed to secure the money for the initial publication of *Hobomok*. Then, when the book received little attention and was selling poorly, she took advantage of her brother's association with the influential George Ticknor by asking if he would write "a few words" because his "judgment would have much weight with those whose taste is law, and [his] notice would induce many to purchase, who would otherwise regard the subject with a very natural indifference." Emboldened because she had been informed that Ticknor had made "flattering observations" about the book, she took this risk because she knew that his "influence" could potentially rescue "the unfortunate book." Child disguises her self-promotional aim behind a deferential mask. In the same sentence that she acknowledges that she has taken an "almost unpardonable" liberty, she assures Ticknor that she is "certain it will afford [him] some pleasure to revive the hopes of a young and disappointed author." Child not only harbored literary ambitions and worked hard to actualize them; she also perceived herself as an author at a time when that term was reserved for men.[17]

These biographical details suggest why Child's first novel is centrally concerned with questions of personal and national identity, and why spatial themes and metaphors are its primary trope. By centering the plot around a young female protagonist who struggles to make a place for herself in a new nation, Child devises a way to explore her own feelings of anger, exile, and exclusion while also participating in a political debate about who gets to claim America as homeland. She effectively personalizes what it means to be deprived of the promises of America because this vision is based on her own feelings and experiences. Like Child, Mary Conant endures familial exile when she is forced to leave her parental home in England to nurse her dying mother in Puritan America. Like Child, Mary Conant is frustrated by her exclusion from an intellectual culture once she is confined to the "dark circle" of gender-determined roles in America (36). And like Child, Mary Conant experiences political exile when she is excluded from her newly adopted country's most sanctified promise—the right to intellectual and emotional freedom.

Child's vision of America in *Hobomok* makes clear that although she inherited a Puritan legacy through birth and history, she did not feel as if she were one of the chosen. On the contrary, excluded from the legacy of America's origin story and its most cherished democratic ideals, she perceived herself as an outcast in what was supposed to be an Edenic land, a country recently liberated from cultural and political tyranny. Her sense of exclusion motivates *Hobomok*'s ultimate fantasy of the restitution of a republican woman's rightful privileges.

In *Hobomok*, Lydia Maria Child's anger emerges into clear view when she addresses issues of exclusion, exile, and patriarchal domination. These textual moments are transformative, for both Child and her female readers. The act of writing an imaginative tale was liberating for Child because she learned how to use her anger creatively and productively. And this ability is what eventually enabled her to become "one of nineteenth-century America's most original writers and reformers."[18] The issues and themes Child addresses in *Hobomok*, Carolyn Karcher notes, "uncannily [predict] her future career."

> Not only does the intermarriage plot foreshadow Child's literal espousal of the Indian cause during the Cherokee removal controversy later in the decade, but it also prefigures the campaign against antimiscegenation laws with which she would inaugurate her career as an antislavery agitator in 1833, and it adumbrates her lifelong conviction, developed with progressively greater political awareness in subsequent writings, that the destiny of the American nation lies in the fusion of its races and cultures. *Hobomok* forecasts Child's commitment to the struggle for women's rights as well— a struggle she would define in the 1840s to include sexual freedom. No less centrally, the novel's condemnation of Calvinist bigotry and its recognition that Protestants, Catholics, Muslims, Hindus, and aboriginal animists must all be "pleasing in the sight of God" points ahead toward the crusade for religious toleration that would culminate in the "eclectic Bible" Child published two years before her death—a Bible featuring a higher proportion of nonChristian than of Christian sacred texts. Finally, *Hobomok* reveals Child's conflicting aspirations toward respectability and marginality, acceptance by her society and rebellion against it, signaling how she would seek to resolve those conflicts—by refashioning her society to conform with her ideals.[19]

For Lydia Maria Child, *Hobomok* was a learning text. Through the act of writing the novel, she learned how to acknowledge anger and imagine retribution. Only after she mastered these lessons did she acquire a firm voice and speak in anger publicly without fear.[20]

For women readers very much like the young Child, Mary Conant's trials in and out of captivity struck a responsive chord. By placing Mary's personal story in a nationalist context, Child prompted her readers to consider whether their relationship to republicanism and American history—as well as their status in the culture at large—was like Mary Conant's. She also telegraphed a masked message to women about anger's utility. By creating the character of Mary Conant, Child offered a model of a virtuous yet covertly angry young woman whose rebellion against white men ultimately enables her to secure a respectable place in her community. While addressing these concerns in a seventeenth-century context created the illusion of distance, Child was well aware that the relevance of her story would not be lost on female readers who were as engaged in the process of defining their relationship to American republicanism as she was.

The Artistry of Anger behind the Mask of a Historical Tale

In *Hobomok*, Lydia Maria Child delineates three heinous oppressions that rob white, middle-class women of their rightful democratic privileges: the denial of women's artistic sovereignty; the ways in which male-authored national mythologies erase women's subjectivity and experience, thereby enforcing patriarchal domination; and the pernicious function of heterosexual love in a society that disallows women any other outlets for their emotions and talents. Examining how Child dramatizes each of these grievances reveals her artistry of anger as well as her political vision.

Hobomok's anonymous publication and narrative structure signal Child's profound anger at women writers' diminished status in the early republic because both place the problem of female authority in bold relief. Child's decision to obscure her gendered identity by replacing it with a nationalist one—the book was published with "by an American" on its title page— confirms that she knew that her novel would be better received if readers thought it was written by a patriotic male citizen.[21] To compound the effect further, she uses the guise of a male narrator rewriting seventeenth-century male-authored texts as a narrative device.[22]

An exchange between the male narrator and a male friend about the writing of historical novels sets the novel in motion. When the friend confesses that another friend's "remarks concerning our early history have half tempted [him] to write a New England novel," he and the narrator then discuss the impossibility of rivaling what Waverly, Scott, and Cooper have already mastered (3). Yet, because the narrator knows that his friend "under an awkward and unprepossessing appearance, concealed more talents than the world was aware of," he decides to "favor the project" by supplying him with "many old, historical pamphlets" (4).

True to his promise, a few weeks later the friend drops off a completed manuscript based on the "old and forgotten manuscripts" of "our earliest history" (4). He leaves the decision of whether it is worthy of publication entirely up to the narrator, who, exercising his prerogative, obviously thinks it is since the story we read is presented as the one his friend has written. Thus, this tale of the ways in which Puritan authoritarianism affects the lives of men and women is supposed to have been written by a modest, talented man, and further, it is a man who ultimately decides it is valuable enough "to give . . . to the public" (4). Making readers believe they are listening to a man's voice that has already been sanctioned by another man's approval, Child devises a strategy to impart her ideas to a culture that believes women do not possess the right, nor the ability, to write a historical novel, let alone address "the public."

Child's decision to disguise her authorship by suggesting that *Hobomok's* original writer and subsequent reviser are men demonstrates her acute awareness of women's lack of authority when they picked up a pen. Nina Baym's reception study of antebellum fiction confirms that Child's strategies were not misguided. According to Baym, reviewers enforced "two entirely different systems of evaluation" that were strictly gender determined. This was especially true, she notes, of their assessment of male and female characters. Unlike male characters, female characters were criticized if they were individualized and praised when they conformed to a "type"—the ultimate "feminine" essence. In other words, female characters were critiqued according to whether they fulfilled gender-prescribed roles, not according to their individual personalities. The same gender biases were applied to women writers. Assumed "less capable of literary artistry because they belonged to the weaker sex" and less wide-ranging because they wrote primarily about their female-centered domestic worlds, women writers were judged lacking from the start.[23] By masking her authorship, Child circumvented a biased reception of her vision. She also courted popular nationalist ideas that the United States needed a literature based on its own history and culture. In devising this solution, Child transformed her anger at exclusion into a useful literary device that enabled her to gain a hearing when—as the poet "Ada" so aptly expressed it a decade later—women were not allowed to " 'cry aloud' . . . [a]nd lift [their] voices in the public ear."[24]

Child's employment of ironic reversals that shame male mythologizers is yet another indication of her anger at gendered constrictions. Indeed, nowhere is this anger more apparent than in her rendering of Puritan America as a kind of captivity for women. Recasting the conventional characters in America's quintessential, nation-building genre—the captivity narrative—Child presents a version of national evolution radically different from those contained in male-authored texts. In Child's vision, it is not "uncivilized, bloodthirsty savages" who impede white America's progress and hold women hostage; it is the beliefs and practices of authoritarian white men. They stunt women's intellectual growth, control their sexuality, and deny them a full range of emotional freedom.

Child introduces this idea from the very beginning by providing two different interpretations of America's progress—one based on patriarchal myth, the other based on lived experience. She does this to demonstrate what happens when history is written based on the former: there is a large discrepancy between myth and experience, especially when the experience is a woman's. In the novel's opening pages, the male narrator explains how his "manuscript" revises existing historical sources. He begins with these observations: "I never view the thriving villages of New England . . . without feeling a glow of national pride, as I say, 'this is my own, my native land.' A long train of associations are connected with her picturesque rivers, as they repose in their peaceful loveliness, the broad and sparkling mirror of the heavens,—and with the cultivated environs of her busy cities, which seem everywhere blushing into a perfect Eden of fruit of flowers" (5).

The narrator begins by proudly claiming America as homeland. The implication is that if he can claim America as his "own . . . native land," he can also become its historian. The Edenic images he uses to describe the "thriving villages" and "busy cities" suggest that, in his view, America's early nineteenth-century economic prosperity has created a modern-day paradise. Indeed, his tremendous pride in his country's accomplishments is underscored by the succinct version of American history that follows: the founding of America was sanctified by God's plan; it is the moral and spiritual "light" that emerged from the "darkness of Europe," thus it leads the "western world" "in the proud and rapid march of freedom"; it is impossible for the heart not to pay "involuntary tribute" to the Puritan fathers' "persevering fortitude" even if, from the vantage point of his "enlightened and liberal age," they may appear to have "exhibited a deep mixture of exclusive, bitter, and morose passions" (5–6). The irony, of course, is that the only way Child, the early nineteenth-century woman, can celebrate mythic America as homeland is by imagining herself as a white male.

The tension between the myth of America as "a perfect Eden" and the reality of its banishment of women is also conveyed textually. After the narrator provides the mega-narrative of American progress, he then notes that because previous historians did not record "the varying tints of domestic detail" that made up the Puritan father's lives, their personal histories can never be known. He quickly adds, however, that there is still a chance to retrieve some of the "details" that have been "concealed by the ivy which clusters around the tablets of our recent history," because they are found in the "old worn-out manuscript" that is the basis of his story (6). Explaining that he has taken "the liberty" of revising a text that was originally "written by one of [his] ancestors who fled with the persecuted nonconformists from the Isle of Wight," he then cavalierly notes that since "[e]very one acquainted with our early history remembers the wretched state in which they found the scanty remnant of their brethren at that place," he will "pass over the young man's dreary account" and provide his own interpretation (6–7).

Child does two things here. First, by introducing the comment about the "wretched state" of the Puritans immediately following the sanctified historical mega-narrative, she juxtaposes the myth of Edenic America with the reality of the lived experience of the first settlers. This contrast is so important to Child that she repeats it again once the seventeenth-century narrative begins in earnest. The first thing the narrator relates is how overwhelming it felt to be arriving "in a new world" that "owed nothing of its unadorned beauty to the power of man" (7). Marveling in fear and awe at the vastness of God's creation, he immediately confronts feelings of insignificance and powerlessness. He "viewed [himself] as a drop in the vast ocean of existence, and shrunk from the contemplation of human nothingness" (7). As soon as his feet touch land, however, America is God's paradise no longer. Even though he had heard "contradictory reports" of what to expect when he arrived, "the scene" at Naumkeak "was far worse than [his] imagination had ever conceived" (7–8). The settlement consists of "six miserable hovels" (7) inhabited by "sickly and half starved" (8) occupants; the food is "unpalatable"; the community is rent with dissension (9). Once again, America is first perceived as mythic Eden, but as soon as reality intrudes it becomes a land of "sickness and distress." It is a vast, untouched "new world" from afar, but once lived in, it becomes "bleak and sterile" (7).

In the same way Child underscores the disjunction between myth and reality by contrasting two versions of America's origin story twice within the novel's opening four pages, she also makes it clear that the story she has taken "the liberty" of revising has not yet been told. Because she announces that she is going to make visible the concealed "domestic details" that previous male-authored texts did not see, or considered too trivial to record, Child intimates that her version of America's origin story is being told from a woman's perspective. Her most important point, however, is that when a woman writes history based on "the varying tints of domestic detail," the gap between male myths and female realities is glaringly exposed. And it is this exposure that impedes unquestioned patriarchal privilege because it makes evident the oppression that has previously been hidden.

Our introduction to the sparkling-eyed Mary immediately after the narrator describes her father's bleak history underscores this point. Mary's strong emotional connection to her past, we learn, is a point of contention between her father and herself. For when "in rapid succession she inquired about the scenes of her youth," her father angrily chastises her not to "look back for the flesh-pots of Egypt" (9). Not only does the father's rebuke suggest that these two characters have a different relationship to their place of origin; it also shows that the father exerts an emotional control over the daughter that oppressively censors her feelings. By having Mr. Conant evoke an Old Testament Biblical passage that condemns the "children of Israel's" refusal to accept the deprivation that is part of God's plan, Child associates the father with disciplinary enforcement.[25] Moreover, by emphasizing Mary's attachment to her past in England, Child informs us that Mary has not claimed America as homeland, nor has America claimed Mary as citizen.

As the plot unfolds, we understand why this is so. In America, Mary is like "[a] lily weighed down by the pitiless pelting of the storm; a violet shedding its soft, rich perfume on bleakness and desolation; a plant which had been fostered and cherished with mild sunshine and gentle dews, removed at once from the hot-house to the desert, and left to unfold its delicate leaves beneath the darkness of the lowering storm" (79). Child uses images of oppression, violence, and stunted growth to signify the frustration of lost potential. Mary Conant is like the richly fragrant plant that needs gentle nurture in order to grow. In her grandfather's home in England, she had "become covetous of mental riches, and worshipped at the shrine of genius"; "there she had been the little idol of the brilliant circle" (78). It was there, too, that she first met Charles Brown "and mingled with him in the graceful evolutions of the dance" (78). But once forcibly removed from the "promise" of the hot-house to the emptiness of the desert because "the stern voice of duty was heard commanding her to depart from her country and kindred," there is no way for Mary to flourish (78).

In yet another vengeful reversal, Child depicts England as the lost paradise and America as the oppressive wasteland. In England, women assume a noble status, participate in a vibrant, intellectual culture, and also love with impunity. In America, they encounter nothing but "bleakness," "desolation," and "the darkness of the lowering storm." Returning to England is the only way Mary can envision regaining her lost privileges. Child evokes this ironic reversal again when Charles Brown is about to be banished. At that time he imagines himself and Mary back in England with "Mary restored to her original rank, and shining amid the loveliest and proudest of the land" (73). Positing England as the lost paradise hopefully to be regained, Child bitingly suggests that Euro-American women need to reassess which of their home-lands actually fosters freedom.

This ironic reversal also implies that when women are deprived of an intellectual life and forced to devote all their energies to "love" in a hostile homeland, they are literally deprived of life. It is significant, for example, that Mrs. Conant, the mother Mary was called away from England to nurse, and Lady Arabella, one of her mother's friends, are literally killed by devotion to their husbands once they come to America. Like Mrs. Conant, Lady Arabella is unable to withstand the sacrifices emotionally bereft Puritan men require of their wives. While "[f]irmness of purpose had been her leading trait from childhood," the conditions in America "tasked it to the utmost" (107).

Child graphically expresses her rage at a system that forces women into deathly domestic captivity by having Mrs. Conant and Lady Arabella both die in the same room within a day of each other. That she believes domineering, unfeeling men are responsible is evident when she has Lady Arabella's husband admit to his complicity in his wife's death. "I could bear all," he cries, "had I not brought you into trials too mighty for your strength. But for my selfish love, you might now be living in ease and comfort" (110). In the same way Mrs. Conant's unconditional love for Mr. Conant, the "rigid Calvinist" (8), ultimately kills her, so, too, does Lady Arabella's "enthusiasm" for "all the plans of her honored husband" (107). Indeed, Mr. Johnson is so dependent on his wife's love that he is unable to live without her—he dies a few weeks later. Child explicitly identifies the cause of these wives' deaths: when women are solely responsible for providing emotional sustenance to selfish and dependent men, they are depleted of both physical and psychic strength.

Child reiterates this point when she pays tribute to the two women immediately following their demise. "There, in that miserable room," she writes, "lay the descendants of two noble houses. Both alike victims to what has always been the source of woman's greatest misery—love—deep and unwearied love" (111). Robbed of status, deprived of comfort, and denied the reciprocity of love, these women are "victims" of heterosexual gender arrangements in which they are the primary emotional laborers.[26] Equally significant, by showing the profound effect Mrs. Conant's suffering has on Mr. Conant's capacity to feel—a "sigh or groan from the woman whom he had so long and sincerely loved, had power to stir up those deep recesses of feeling, which had for years been sealed within his soul"—Child also suggests that in order to effect the equivalent of an American revolution in men's ability to be emotionally expressive, the lives of their wives must be sacrificed (108).

Child's portrayal of Mrs. Conant and Lady Arabella as martyrs to the cause of "deep and unwearied love" reveals her anger at white patriarchal gender arrangements that forced women like herself into a singular sub-servient role. As wives and mothers, women were supposed to ensure the smooth functioning of a virtuous republic by instilling proper values in a pious domestic atmosphere. Because they were considered more spiritual and loving, their primary contribution to the building of America was through their moral influence on the nation's future male citizens. The imaginative world that Child creates in *Hobomok* is a response to the ideology that characterized women's political participation strictly in terms of domestic roles. When love is the only outlet a woman has to express her creative impulses and political beliefs, Child argues, she is denied emotional and political freedom. Hence Child envisions heterosexual love in a patriarchal culture as a kind of deadly captivity because women are literally killed by "love—deep and unwearied love." As a result, the question of how to negotiate love within marriage—the most important source of economic solvency for women of her class—and still maintain a self in a nation that denies women citizenship is one of her greatest concerns.

Child explores this question by using a spatial metaphor that had a great deal of meaning to men and women in the early nineteenth century. Over and over again throughout the novel, the tension between freedom and captivity, individualism and community, duty and desire is symbolized by a circle motif. Mary is either attempting to create her own circle—symbolic of controlling her own fate—or she is encircled by the tyrannical patriarchal culture.[27] By invoking one of the nineteenth-century's most cherished symbols of gender difference—the separate spheres of men and women—Child critiques a system of social relations that confines women to separate and unequal spheres of freedom. By using this culturally resonant imagery to its maximum potential, she identifies a problem as well as suggests a solution.

Choosing one's marriage partner, Child suggests, is one way women can resist stultifying emotional enclosure. Because Mary's maternal grandfather objected to her mother's relationship with her father in much the same way that Mary's father objects to her own with Charles Brown, it is clear that Child sees paternal interference in love as an urgent problem that a younger generation of republican-minded women must rectify. And in order to break through the boundaries of this encirclement, Child maintains, women must enter courageously the "dark forests" of unknown worlds and risk performing their own courtship rituals (12). When they do this, they can control their own sexuality.

In one of the novel's most spectacularly imagined scenes, the narrator observes Mary "flitt[ing] by the corner of the house" in the "lonely hour of the night" mysteriously "plung[ing] into the thicket" (13). His curiosity aroused, he secretly follows her, and then witnesses what Carolyn Karcher notes "can only be called a ritual of witchcraft."[28] This is how the narrator describes what he saw:

> She had stopped near a small brook, and when I first discovered her, she had stooped beside it, and taking a knife from her pocket, she opened a vein in her little arm, and dipping a feather in the blood, wrote something on a piece of white cloth, which was spread before her. She rose with a face pale as marble, and looking round timidly, she muttered a few words too low to meet my ear; then taking a stick and marking out a large circle on the margin of the stream, she stept into the magic ring, walked round three times with measured tread, then carefully retraced her steps backward, speaking all the while in a distinct but trembling voice. The following were the only words I could hear,
>
> Whoever's to claim a husband's power,
> Come to me in the moonlight hour.
> And again,—
> Whoe'er my bridegroom is to be,
> Step in the circle after me.
> She looked round anxiously as she completed the ceremony; and I almost echoed her involuntary shriek of terror, when I saw a young Indian spring forward into the centre. (13)

As if placing the "young Indian" in the "centre" of her invocation is not shocking enough, Child also includes the other desired lover—Charles Brown—in this highly charged sexual reverie. While Mary was "retreating from the woods," the narrator reports, "a third person made his appearance . . . young Brown." Upon seeing him, "Mary eagerly caught his arm, and seemed glad amid her terror and agitation, to seek the shelter of his offered protection" (14). More than anything else, this scene exposes Child's ambivalence about desiring the forbidden.[29] On the one hand, she realizes that in order for women to break the constricting boundaries of Euro-American social conventions, they have to enter unknown worlds inhabited by nonwhite men. On the other hand, however, she is unwilling to relinquish the fantasy of finding shelter in civilized white men's arms. Yet, as Carolyn Karcher argues, by imagining both men as objects of desire, Child imaginatively resolves the conflict: she envisions freedom and protection as simultaneous, not mutually exclusive states of being.[30]

When the boundaries of the heterosexual circle are opened up, Child suggests, there are possibilities for different kinds of couplings that cannot be contained within the confines of a separate and unequal sphere. By making Mary, Charles Brown, and Hobomok a trio connected to each other by love, Child creates a triangular arrangement in which each of the participants is a partner in an emotional exchange that can assume myriad variations. She imagines a new spatial metaphor—a triangle—to accommodate an imaginative vision that reshapes popular notions of women's emotional subservience.

It is worth noting, however, that Child must take Mary out of a white male-dominated world in order to do so. To create a "magic ring" in which a man of her choice assumes the center, Mary must venture into the spaciousness of nature, which is the opposite of a claustrophobic Euro-American culture. Indeed, Mary "mark[s] out a large circle on the margin of the stream" because it is only on the edge of her culture that she can attempt to secure emotional and sexual freedom. Child also makes it clear that in addition to physical space, Mary needs literate space to achieve self-determination. Before she creates the "magic ring," Mary uses her own blood to "[write] something on a piece of white cloth which was spread before her." Laden with birth imagery, this gesture suggests that women like Mary must rely on themselves to be sources of creation. Using her blood as ink, Mary attempts to control her own destiny by inscribing her own fate. Freed from the house, with language as a powerful tool, Mary attempts to write her own plot, not follow the one her culture has predetermined.[31]

Here, as in other places in the novel, Child's emphasis on the importance of writing reveals her anger at a patriarchal system that denies women literacy in order to maintain domination. By demonstrating that the written word rectifies untruths and revises male-authored versions of history, Child affirms that writing is a powerful weapon against masculine oppression. One of the ways she illustrates this point is by dramatizing what happens when Mary's close friend, Sally Oldham, is desired by two men and one attempts to slander the other in public. Sally defends the favored lover by providing written testimony of her role in the affair. Because she does not know how to write, however, she solicits Mary to write the letter for her. Although Sally's "impudent" father amends the letter by adding his criticisms "respecting Churche Govermente," "the elders" take "no notice of [his] advice" because he is not duly subservient. But because "Sally's testimony was so simple and decisive," the slandered lover is exonerated (55–56). Thus writing not only allows women the opportunity to voice their desires through language; it also provides a way for them to testify against personal and social injustice.

For Mary, writing with her own blood certainly allows her to control her sexual destiny: she eventually marries both the "young Indian" and Charles Brown. Yet even though she is able to stake out this physical, literate, and sexual space at the start, it becomes increasingly difficult for her to control her own fate, especially when death, marriage, and banishment deprive her of her only beloved community. Indeed, with her mother and Lady Arabella dead, her best friend, Sally, married and relocated, and her lover, Charles Brown, exiled and believed dead, Mary's situation becomes more and more circumscribed. "With none," Child writes, "had Mary any thing like communion" (114). Without the "cheering influence" and "firm support" of her women friends, as well as the "mild, soothing spirit of her mother," unless Mary wrests control over her own life she, too, will live out her mother's and Lady Arabella's fate. In bold and vivid detail, the cautionary tale of what Mary must avoid is dramatized in one of the novel's most strikingly symbolic scenes—that of a deer hunt.

When Mary learns that a group of Indian men are going to "hunt by torch-light," she is greatly excited by the idea of witnessing something so dramatic. "Oh, they are coming out by torch-light," exclaimed Mary, "as Hobomok says the western Indians do. How I do wish I could see them hunt by torch-light" (87). In his characteristic fashion, Mary's father sternly refuses Mary's desire: "A pretty sight truly . . . to see you out at midnight with twenty hunters" (87). But when Mrs. Conant gently persuades him that she doesn't see any "harm" in Mary going, especially since "there are few such gratifications in the wilderness," he relents (87). Following Mrs. Conant's suggestion, Mary invites some other "young women," and with Mr. Conant holding "the rein of Mary's horse" and Hobomok walking by her side, the party sets off (87–88).

Child describes the scene as a harmonious pageant of exquisite contrasts. Not only is there "the contrast of heathen and christian, social and savage, elegance and strength, fierceness and timidity"; when the group of whites and Indians stand together "in the loneliness and solitude of nature," there is also a contrast of stillness and movement (89). It is a frozen night of "glittering beauty," yet "the trees danced to the shrill music of the winds" (88). "The mellow light of moon and star looked down upon the woods," yet "[I]t seemed as if the sylphs and fairies . . . [who] peopled the mountain and the stream, had all assembled . . . on the great altar of nature" (88).

As soon as the hunters arrive, however, nature's setting is a magical pageant no longer. Entering with their phallic torches held high, they disrupt the delicate balance of stasis and movement, the cyclical rhythms of light and dark, life and death. The "lurid glare" of their torches intrudes upon the "mild, tranquil light of the evening" (88). "[T]he unwonted glow of [the] artificial rays" is the deadly weapon that will "bewitch" the deer, making them vulnerable to attack (89). For as soon as the deer see the man-made light, they become transfixed, paralyzed in their tracks. Once the "majesty" of nature is dethroned by male hunters, the inhabitants that enjoy freedom under her protective domain are easily lured by trickery into mortal danger (88).[32]

Child's description of how Mary reacts when she witnesses the killing of two deer makes it clear that the deer are symbolic representations of women, and that the "bewitching" artificial light is a symbolic representation of an unequal heterosexual love that blinds, tricks, and ultimately destroys its female "victims." Like the deer who "saw the forms of men, and knew they were his enemies," but were mesmerized into paralysis because of the "powerful . . . fascination of the torches," women, too, risk losing rationality when they succumb to a "bewitching" phallic love (89). It is highly significant indeed that when Hobomok—wanting to prove his prowess to Mary—takes aim, "Mary touch[es] his shoulder," saying "Don't kill it, Hobomok—don't" (88). But it is too late because a "weapon" from Hobomok's "hand . . . seldom missed its mark." When the deer received the mortal arrow it "sprung high into the air, its beautiful white breast was displayed for an instant, a faint, mournful sound was heard—and Hobomok stept forward to seize the victim he had wounded. As he brought it up to Mary, the glossy brown of its slender sides was heaving with the last agonies of life, and she turned away from the painful sight" (89).

The juxtaposition between female victimization and male conquest establishes a direct link to Mrs. Conant's and Lady Arabella's death scene. The wounded deer has a "beautiful white breast" and "slender sides"; it is a "victim" of male brutality in the same way Mrs. Conant and Lady Arabella are. Although Hobomok is an Indian "cast in nature's noblest mould" whose "long residence with the white inhabitants of Plymouth had changed his natural fierceness of manner into haughty, dignified reserve," his actions in this scene are violent, cruel, and anti-female (36). He "seizes[s] the victim he [has] wounded" in order to win Mary's approbation. Like the "artificial light" that is associated with the deer's demise, Mrs. Conant is described as "sinking away, like a decaying lamp" while she lies dying (92). Like the second wounded deer that "utter[s] a piercing cry" (89), Mary, too, "utter[s] an involuntary shriek" the moment her mother dies (109).

To reinforce the horror of male brutality, Child once again uses a doubling technique that resonates with nuanced meanings. Seconds later, another deer is "bound by the same bewitching spell" (89). Only this time, the first Indian does "not effect his purpose entirely; for the creature uttered a piercing cry, and bounded forward with incredible swiftness" (89). Yet before the deer can escape, another Indian "rush[es] before his companion" and "bur[ies] his knife deep in the bosom of the wounded deer" (89). An argument then ensues as to which of the men gets to claim the dead deer as theirs.

> "It's mine," exclaimed he, in Indian language, "It's mine, for I killed it."
> "Tisn't yours," reported the other, furiously; "the deer hadn't run ten rods; and a hunter never gave up a beast under that." (90)

Even though "the girls could not understand what was spoken by the contending savages," they sensed a brawl was about to begin, and so Mary asks Mr. Conant "to guide them homeward." Mr. Conant returns just as "the others were preparing a new set of flambeaux for a fresh attack" (90).

In this remarkable scene Child depicts a cautionary tale in spotlighted relief, for the deer hunt by torch-light metaphorically encapsulates women's relationship to men in an America "where the heartes of men are as hard and sterile as their unploughed soile" (79). Like the deer "bewitched" by the "artificial rays" of men's torches, Mary is at first "bewitched" by the idea of male sport. But once she witnesses what happens to the deer, "she turns away from the painful sight" (89). Mary now understands what happens to women when they attempt to partake in a male-defined pageant of power. Her revelation leads to an important question about women's options in a patriarchal culture: where are women like Mary to turn in their quest for intellectual, emotional, and sexual fulfillment if they are imprisoned in a deathly, constricted circle that regards murdered women as trophies of male conquest?

Child's creation of Hobomok suggests an answer: Mary can escape white patriarchal captivity by marrying an Indian. Yet Child envisions Hobomok as far more than a pathway to Mary's liberation. He is also a target for her displaced anger at white men as well as a weapon of revenge against them. Hobomok's complex characterization reveals the ways in which Child's attitudes about race affect her vision of gender relations. Devising a drama in which whites watch Indians perform is the first clue that, in Child's imagination, Indians have the potential to provide pleasure. It is important to remember, however, that Mary and her friends had to obtain special permission to attend the event in the first place. Denied access to public sites of work and leisure that are male defined, the young women are not white men's equals. What becomes evident then is that while Child perceives white men and women as united by race—in relation to the Indian performers, they are spectators speaking a different language—when gender is taken into account, white men and women are disunited by unequal power relations. Nevertheless, the Indian men are depicted as mythic actors whose primary function is to entertain whites in "a strange romantic scene" (88). With a "figure [that] might well have been mistaken for the fabled deity of the chase," Hobomok and his associates are convenient markers of difference, men set apart from whites, white men in particular (88).[33]

Yet, what makes Child's vision complex are the ways in which she uses racialized fantasies to express anger indirectly at the white men she believes are responsible for her own oppression. To begin with, the fact that it is Indian men who indulge in ritual rites of conquest over prizes that are gendered female suggests that Child believes all men embrace the same attitudes about women. Whether the heartless male hunter is civilized or savage, when he invades nature—the female "majesty"—he intrudes upon her natural habitat, indulges in an impulse to conquer, and then triumphs in his prowess. But this vision of a hegemonic maleness that transcends racial barriers contrasts sharply with Child's other vision of maleness that Hobomok also embodies. He is a generous, attentive, loving man who is so much in sympathy and sensibility a part of the female world that he finds voice only in the company of women. "Hobomok seldom spoke in Mr. Conant's presence," Child informs us, "save in reply to his questions. . . . [B]ut with Mary and her mother, he felt no such restraint, and there he was all eloquence" (85). When Hobomok is in a woman's world, there are no barriers to communication. But when he takes part in a male ritual in which women are excluded and symbolically victimized, he speaks a language that Mary and her female friends find incomprehensible.

Child's contradictory portrait of Hobomok as both male hunter and sensitive lover is more understandable when we consider how she expresses anger indirectly at men of her own race and class. Although it is the white fathers, husbands, and lovers who force women into deerlike vulnerability throughout the course of the text, Child never once directly identifies them as the source of the problem. Instead, she literally has the Indian men act out the behavior she finds most repugnant in white men. Doing so allows her to find a culturally acceptable and emotionally safe way to express rage at the men who oppress her. Child displaces her anger at white men onto men of color.

Yet, at the same time that Child imaginatively uses Hobomok to signal her rage at women's intellectual, emotional, and artistic confinement, she also uses him to imagine a new kind of sensitive man who will partner her liberation. Hobomok's dual purpose exposes Child's ambivalent relationship to the racialized logic of her time: on the one hand, she uses the dispossessed "other" for her own purposes—primarily as a safe vehicle through which she can confront and express forbidden rage in an unequal power relationship. On the other hand, however, she identifies with the plight of powerless "others" who are excluded from the promise of a democratic America. Indeed, the identification is so strong that she envisions an alliance between white women and "others"—a marriage if you will—as a way of democratizing interpersonal relations. And it is these relations, Child believes, that will ultimately democratize the nation.[34]

But because Child imagines the alliance between Mary Conant and Hobomok as inherently unequal, she is much more interested in what the alliance will achieve for her white female protagonist, rather than in the idea of the alliance itself. Indeed, the relationship between Mary and Hobomok reveals Child's concern about gender oppression, not racial oppression. The most striking characteristic of Mary's and Hobomok's relationship is that it is structured along the same lines of dominance and subservience as that of white men in relation to white women, only in their case the power differential is ironically reversed: Mary assumes the position of the white man, and Hobomok the position of the white woman. Child not only creates a place of refuge from white male tyranny by envisioning a relationship between a white woman and a cultural "other"; she also gets revenge by insinuating that white male nation-builders are inadequate when compared to "uncivilized savages."

As an attentive adoring man who values tender feelings, Hobomok possesses the qualities white men lack. His greatest attraction is that he willingly relinquishes his own desires to gratify those of his beloved. As he says during their wedding ceremony, "Hobomok love [Mary] like as better than himself" (125). It is he, not Mary, who assumes the subservient and self-sacrificing position in the relationship. Full of a highly suggestive sexual "vigor and elasticity," it is he who provides "the flattery of devoted attention," something "a woman's heart loves . . . let it come from what source it may" (84). It is he who "break[s] the monotony" of Mary's pained existence after Charles Brown is banished (84); he who respects Mary's need for psychic and physical space by "silently remov[ing] a short distance from her" when they are together (121).

Most important, it is Hobomok's "idolatrous" love that gives Mary solace when she is deprived of all other sources of parental, platonic, and erotic loving. She agrees to marry Hobomok when "she remembered the idolatry he had always paid her, and in the desolation of the moment, she felt as if he were the only being in the wide world who was left to love her" (121). In this fantasy of devotional, unconditional love, Mary is the recipient; thus she is in control. Because Mary is in the more powerful position, she is not required to sacrifice herself or her desires to maintain the relationship. On the contrary, because her powerful status protects her psychic claims, Hobomok must assume the role that she, as a white woman, would normally be expected to play if she were in a relationship with a white man.

Child's repeated use of the word "reverence" when she describes Hobomok's feelings for Mary is the most telling indication of her wishful reversal. Compared to the "obtrusively officious" Mr. Thomas Graves and the "harshness" of Mr. Conant (47), "whenever Hobomok gazed upon Mary, it was with an expression in which reverence was strikingly predominant" (17). In stark contrast to the self-centered claims white men make on women, Hobomok exhibits a "spirit of devotion" (33) characterized as "unlimited reverence" (84) both before and after he and Mary are married. Child's repeated use of a term that connotes an unequal relationship between an imperial ruler and an obedient subject exposes Child's fantasy of what it would be like to be in the more powerful position in a heterosexual love relationship.[35] It also reveals how she uses the representation of Hobomok to transform her anger at female powerlessness into a political vision of social change. By imagining Mary in the more powerful position, Child vicariously experiences what it is like to use power in both the personal and political realms. At the same time, however, her fantasy of being revered by a man of color also shows that she does not confront her anger at white men directly. The real target of her anger is masked behind a titillating fantasy of power and revenge achieved at the expense of "otherized" men.[36]

Child's depiction of Mary's relationship with Charles Brown makes it clear why she uses her "other" relationship with Hobomok as a foil. Put simply, in relation to Charles it is Mary who is expected to assume the female role of subservient, self-sacrificing partner. Child demonstrates how this expectation impacts on the dynamics of their relationship in several different instances. Early in the narrative, for example, when Mary and Charles discuss Mr. and Mrs. Conant's relationship, he wonders if she would be willing to "endure" what Mrs. Conant has for the sake of love. "Do you think you could endure so much for me, Mary?" he asks (49). The treacherous implications of his question are evident in Mrs. Conant's death scene. In yet another example, he writes a letter to Mary after he is banished in which he praises her "dutiful" self-sacrificing behavior. "God willing, I would have shared any difficulties with you, soe as I might have called you wife; but I loved you the better in that you forgot not your dutie to your mother in your love for me" (103).

The most telling example, however, is the interaction between Charles and Mary after Charles returns and learns that Mary has married Hobomok in his absence. When Mary first sees Charles, she gets on her knees and begs forgiveness. In this important denouement, Child depicts the rebellious young woman in the posture of the repentant, reverential subject asking mercy of the Godlike ruling king, her white male lover.

> In an instant she was at the feet of her lover, clasping his knees with a pale imploring countenance, as she said,
>
> "Can you forgive me, Charles,—lost and humbled as I have been?"
>
> "The Lord judge you according to your temptations, my dear Mary," replied he, as he raised her to his bosom, and wept over her in silence. (148)

The psychological and social power Charles wields over Mary is expressed, once again, in spatial terms and metaphors. Shamed because she allowed herself to pursue her own desires, Mary is morally lower than Charles because she veered from her socially prescribed place. Although Charles has the authority to raise her back to her former status, Child makes it clear that, within the parameters of their newly reestablished relationship, Mary has less power. Instead of weeping with her and sharing her grief on equal terms, her future husband weeps "over her," thus maintaining a position of socially sanctioned masculine dominance.

Child's surprising reinscription of unequal gender relations can best be understood by applying Susan Harris's theory that the subversive middles of nineteenth-century women's texts undercut their traditional endings.[37] In psychological terms, the narrative design of *Hobomok* consists of three stages: the first is Mary's increasing anxiety, disillusionment, and isolation; the second is her self-imposed exile to pursue her own desires; and the third is the reclamation of a newly envisioned homeland that requires erasing any trace of the struggle it took to establish it. Once Mary is reinstated in white culture, she is the beneficiary of an inheritance from her English grandfather, half of which is used to provide her son—adopted by Charles—with an English education. The boy's "father was seldom spoken of; and by degrees his Indian appellation was silently omitted" (150). What is remembered, however, are the positive effects of Hobomok's sacrifice. Mary cherishes memories of Hobomok's "devoted, romantic love" because it enabled her to experience what it would be like to have male power. The culture remembers "his faithful services" "with gratitude" because his self-sacrifice ensured the building of the American empire (150). Hobomok's sacrifice assists the white daughter as well as her culture.

Child not only examines what is culturally forbidden in the text's middle; she also uses a "middle" male figure to fantasize about a loving family life not bound by patriarchal strictures. For although Child depicts Mary in the more powerful, traditionally male position and makes it clear that Charles Brown is the favored lover, she describes Hobomok's and Mary's daily married life positively. The magnitude of Hobomok's love affects Mary's feelings—"by degrees [she] gave way to its influence, until she welcomed his return with something like affection" (135). In time, he proves to be such a loving and considerate husband, father, and provider, that Mary unabashedly announces to her friend Sally that contrary to common belief, she is far from miserable. "I speak truly," she says, "when I say that every day I live with that kind, noble-hearted creature, the better I love him" (137). Child uses Mary's and Hobomok's marriage as a way of imagining what life could be like with a "kind, noble-hearted" man. The "other" marriage with a "middle" figure who embodies both male and female qualities—which occurs in the middle portion of the text—allows Child to explore an alternative vision of love within heterosexual marriage.[38]

Nevertheless, Child's ultimate ambivalence about a woman's right to express anger at her oppressors is what *Hobomok*'s traditional ending reveals more than anything else. Although Child envisions Puritan America as a kind of deathly captivity for women, she remains ambivalent about how they should exercise emotional freedom once they secure it. Because she has internalized her culture's belief that anger and womanhood are mutually exclusive, she can not grant her heroic female protagonist angry feelings. In the imaginative vision of the twenty-two-year-old Child, anger is a male prerogative, no matter how socially and personally destructive its costs. For women, anger causes turmoil.

Nowhere is Child's ambivalence about anger more evident than in the way in which she creates doubles for both her main protagonists. For by portraying different styles of expression in psychically linked characters, she engages in an internal dialogue about who she believes has the right to express anger, and under what circumstances the anger is socially permissible. Child's different characterizations of the female doubles are especially revealing in this regard. By juxtaposing Mary Conant's behavior and that of her double, the "roguish damsel" Sally Oldham, Child suggests that a woman of "noble" status is not permitted to express anger openly, especially to a male authority figure (21). Compared to the rambunctious and boisterous Sally, Mary is saintly, demure, and heroically self-repressive. While Sally doesn't hesitate to strike an abusive suitor when he attempts to fondle her, Mary reacts to anger-provoking situations by expressing anger indirectly. When Charles Brown comes to bid his supposed final farewell, for example, and Mr. Conant rudely throws him out of the house, Mary reacts by bursting into tears and burning her father's dinner. Mary's two responses are classic manifestations of repressed anger.[39]

The difference between Mary's behavior in relation to Charles's is also significant. While Child conveys how difficult it is for Charles to suppress his indignation during this same scene—"Pride was struggling hard for utterance . . . but for Mary's sake it was repressed" (77)—Mary's feelings are not mentioned. On the contrary, Child sidesteps the issue of Mary's anger by describing how she "rushed into her apartment, . . . [hid] her face in the bed clothes [and] gave free vent to her tears" (77). The only time Child allows Mary to feel anger openly at her father is when "there was a partial derange-ment of [her] faculties" (120). When she believes that Charles Brown has been killed, "[I]n the unreasonableness of mingled grief and anger, she accused her father as the sole cause of her present misery" (122). In such a "stupefying" state, Mary no longer controls her feelings; thus her anger is excusable.

The key to why Mary can not express anger openly at male authority figures but her double, Sally Oldham, can, lies in Child's perception of their different class positions. Whereas Sally is an "untutored" daughter of a rebellious father who lives on the outskirts of the community, Mary is a refined, well-educated daughter of one of the colony's rulers (36). The im-plication is that the more removed a woman is from the social conventions of civilization, the more emotional room she has to maneuver. Sally's forthright response to her insensitive suitor demonstrates this point. Yet it is important to note that the only reason Child condones Sally's anger at Mr. Graves is because he tries to take advantage of her womanly virtue.

> "I tell you sir," rejoined the angry damsel, "that I am weary of your unsavory discourse; and if husbands like you, grew by hundreds on the lowest boughs of trees, they might stay there till doomsday before I'd stop to pluck 'em therefrom."
> "But you'll let me take the milk across for you," continued the persever-ing suitor, as she stept upon a narrow board that was laid across a deep ditch. Sally, in the wickedness of her heart, held out the pail to him; but just as he was in the act of taking it, she managed by a gentle motion, to place him ancle-deep in the mud below; then turning round for an instant, with a loud and provoking laugh, she soon disappeared. (23)

It is significant that Child portrays Sally Oldham and not Mary Conant as the "angry damsel" who harbors "wickedness of heart," even if she intends these descriptions to be humorous (24). Compared to Mary's "habitual sweetness of disposition," Sally is mischievous, sassy, and unrestrained (46). While Mary is self-controlled and disciplined, Sally is willful and impetuous. These contrasting characterizations suggest that in the same way Child imagines Indians acting out the most heinous behavior of white men, she also imagines another "otherized" character—a woman "so vastly [Mary's] inferior"—acting out behavior that threatens the social fabric (136).

Like the female doubles, the male doubles also reveal Child's ideas about who has the right to express anger, and in what circumstances. Charles Brown reacts with righteous indignation when he learns that the ruling elders have decided to banish him. He "scornfully" accuses the council of hypocrisy by reminding them that "It is easy to talk about conscience and humility, but wherein have you shown it, in that you judge the consciences of your brethren?" (72). He leaves threatening vengeance: "There are those who can tell of your evil practices, and they shall be told in a voice of thunder" (73). Although he later admits to the ever conciliatory Mary that his "unruly tongue led [him] far beyond [his] reason in this matter," it is clear that, in Child's view, he has every right to feel anger, express anger, and use it as a weapon in a political fray (75).

Hobomok's relation to anger, on the other hand, is more complex because he acts out both "Indian" and female responses. When he is constructed as Indian, he expresses anger unproblematically. Engaging in typically "savage" behavior, he gets into a highly charged confrontation with another Indian man, Corbitant, over the issue of loyalty to whites. When Corbitant accuses Hobomok of caring more for the "tears [of] the white-faced daughter of Conant" than avenging the blood of his own kinswoman, Hobomok responds by "lift[ing] his tomahawk in wrath" (31). Only the intervention of another Indian, a wise old fatherly chief, prevents Hobomok's anger from turning into physical violence. On the other hand, however, when Hobomok is constructed as embodying a female sensibility, he is heroically repressive. When confronted with Brown's reappearance, for example, his decision to relinquish his own claims on Mary and his son is dutifully swift. Although he briefly considers taking his "rival's" life, when he puts Mary's desires before his own he concludes that "[t]he sacrifice must be made to her" (139).

Hobomok endures his loss with stoic sadness; that he may be feeling angry at Charles Brown and his own powerlessness is alluded to only when he is constructed as a potentially "savage" Indian. When first asked about Mary, for example, Hobomok has such "a strange mixture of sorrow and fierceness" in his eyes that Brown fears for his life (138). But once he begins to think like a woman, he represses his feelings and vanishes with "a bursting heart." He experiences anger like a woman as well. After "musing on all he had enjoyed and lost," Child informs us, Hobomok "sprung upon his feet, as if stung with torture he could no longer endure, and seizing his bow, he pursued with delirious eagerness every animal which came within his view" (140). In the same way Mary's tears and burnt dinner signal repressed anger, so, too, does Hobomok's frenzied hunting of deer. Since deer symbolize women, he kills all the women he can find. In a final noble gesture, he leaves the "largest deer" for Mary and his son with a note written for him by the "Governor of New Plimouth," informing the community that his marriage to Mary has been legally dissolved (146). Once again, the hunted deer symbolically represents female victimization and sacrifice, only this time it is Hobomok who must "turn away from the painful sight" (189) so that "Mary may be happie" (146) in her reconstituted community.

In Child's imagination the right to express anger is integrally related to a person's gender, race, and class status. She never questions whether it is appropriate for Charles Brown, Mr. Conant, or Mr. Oldham to feel anger; because they are powerful white men, their anger is taken for granted. Although she infers that they should not abuse these feelings because when they do they oppress women, the right to feel and express anger is not at issue. Child's view of whether women have the same right is more complicated. Her creation of Sally suggests that it is easier for her to imagine a woman she perceives as socially inferior expressing anger directly at men, rather than a refined white woman like her protagonist Mary Conant, who is modeled on herself.

To Child, anger and its expression are fundamentally linked to issues of power and social position. Moreover, her creation of both doubles as non-writers suggests that, in her mind, in the same way anger and power are related, so too are literacy and cultural visibility. The "other" sides of Mary and Charles—Sally and Hobomok—need to have a more powerful person write their stories for them when their versions of truth are at stake. In order to secure an historical legacy in a culture built on the power of the word, Child implies, the ability to write is a crucial tool. Once again, Child reiterates the importance of literacy when the question of whether women, African Americans, Native Americans, and the poor should be educated is being heatedly debated.[40] Ironically, however, it is also the "other" sides of Mary and Charles who have the right to act out anger in the same way that white men can, precisely because of their social marginalization. Given these circumstances, it is understandable why Child believed that white women like her protagonist and herself could not claim anger openly as the basis of a cultural critique. If they do, they risk permanent exile from their privileged status as literate daughters of men in power.

The complex dialogue about anger, rebellion, and literacy that the doubled characterizations of Mary/Sally and Charles/Hobomok reveal, betrays more than anything else Child's ultimate ambivalence about transgressing cultural boundaries. While on the one hand *Hobomok* conveys profound anger at the failed promises of democratic America by suggesting that intellectual white women need to conduct their own forms of revolution, on the other hand, the text is a loving embrace of the idea of America as Edenic homeland. Because Child revises male-authored historical texts, as opposed to conceptualizing new ones, she does not want to relinquish the fundamental idea of America that those texts encode. On the contrary, she wants to expand their limited gendered terrain. Her greatest wish is to write white women into the received historical narratives as well as the republican ideal. The irreconcilable tension between the desire to belong to an America that provides limitless gendered space for intellectual women, and the reality of psychological and material exile, compelled Child to explore what both she and her culture regarded as forbidden. The result is an artistry of anger that masks its own intentions.

Embracing a politics of moral emotionalism made this artistry possible. Clearly, Child believes that because women are endowed with a greater capacity to feel, they can envision a truly democratic model of social relations. The fantasy of "rigid" Calvinist men transformed into sensitive and loving community members shows that Child values female-styled emotionalism so much that it is the foundation upon which she bases her vision of a democratic America. To her mind, men's emotional rigidity is oppressive and anti-democratic; only when men are as emotionally expressive as women will America realize its Edenic potential. On the other hand, however, Child's difficulty with the direct expression of anger reveals the limitations of the politics of moral emotionalism. Since women are supposed to be more loving, moral, virtuous, and pious than men, for them to express anger publicly is equivalent to acting like men in the marketplace. If they behave in such an unwomanly fashion, the very basis of their authority is undermined. Thus, when women like Child use the politics of moral emotionalism to empower themselves as intellectuals, activists, and writers, both their critiques and their imaginative visions are necessarily circumscribed.

These limitations are best illustrated in Child's characterization of Hobomok as both the martyred enabler of white civilization and the exiled victim who is robbed of identity, homeland, and history. On the one hand, Child admires the strength and determination it takes for Hobomok to sacrifice his own desires so that a civilized, literate community can take root and flourish. On the other hand, however, she is painfully aware that such sacrifices ultimately lead to death of spirit and erasure from the public record.

Child's ambivalent characterization of Hobomok shows how she used the notion of a racialized "other" to come to terms with her conflicted feelings about anger, rebellion, and cultural transgression. By imagining an Indian as the victim who gets cast out of America's paradise, Child does not have to sacrifice the idea of America as a promised homeland for white women. Because Hobomok performs Mary's gendered function for her, she can reenter the culture assured of the right to inherit America's democratic legacy. Imaginatively inhabiting racialized space allows Child to reclaim the Eden of republicanism.

While in one sense this conventional happy ending proposes that there will be no more need for Mary to rebel once she assumes a space of her own in an unrestricted culture, in another, it exposes the anger that remains unresolved—and unresolvable—given the limitations of Lydia Maria Child's culture, politics, and imaginative vision. The novel's concluding fantasy of reconciliation—not only between white men and women, but also between competing national origins—indicates how valiantly Child was striving to resolve the central contradiction of her existence: how to be an intellectual woman in a republican nation that denies women citizenship and subjectivity. By having Mary inherit money from her English grandfather, which subsidizes her son's education in both America and England, Child claims America as homeland for a protagonist who can be an educated woman, loving mother, and virtuous citizen in a nation that does not recognize Native Americans as part of its heritage.

Hobomok's happy ending poignantly reveals that the closest the twenty-two-year-old Child can come to resolving the republican woman's conflict is by imagining culturally marginalized "others" in a contested America. Creating Indian men and lower-class women characters allows her to explore culturally forbidden ideas and feelings. While these imaginings inspire Child to envision a nation that includes a space for refined and superior intellectual white women—who secretly wish they did not have to remember their previously exiled state—they do not inspire her to envision a nation with radically transformed race relations. For that vision of America as homeland, it is necessary to turn to Child's contemporary, Maria W. Stewart.

FIVE

Maria W. Stewart's Inspired Wrath

My friends, I have been brought to consider that it is because the Lord he is God, that I have not been consumed. It is because that his tender compassion fails not, that I am not now in hell lifting up my eyes in torments, where the worm dieth not, and where the fire is not quenched. And I cannot help but exclaim, glory to God that I am yet a prisoner of hope. I rejoice that I have been formed a rational and accountable creature, and that ever I was born to be born again.

—Meditation III, from *Productions of Mrs. Maria W. Stewart* (1832)

Maria W. Stewart was so profoundly embittered by the broken promises of American republicanism that she built her own version of the nation through her writings. A self-proclaimed "prisoner of hope," Stewart was unwilling to accept invisibility and marginalization in the stories white Americans told about themselves and their history. In speeches, essays, meditations, prayers, and autobiographical writings, she provides a counter interpretation of history, truth, morality, and freedom that lambastes the pernicious effects of racial oppression.[1] Adopting the rhetoric and stance of an angry God makes her artistry of anger possible.

Born a "free" black in 1803, just one year after Lydia Maria Child, Maria W. Stewart also came of age when postrevolutionary optimism about rights, freedom, self-rule, and artistic sovereignty infused every aspect of American cultural life. As "one of the wretched and miserable daughters of the descendents of fallen Africa," however, she was daily reminded that those prospects were meant for white people only (55). Denied respect, educational opportunities, and economic prosperity, she and her "free" black peers were exiled from an America that was supposedly a beacon of democracy. Maria W. Stewart's anger at this exclusion inspired a boldly vengeful artistry. Relentlessly invoking the language and images of republicanism, she uses America's most cherished ideals to expose its hypocrisy.

When Maria W. Stewart stands behind the mask of an angry God, it is clear what she wants her anger to accomplish. Enraged that the "powerful force of prejudice" has denied the promise of peace, prosperity, and the pursuit of happiness to the "sons and daughters of Africa," she urges the black community to demand the privileges of white America for themselves. The language and themes of republicanism run like a leitmotif through her texts, but in her vision concepts such as independence and freedom take on added meaning. When applied to the black community, republican rhetoric justifies alternative nation-building. Appropriating its logic and vocabulary, Stewart uses republican rhetoric to agitate for black people's political, economic, and cultural rights. By expanding the discourse of republicanism to include the "sons and daughters of Africa," Stewart creates an alternative America and claims it as homeland.

As a black woman who had been raised as a white man's servant, Stewart has neither the leisure nor the luxury of writing fiction behind a deceptive cover. Disguising her presence is impossible because she has to deliver her message herself. Exiled from the white world, the black community is her audience. Stewart insists that she and her listeners share the same plight, and that her main purpose is to engender a God-believing community so that everyone in it will flourish. When African Americans "awake" and trust God and his judgments, Stewart exhorts, the "day of deliverance [will come and] God will provide a way for [community members] to escape, and fight his own battles" (80). God's "own battles" are the struggles to achieve equality and freedom for the people "He hath formed and fashioned . . . in his own glorious image" (4). Committed to the elevation of her race and the abolition of slavery, Stewart's texts are direct, purposeful, and insistent. The essays are written in the form of letters; the speeches are addressed to specific audiences; and the meditations engage her God in a one-to-one relationship.

Appealing, lamenting, cajoling, reprimanding, and encouraging, her narrative strategy is both thunderously Godlike and intimately parental.

Evangelicalism enabled Stewart to fashion herself as an inspired leader who was practicing an artistry of anger because she was faithfully obeying God's command. For "free" African Americans like Stewart, evangelicalism was an especially liberating theology: it offered parables of heroic behavior, moral justification for righteous anger, and a resonant vocabulary for its expression. Equally significant, the spiritual concept of conversion permitted the formulation of a secular politics of social change: in the same way sinners could be converted into saints, so, too, could America be converted into a righteous nation. For women, as Stewart's example demonstrates, evangelicalism had even greater benefits: it unwittingly promoted gender emancipation. It sanctioned women's literacy, provided them with opportunities to assume power in institutions outside their own homes as well as the ones in which they labored, and enabled them to transcend hierarchical race and gender power arrangements. By claiming that God had sanctioned their leadership, women bypassed patriarchal prohibitions and authorized their role as his holy warriors.

It is yet another nineteenth-century irony, however, that at the same time evangelicalism facilitated women's individual and political empowerment, it also negated their subjectivity and delimited their power. When women are God's handmaidens and ventriloquists, they can not act or speak for themselves. God wills their actions and their utterances for his specifically designated purposes. Thus God is the ultimate patriarchal authority, determining when and how women speak, as well as what they say when they do. Internalizing this conception of their divine mission, evangelical women experience profound anxiety if they believe they are speaking, acting, or feeling for themselves. All their psychic and social actions must be God's wishes, not their own.

There is no better example of this phenomenon than the way in which Maria W. Stewart relies on God to express anger for her. Whether it is anger at racial injustice or personal "enemies" who "wrongfully persecute" her, Stewart calls upon God and asks him to express the anger she believes she should not feel. In one of her meditations, for example, she alludes to many anger-provoking situations—"troubles," "distresses," and "wrongful persecutions"—yet it is God's anger that she acknowledges, not her own.

Lord, when mine enemies multiplied themselves against me, then I cried unto thee in my trouble, and thou didst deliver me from all my distresses.

Thou didst behold from thy holy habitation, that I was wrongfully persecuted, and that there was none to help. Then was thine anger kindled, and thy wrath waxed hot against mine adversaries, and thine own arm saved me, and thine own right arm wrought salvation. Thou didst vindicate my cause in the presence of mine enemies. (47–48)

Although the meditation enables Stewart to express relief that God vindicates her angry feelings, strikingly absent is any suggestion that she feels anger herself. Because Stewart believes she is not entitled to feel her own anger, God must feel it for her.

Maria W. Stewart's texts encode important information about African American women's access to anger through evangelicalism. On the one hand, because evangelicalism aided African American freedom struggles, it offered women the opportunity to utilize two liberatory discourses simultaneously. The evangelical belief that all human beings—regardless of their skin color—could find salvation through God's grace confirmed black people's humanity. Equally significant, the conjoining of the evangelical and black liberation movements offered women models for angered expression that they could fruitfully adopt and transform. Maria W. Stewart is a perfect case in point. As Marilyn Richardson notes, not only did "Stewart's initial political arguments [grow] out of [an independent] black protest and abolition tradition . . . which carried forward themes prevalent in the progressive black political climate of the day," she also found her most "profound and enduring" influence in David Walker, one of Boston's most radical, deeply religious, and outspoken abolitionists. The author of the militant text entitled *Walker's Appeal, In Four Articles; Together With A Preamble, To the Colored Citizens of the World, But In Particular, and Very Expressly, To Those of the United States Of America*, he was, according to Richardson, Stewart's "political and intellectual mentor."[2]

Following Walker's lead, Stewart stands boldly in front of an audience and ridicules American hypocrisy. In contrast to white women who express anger indirectly at white men, Stewart fearlessly prophesizes their doom: "O, ye great and mighty men of America, ye rich and powerful ones . . . You may kill, tyrannize, and oppress as much as you choose, until our cry shall come up before the throne of God; for I am firmly persuaded, that he will not suffer you to quell the proud, fearless and undaunted spirits of the Africans forever; for in his own time, he is able to plead our cause against you, and to pour out upon you the ten plagues of Egypt" (19). With God and the Bible in assistance, Stewart has no problem visualizing retribution for the "great and mighty men" who oppress her. Working within the Black Jeremiad tradition, she adds her threats to those of black men. Warning whites "that many powerful sons and daughters of Africa will shortly arise . . . and declare by Him that sitteth upon the throne, that they shall have their rights" (71), she uses black people's collective anger to warn her oppressors that their actions will have dire consequences.[3]

At the same time that evangelicalism provides an essential opening for women to express righteous indignation alongside men, however, it also reinscribes patriarchal power. The gendered nature of postrevolutionary evangelical discourse, Susan Juster argues, demonstrates that misogynistic ideas about women had become a fundamental part of the ideology. Because the evangelical church "needed a more masculine image," the discourse was infused with "patriarchal language and structures." Disorder and sin were "metaphorically 'feminized' "; thus women were associated with transgressive behavior that needed to be eradicated by temporal Godlike fathers.[4]

Amy Swerdlow's study of the Ladies' New York City Anti-Slavery Society also suggests why evangelical Christianity reinforced patriarchal authority. White, middle-class evangelicals championed "the 'God-given' hierarchical family structure" because they believed that "[t]he church-going Christian family, with the mother in her proper and secondary sphere as religious and moral guardian, was . . . the best protection from the poor, the morally depraved, and the non-Protestant immigrants." By enforcing traditional gender arrangements in order to maintain class privilege, evangelicalism reinforced the notion that women should be self-sacrificing instruments of middle-class social control. Swerdlow theorizes that the white women who belonged to the Ladies' New York City Anti-Slavery Society did not support woman's rights because they were "[t]rained for benevolence and giving." Thus they "could not justify 'selfish' demands on [their] own behalf—especially since these demands threatened the deferential order of the whole society and could undermine [their] own and [their] children's privileged economic and social position." Because evangelical ideology reified notions of female subordination and upheld class inequity, it did not provide a respite from gender and class oppression in the secular world. On the contrary, evangelicalism buttressed patriarchal domination in religious culture and life.[5]

Spiritual autobiographies written by African American women tellingly reveal their response to evangelicalism's limitations. In these texts the recurring tension between the sacred and the profane signals the problem women faced when they attempted to transcend gender constrictions by adopting a sacred identity and community. When evangelical women such as Maria W. Stewart, Jarena Lee, and Zilpha Elaw stand before their audiences as God's instrument, messenger, and handmaiden, they can not escape secular ideologies and practices: their writing is a commodity in the public marketplace; they are judged by their gender and their skin color, not by the integrity of their characters; and their actions are interpreted based on the belief that leadership and womanhood are mutually exclusive. Thus, the secular world constantly intrudes. Indeed, although evangelical women valiantly attempt to create a community, economy, and government in the sacred world, such alternative nation-building is always compromised by secular concerns. The would-be architects precariously straddle a sacred and a secular world, and ideologies of gender confine them in both.

Maria W. Stewart's life and texts exemplify this occurrence in painstaking detail. The story that they tell, and the one I track here, is of a profoundly angry woman who turned to spirituality for refuge, opportunity, and empowerment. Living and working in a secular world stratified by race, class, and gender hierarchies, for Stewart the sacred world promised a community not torn asunder by poverty, death, and alienation. It also offered the love and protection of a God who accepted all people as worthy of divine grace. Furthermore, membership in the sacred world provided a way to transcend gendered boundaries. As an evangelist, Stewart utilized both a feminine and a masculine sensibility. On the one hand, she imbued popular dominant-culture beliefs about women's greater morality with radical potential by showing how these ideas were instrumental to racial struggle. On the other hand, she stood behind the mask of a patriarchal God in order to authorize her masculine-styled artistry of anger.

In the end, however, Maria W. Stewart was betrayed by the sacred world in the same way she and her "free" black peers were betrayed by the nation. Because ideologies of gender subordination were as salient in the sacred world as they were in the secular, the sacred world was far from an egalitarian haven. Self-imposed anxiety conjoined with hostility from white culture and her own community made it impossible for Stewart to maintain her newly fashioned masculine-styled identity. Strictures against powerful, angry, vocal women conspired against her. So, too, did her own beliefs about gender difference. Assaulted from every direction, Maria W. Stewart was eventually forced to relinquish her patriarchal God persona, and she reentered the secular world an angry, vulnerable woman.[6]

The Personal Sources of Maria W. Stewart's Public Anger

Biographical information about Maria W. Stewart is scant; the little that is known comes from Stewart herself. The scarcity ironically reveals the enormity of what must have been a major source of Stewart's anger and pain: her frustrated desire to create herself as an enduring historical subject. That desire is evidenced in the autobiographical details contained in her texts, and the rudimentary memoir she included in the "new and enlarged edition" of her work, which she published shortly before her death in 1879. Entitled "Sufferings During the War," the memoir consists of five brief chapters that chronicle Stewart's efforts to make a living, find a home, and work for the black community through institutionalized religious networks. In the text, Stewart presents herself as a long-suffering, virtuous "heroine" who maintains her faith in God as she negotiates poverty, treachery, and alienation.[7]

Deprivation, betrayal, loss, and dislocation are key themes in Maria Stewart's autobiography, as well as in the story of her life. According to her own account, she was deprived of parental sustenance, the experience of childhood, and the privileges of an education. In her words, she "was left an orphan at five years of age; was bound out in a clergyman's family; had the seeds of piety and virtue early sown in [her] mind; but was deprived of the advantages of education, though [her] soul thirsted for knowledge" (3). In one of the letters contained in the 1879 text, a friend reiterates the deprivation theme, consciously connecting it to racial discrimination. "I have no doubt if she could have had the advantages of an early education and an opportunity to have developed her superior intellect, she would have been the equal, if not the superior, of her sisters of the more favorable race."[8]

Privation, bereavement, and displacement are also key themes in the story of Stewart's later life. Living in Boston's abolitionist community in the 1820s and 1830s, she married a much older, prosperous businessman in 1826 when she was twenty-three years old. Like many other women of her era, however, she lost her newly acquired middle-class status when her husband died three years later and white executors "literally robbed and cheated her out of every cent" of her husband's inheritance. Defrauded "of what should have amounted to a substantial" sum, Stewart was left, in her friend Louise Hatton's words, "entirely alone in the world—without mother, father, sister, or brother—in fact, not a living relative in the world to care for her."[9]

One year after her husband's death, Stewart suffered another traumatic loss, that of her friend and mentor, David Walker. It was during this period that she experienced conversion and launched her career as a speaker, writer, and reformer. She lectured in Boston between 1831 and 1833 and published her work in the newly established abolitionist newspaper, the *Liberator*. In 1834 she moved to New York City where she became a teacher and continued to participate in antislavery and African American self-help organizations. Whether her exile from Boston was self-willed or imposed by members of her community is unknown. After she "lost [her] position at Williamsburg, Long Island" in 1852, she left New York and moved to Baltimore where she opened a school.[10] During the Civil War, she relocated to Washington, opened a Sunday school, and worked as a matron in the Freedman's Hospital.

Meeting Maria W. Stewart at some point during these years, Louise Hatton recalled that she "at once became deeply interested in her, because there was a quiet sadness and melancholy of expression which, to a close observer, denoted a life of sorrow and disappointment." Sadness, sorrow, and disappointment are feelings that engender anger. "Many were the bitter tears I shed to think I had left all my friends at the North and had come here among strangers. Oh! Many were the tears I shed!" Stewart exclaims in the first chapter of her memoir. The "bitter tears," exasperated "Oh," and two exclamation points are classic expressions of antebellum women's coded anger. Anger, betrayal, and the search for community are paramount in the story of Maria Stewart's life.[11]

So is her desire to be a writer. And it is this element of her biography that provides an important clue to what must have been another source of Maria Stewart's profound anger and pain: thwarted authorship. The testimony of her contemporaries as well as internal textual evidence confirm that Stewart harbored literary ambitions. In a letter included in the 1879 text, for example, abolitionist editor William Lloyd Garrison remembers how Stewart asked him for "criticism and friendly advice" on a "manuscript embodying [her] devotional thoughts and aspirations." In another letter, the Episcopal minister Alexander Crummell recalled "the great surprise of both [his] friends and [himself] at finding in New York a young woman of [his] own people full of literary aspiration and ambitious authorship." He then notes how rare such "aspirations" were for black women at that time. Forty years later, his perception is that "in those days" "the desire for learning was almost exclusively confined to colored young men. [Although] [t]here were a few young women in New York who thought of these higher things, . . . it was a surprise to find another added to their number."[12]

Alexander Crummell knew about Stewart's "literary aspiration" because of her membership in a black women's literary association in New York City, The Ladies Literary Society. This society, and others like it in Boston, Philadelphia, and Providence, were organized by middle-class black women who believed that self-improvement was one way to "break down the strong barrier of prejudice." Devoted to "mutual improvement in literature and morals," the women met in each other's homes where they discussed literature, current events, and their own literary efforts. Considering that Stewart uses an image of bodily hunger to convey her "thirst for knowledge," it is appropriate that she joined a group of women who referred to their meetings as "mental feasts."[13]

Maria W. Stewart wanted more than to imbibe knowledge, however. She also wanted to create it. The most telling evidence of her literary ambition is contained in the publication history of her texts. Although Stewart pursued every available opportunity to promote her work, she was unable to sustain a literary career. Racial discrimination, poverty, and gendered vulnerability made it impossible. As a result, her canon consists of just one text, the 1835 *Productions*, which she republished forty-four years later in 1879 as the *Meditations From The Pen of Mrs. Maria W. Stewart*. While the later edition does contain some new material, it is essentially the same text.[14] In the preface to the 1879 edition, Stewart hints at why she has been unable to pursue authorship. Referring to herself as an "unworthy author," she informs her readers that in the intervening years when "[t]he work was suppressed," "the author was struggling . . . in widowhood and sorrow to maintain her dignity and standing as a woman and a Christian in poverty's dark shade." No longer wearing her angry God mask, Stewart speaks in a conventionally feminine, self-effacing mode. She relates that her text and God's message are now miraculously resurrected because her friend, Louise Hatton, has vindicated her right to receive her late husband's government pension, compensation for his service in the War of 1812. Stewart's comments explain why there are so many silences in her creative life.[15]

Maria Stewart's frustrated desire to become a writer surely must have engendered profound anger. Although she left no record of her personal feelings, her conversion into a holy warrior suggests that she found a fruitful avenue for expressing her personal pain and anger in evangelical activism. As a religious soldier fighting for the rights and freedom of the "benighted sons and daughters of Africa," Stewart submerged her own anger into the collective anger of the race (11). Transmuting her personal anger into political activism made it possible for her "to succor the outcast, reclaim the wanderer, and lift up the fallen."[16] No longer a desolate woman wallowing in her own pain, Stewart the religious crusader was one among many using God's wrath to foster virtue and righteousness.

Maria W. Stewart as Holy Warrior: Public Activism and Social Change

Marilyn Richardson notes that "religious faith and [David] Walker's political analyses provided a theoretical foundation upon which Stewart constructed a model of struggle for social justice."[17] There is yet another force fundamental to Stewart's thinking that Richardson does not name: the ideology of moral emotionalism. Maria W. Stewart's belief in women's greater moral virtue and emotionality significantly affects the formulation of her political program. She not only uses this belief to justify her own and other women's public activism; she also uses it as the basis of a philosophy of social change.

Fusing three different discourses—evangelical, abolitionist, and ideologies of gender difference—Stewart creates a new kind of discourse, one that incorporates both a female-gendered and a male-gendered sensibility. This fusion allows her to participate in both worlds simultaneously: she can appropriate the stance of an angry, patriarchal God while still viewing the world from a female perspective.[18]

Stewart, like other evangelical women, believes that women are closer to God. She articulates this view when she declares that the lines of communication between God and women are more open than are those between God and men. In her 1833 "Farewell Address," she informs her audience that there is "[a] belief . . . that the Deity more readily communicates himself to women, [which] has at one time or other, prevailed in every quarter of the earth" (76). The "Deity" has chosen Stewart as his emissary, for it is she whom he "commanded to come out from the world and be separate" (73); it is she whom he has selected to profess his teachings. Although Stewart tells her audience that she is "sensible of [her] ignorance," in the next breath she assures them that every controversial word she says has been divinely transmitted: "[S]uch knowledge as God has given to me, I impart to you" (6).

Women's intimate relationship with God, Stewart believes, makes them more receptive to his message. When she addresses women directly, offering the kind of domestic advice that was so prevalent at the time, she points to women's ability to give and receive "influence" as their unique capacity. The idea that women's primary role is to instill future generations with moral values is a commonly held belief; in Stewart's interpretation, however, it takes on added meaning. Whereas in periodicals designed to appeal to an increasingly literate, middle-class, white female readership—such as the extraordinarily popular *Ladies Magazine* begun in 1828—Sarah Hale and other promulgators of the doctrine of influence stressed that it should be "secret and silent," Stewart imbues the concept with connotations of openness and expression.[19] For her, woman's influence means not only causing an effect through model behavior; it also means acting as a righteous God-like medium.

Like many other women in the nineteenth century, Maria W. Stewart uses the doctrine of influence to invest women's culturally devalued gendered qualities with power and importance. By elaborating an ideology of gendered superiority, Stewart and others countered the notion that they were inferior appendages of men, and were incapable of exercising their own form of virtue. The undefined, awesome "influence" supposedly made men regard women "with an air, a reverence, and an affection which before [they] knew not [they] possessed." It assured women that they, too, had a crucial role to play in the building of the new nation.[20]

Because Stewart believes black women occupy a privileged position in relation to God, as well as in their families and community, she "calls" on them to make use of their specially endowed, gendered powers. In an emotional plea, she appeals to their sense of responsibility by underscoring how important their domestic role as wives and mothers is to the attainment of racial uplift.

> O woman, woman! upon you I call; for upon your exertions almost entirely depends whether the rising generation shall be any thing more than we have been or not. O woman, woman! your example is powerful, your influence great; it extends over your husbands and over your children, and throughout the circle of your acquaintance. Then let me exhort you to cultivate among yourselves a spirit of Christian love and unity, having charity one for another, without which all our goodness is as sounding brass, and as a tinkling cymbal. (62–63)

A typical evangelist, Stewart uses heightened emotion to inspire conversion. In this case, however, the heightened emotion is both a rhetorical style and the basis for an argument. Because women's presumed greater emotionality allows them direct access to God and his righteousness, they must communicate God's values to their husbands, children, and the culture at large. Once mothers "create in the minds of [their] little girls and boys a thirst for knowledge, the love of virtue, the abhorrence of vice, and the cultivation of a pure heart" (13), they inspire their children, as well as their "brethren" to fight for "freedom's cause" (7). Mothers have the special responsibility of bringing all those within their sphere of "influence" closer to "religion and the pure principles of morality" (3), the building blocks of progress. In Stewart's mind, morality is infused with—indeed, dependent upon—a sense of emotional communication that is fluid, open, and interactive. Thus, to her, women are key to a truly democratic America, for it is they who have the power to inspire self-worth, community building, and a zealous commitment to racial freedom.

Stewart's political program is grounded in moral emotionalism's central tenet, that female-styled expressivity is crucial to political progress. To free the nation from racism, African Americans must collectively feel indignation. They must do so in the privacy of prayer as well in the public arena of social interaction. In order to perform the work of racial uplift, men and women must be converted through a heart that is "wise and understanding" (11). With the help and protection of a righteous God who inspires "the pure principles of piety, morality, and virtue," African Americans will unite in their struggle for liberty, education, and achievement, and as a result "the chains of slavery and ignorance [will] burst" (6). For Stewart, conversion has both a religious and a secular meaning: when men and women are converted to God through the practice of moral feeling, they are also converted to the cause of African American liberty.

Because Stewart's argument for racial equality is based on the belief that "it is not the color of the skin that makes the man or the woman, but the principle formed in the soul" (78), it is understandable why she values morality so highly: it is integrally related to the attainment of freedom. Only when "the American free people of color . . . turn their attention more assiduously to moral worth and intellectual improvement," Stewart contends, will "prejudice . . . gradually diminish" because then "whites would be compelled to say, unloose those fetters!" (52). In Stewart's view, moral emotionalism, religious belief, and the pursuit of social justice are inextricably linked.

The importance Stewart places on "feeling," and the way she envisions its relationship to revolutionary moral activity is evident in the opening line of her first published text, "Religion and The Pure Principles of Morality."[21] The first word the reader encounters is "feeling," and the first sentence in which it appears emphasizes its connection to public moral action: "Feeling a deep solemnity of soul, in view of our wretched and degraded situation, and sensible of the gross ignorance that prevails among us, I have thought proper thus publicly to express my sentiments before you" (3).

Establishing a relationship between feeling and activism, Stewart justifies her entrance into the public sphere as a necessary consequence of despair. In her formulation, feeling ignites a series of chain reactions that result in the public expression of discontent. Feeling solemnity motivates awareness of the "wretched and degraded situation" of racial oppression; this awareness motivates assertion of the authoritative self; and the authoritative self then creates a public consciousness by explicitly expressing the original discontented feelings. To Maria W. Stewart, female-styled moral emotionalism is revolutionary. It enables her to critique her culture, her community, and the nation that disowns her, and it inspires other black women to do the same.

Because moral emotionalism reinforces religious fervor, it encourages women's intimate relationship with God. For Maria W. Stewart, this sacred bond is especially liberating. Incorporating both feminine and masculine features, Stewart's God satisfies all her desires. Committed to righteousness, he is loving, protective, and wise, and he also vindictively punishes his enemies. Because "it is God alone that has inspired [Stewart's] heart to feel for Afric's woes" (20), it is he to whom she is ultimately responsible. Concessions to male authority are no longer required. When God asks Stewart to work for racial justice in the public sphere, she obeys willingly: "Methinks I heard a spiritual interrogation—'Who shall go forward, and take off the reproach that is cast upon the people of color? Shall it be a woman?' And my heart made this reply—'If it is thy will, be it even so, Lord Jesus!' " (51) Because God "has fired [her] soul with a holy zeal for his cause," she has assumed leadership in the community; because he has "inspired [her] heart to publish . . . meditations," she has become an author (59). In her last speech, she describes how her conversion led to a vivid imaginary experience: "[I]n imagination," she tells her audience, "I found myself sitting at the feet of Jesus, clothed in my right mind" (73). "Sitting at the feet of Jesus" with her most basic needs taken care of, Stewart imagines controlling her own destiny. Before "she consecrated [her] soul and body, and all the powers of [her] mind to his service," she had been "like a ship tossed to and fro, in a storm at sea" (73), whereas at God's feet she finds meaning, purpose, and empowerment.[22]

Most important, Stewart's conception of God gives her a way to act on her convictions without threatening her womanhood. Because she has been chosen to speak for a God who is as full of wrath as he is of mercy, she is granted the authority to use his language, style, and tactics. In other words, God gives Stewart permission to feel and speak anger as a religious leader in a culture that equates anger with manhood. Her God's emotional expansiveness legitimates her own. In addition to being the great enabler without whom "we can do nothing" (34), Stewart's God is stern and authoritarian, but only because of his "infinite love" (36) for his children: "[T]hough he chastens and corrects, it is for the soul's best interest" (79). Endowed with socially responsible qualities, he is a "physician" who "alone can heal . . . maladies" (36), an empathetic reformer who "vindicate[s] the cause of the poor and the needy" (49), and a loyal and reliable community member "that sticketh closer than a brother" (79). A "compassionate Redeemer" (36), who is a "prayer-hearing and prayer-answering God" (49), he is a "parent of mercies" (49) who passionately loves and protects his children.

On the other hand, Stewart's God is also capable of great wrath when his plans are thwarted and his commandments disobeyed. Indeed, "the fierceness of his anger" (37–38) can be so terrible, Stewart is thankful that he "remembers mercy" when he is enraged (65). She begs him to "turn away from us thy fierce anger, and pardon this our iniquity, and lift upon us more the light of thy reconciled countenance, and the joy of thy salvation" (29). The threat of God's mighty anger is as powerful as the promise of his redeeming love.

As God's specially chosen emissary, Stewart is granted access to his expansive repertoire. With such a wide range of emotional expressions and postures to choose from, she can exhort her community to action and prayer using a number of different strategies. Indeed, once she is no longer restricted to female gendered language and tactics, confrontational—even acrimonious—methods become possible. When she is commanded to inspire faith and promote social activism in God's name, gender constrictions no longer hamper her. Moreover, not only does God allow her to disregard gender norms and speak anger for him; he also protects her from the anger of others. "I fear neither men nor devils"; she assures her audience, "for the God in whom I trust is able to deliver me from the rage and malice of my enemies, and from them that rise up against me" (57). Even anger turned into physical violence is not threatening because "with the help of God, I am resolved to withstand the fiery darts of the devil, and the assaults of wicked men" (56). Stewart allows herself to feel and express anger at her oppressors by adopting the posture of God himself.

Nowhere is this more evident than in the way in which Stewart uses anger to make her audience aware of their potential. Just as God's anger forces his chosen people and their enemies to recognize that their transgressive behavior will have dire consequences, Stewart's anger forces her audience to recognize that they have the power to change their victimized state. This strategy is best illustrated in her most militant speech, "An Address Delivered at the African Masonic Hall." In this speech, Stewart addresses "her brethren" directly, pointedly castigating their lack of leadership, courage, and moral worth. This state of affairs makes her so angry, she tells them, her soul is "fired" "with a holy indignation" that compels her to express publicly her criticism as well as her political program (64). Stewart's anger, like God's, not only forces her to confront the men of her community; it also forces the men to confront their own inadequacies.

Beginning and ending with the same provocative line, Stewart goads the men in her audience by assuming a Godlike authority: "African rights and liberty is a subject that ought to fire the breast of every free man of color in these United States, and excite in his bosom a lively, deep, decided and heartfelt interest" (63, 72). Stewart tells men not only what they should be thinking about, but also how they "ought" to feel, and what they should do with those feelings—turn them into resistant action. After chastising their lack of initiative and vision, by the end of the speech, she exhorts "every man of color throughout the United States, who possesses the spirit and principles of a man, [to] sign a petition to Congress" (70). The concluding repetition of the opening line shows how Stewart crafted the speech so that it would give concrete form to the message it delivers: in order to counter dissipation and build leadership, the problem has to be identified, and a plan of action has to be executed. Beginning and ending with a statement of the problem and what "ought" to be done about it, Stewart insists that the community never lose sight of the urgency of struggle.

Influenced by an evangelical tradition in which the manipulation of feeling—especially terror—is a primary tool, Stewart employs the same tactics, only she targets different emotions: in order to "convert" men to God's cause, she raises their political consciousness by provoking them into anger. In one of her boldest maneuvers, she challenges their manhood: "If you are men," she chides, prove it, "convince [whites] that you possess the spirit of men" (64). She sarcastically berates their political inaction and lets them know in no uncertain terms that their lack of willpower, courage, and ambition "causes [her] blood to boil":

> I am sensible that there are many highly intelligent gentlemen of color in these United States, in the force of whose arguments, doubtless, I should discover my inferiority; but if they are blest with wit and talent, friends and fortune, why have they not made themselves men of eminence, by striving to take all the reproach that is cast upon the people of color, and in endeavoring to alleviate the woes of their brethren in bondage? Talk, without effort, is nothing; you are abundantly capable, gentleman, of making yourselves men of distinction; and this gross neglect, on your part, causes my blood to boil within me. Here is the grand cause which hinders the rise and progress of people of color. It is their want of laudable ambition and requisite courage. (64–65)

In this passage, Stewart assumes the condescending stance of a paternal God in order to shame and scold her ignorant and wayward children. Yet, in Stewart's deft strategy, not only are the "sons of Africa" subjected to anger; they are also encouraged to become angered subjects. Confronting them with a list of indignities, Stewart wants men to feel anger and then channel it into useful action. The connection between feeling and political agency is imperative. Unless men "feel for [themselves] and [their] little ones, and exhibit the spirits of men," political change will be impossible (21). Thus, for Stewart, the "arousal" of men's anger is key to effecting political change, for it will "fire" their "souls" "with a holy zeal for freedom's cause" (7). Anger in and of itself is not what is most important; it is that it leads to impassioned and committed activism. Indeed, each of Stewart's angry texts contains what can be regarded as anger's antidote—a self-help program that results from the recognition and expression of despair. Considered from this vantage point, when Stewart expresses anger—whether it is directed at her own community, at the white Americans who oppress and exploit, or at the other "nations of the earth" that "hiss" and "reproach"—it is a sign of hope because it maintains that change will result.

Behind the mask of an angry God, Stewart disrupts complacency, forces confrontation, and inspires immediate action. Exposing the hypocrisy of an America that celebrates expansiveness and freedom is central to her artistry. Nowhere is this more evident than in her vision of America as a gaping absence as opposed to an ever-expanding presence. Over and over again throughout the texts, betrayal, barrenness, and lack are recurring motifs; images of stunted growth and confinement concretize limitation and lack of opportunity; and the enervated lives of blacks are set in stark contrast against the decadent, self-satisfied spoils of whites. Far from containing endless economic, political, and social possibilities, or providing a space where a divine self can find free reign in an intimate relationship with nature, Stewart's America is rigid, stymied, and bedeviled by whites. And the only source of liberation is religion, for it is in committed faith that endless possibility resides, not in a severely flawed republican nation. In her words: "Religion is the most glorious theme that mortals can converse upon . . . Earth, with its brilliant attractions, appears mean and sordid when compared to it. It is that fountain that has no end, and those that drink thereof shall never thirst; for it is, indeed, a well of water springing up in the soul unto everlasting life" (80). In a society that deprives black Americans of their most fundamental rights, religion provides intellectual nourishment and imaginative spaciousness. Religion satisfies the "thirst" for the promises America denies.

Excluded from sources of power, Stewart stands outside the nation's borders and fearlessly discloses its falsehoods. America is not a united nation where all its inhabitants share the same history, privileges, and agenda for the future. Unlike white women writers such as Lydia Maria Child who have a stake in rewriting a Puritan-authored usable past to secure a position for themselves within it, Stewart shows how African Americans have to find a different source of authority for both their origin story and their definitions of progress. Her version of history begins at the present moment:

> This is the land of freedom. The press is at liberty. Every man has a right to express his opinion. Many think, because your skins are tinged with a

sable hue, that you are an inferior race of beings, but God does not consider you as such. He hath formed and fashioned you in his own glorious image, and hath bestowed upon you reason and strong powers of intellect. He hath made you to have dominion over the beasts of the field, the fowls of the air, and the fish of the sea. He hath crowned you with glory and honor; hath made you but a little lower than the angels; and according to the Constitution of these United States, he hath made all men free and equal. (4–5)

In order to argue that African Americans are sanctified human beings, Stewart uses the Biblical origin story in Genesis to invoke God as the ultimate historian, and the Constitution—America's secularized Bible of Liberty—to create a version of American history in which African Americans have an equal claim to the land of liberty.

Because the people whose skins "are tinged with a sable hue" are regarded as inhuman, Stewart's America is rent down the middle—one half is inhabited by envious and greedy whites, the other half by degraded and exploited blacks. And these two Americas, she repeatedly points out, are in an ugly moral and economic battle over rights, resources, and inheritances. When she explains, for example, why she thinks "distinguished" black men have not made themselves "influential," she uses religious images to draw a picture of America in which power-hungry, deceitful whites prevent aspiring, deserving blacks from attaining "the highest place in the synagogue, and the uppermost seats of the feast":

> The reason why our distinguished men have not made themselves more influential is, because they fear that the strong current of opposition through which they must pass, would cause their downfall and prove their overthrow. And what gives rise to this opposition? Envy. And what has it amounted to? Nothing. And who are the cause of it? Our whited sepulchres, who want to be great, and don't know how; who love to be called of men "Rabbi, Rabbi," who put on false sanctity, and humble themselves to their brethren, for the sake of acquiring the highest place in the synagogue, and the uppermost seats of the feast. (70)

In yet another embittered passage, Stewart shows how "the strong current of opposition" between the "white sepulchres" and the "benighted sons and daughters of Africa" stratifies the nation into two distinct groups: the haves and the have-nots. Practicing her artistry of anger most effectively, she invokes images of progress and expansionism only to prove their emptiness. She makes absence literally visible when she commands her audience to "see" the extent of their lack: "Cast your eyes about, look as far as you can see"; she exhorts, "all, all is owned by the lordly white, except here and there a lowly dwelling which the man of color, midst deprivations, fraud and opposition, has been scarce able to procure" (66–67). The repetition of the expansive "all"—which connotes the physical terrain of America itself—juxtaposed with the "lowly dwelling" and the meager "scarce" vividly conveys the economic, social, and psychic position of blacks in an America controlled "by the lordly white."

Stewart repeatedly shows why the inhabitants of white America thrive while the inhabitants of black America remain in arid and infertile soil. Using images of confinement, emptiness, and loss, she dramatizes how systematic educational and employment activities "[deaden] the energies of the soul, and [benumb] the faculties of the mind" (53). In a strikingly forthright attack, she underscores the hypocrisy of westward expansionism by invoking geographical metaphors. "[I]deas become confined," she writes, "the mind barren, and, like the scorching sands of Arabia, produces nothing; or, like the uncultivated soil, brings forth thorns and thistles" (53–54). In one of her angriest passages, she stresses that deprivation of education, respect, and dignified labor cause what she sees as black ineptitude, not a flawed intellectual constitution.

> White Americans, by their prudence, economy and exertions, have sprung up and become one of the most flourishing nations in the world, distinguished for their knowledge of the arts and sciences, for their polite literature. While our minds are vacant, and starving for want of knowledge, theirs are filled to overflowing. Most of our color have been taught to stand in fear of the white man, from their earliest infancy, to work as soon as they could walk, and call "master," before they scarce could lisp the name of *mother*. (Stewart's emphasis, 66)

The "vacant," "starving" minds of blacks set against the "overflowing" minds of whites renders a jarring image of deprivation that is glaringly inconsistent with the rhetoric of equality. Even more pointed is the way in which Stewart dramatizes the abnormal stunting of the human life cycle by a slave labor system that is as operative for "free" blacks in the North as it is for those enslaved in the South. By juxtaposing "master" and "mother" in the same sentence, Stewart shows how black women are denied the sanctified right of mothering. When a child grows into adulthood with a "master" and not a mother, Stewart insists, he or she will be robbed of the "natural force and energy" that cultivation of the intellect requires (66).

Because Stewart believes that "there are no chains so galling as the chains of ignorance—no fetters so binding as those that bind the soul, and exclude it from the vast field of useful and scientific knowledge" (52), she finds the denial of education to black Americans particularly reprehensible. When she recounts her own experience, mourning her limitations in a personal lament, her anger and pain are poignantly expressed: "O, had I received the advantages of early education, my ideas would, ere now, have expanded far and wide; but, alas! I possess nothing but moral capability—no teachings but the teachings of the Holy Spirit" (52). Once again, Stewart invokes republican rhetoric to expose the hypocrisy of an America that continues to enchain part of its population. Using the language and images of slavery—chains, fetters, and bindings—she shows how the condition of "free" blacks in the North is "but little better than" "southern slavery" (51–52).

An economic system that delegates "head-work" to one segment of the population and "drudgery" to another is why "free" blacks feel as if they are performing slave labor (17). Repeatedly emphasizing how white Americans have "enriched" themselves by exploiting the "toils," "labors," "blood," and "tears" of black men and women, Stewart vents anger at a system that forces black Americans to "[drag] out a miserable existence of servitude from the cradle to the grave" (54). Referring once again to the way in which white Americans hideously maim the African American life cycle for their own benefit, Stewart explains why it has such deadening consequences. "[H]ard labor irritates our tempers and sours our dispositions," she notes, "the whole system becomes worn out with toil and fatigue; nature herself becomes almost exhausted, and we care but little whether we live or die" (54). What is most enraging is that this "hard labor" built the America that denies blacks the right to benefit from what is rightfully theirs. Using the Biblical story of King Solomon to illustrate this point, Stewart utilizes striking contrasts between emptiness and fullness to convey her indignation.

> Like king Solomon, who put neither nail nor hammer to the temple, yet received the praise; so also have the white Americans gained themselves a name, like the names of the great men that are in the earth, while in reality we have been their principal foundation and support. We have pursued the shadow, they have obtained the substance; we have performed the labor, they have received the profits; we have planted the vines, they have eaten the fruits of them. (67)

In this passage, the grammatical structure of the sentences dramatizes Stewart's point. The repeated, paired use of the "we" and "they" pronouns signifies the divide between white and black Americas. At the same time, however, by structuring the last sentence into two clauses, one connected to the other by a comma, Stewart conveys the complex interrelationship between the two Americas. Because both clauses contain equally active verb structures, yet blacks provide the resources and whites receive the rewards, Stewart demonstrates the structured injustice of black/white social relations through the positioning of subject/verb clauses.

Stewart's critique does not gloss over the special problems of black women who are compelled to labor in such a system. Indeed, her sensitivity to economic discrimination against black women reveals her anger at white women who perpetuate racist employment practices because they are unwilling to risk "losing the public patronage" (52). She relates how when she asked "several individuals of [her] sex, who transact business for themselves," if they would be willing to "grant" young black women "an equal opportunity with others," they replied that although they didn't have a personal "objection," they feared losing customers (52). From the way Stewart unleashes her anger at white women, it is clear that, to her, they signify what black women are denied. Particularly incensed that "the fair daughters of Africa [are] compelled to bury their minds and talents beneath a load of iron pots and kettles" (16), she encourages both men and women to make it possible for women to assume dignified roles as "American ladies" whose primary responsibility is instilling their children with liberating moral values (15).

Directly appealing to white women, which is meant more for her black audience than her "fairer sisters," Stewart invokes Biblical language and dissonant oppositions to convey her indignation:

> O, ye fairer sisters, whose hands are never soiled, whose nerves and muscles are never strained, go learn by experience! Had we had the opportunity that you have had, to improve our moral and mental faculties, what would have hindered our intellects from being as bright, and our manners from being as dignified as yours? Had it been our lot to have been nursed in the lap of affluence and ease, and to have basked beneath the smiles and sunshine of fortune, should we not have naturally supposed that we were never made to toil? . . . Have pity upon us, have pity upon us, O ye who have hearts to feel for other's woes; for the hand of God has touched us. (54–55)

Stewart evidently understands class inequality in racial terms. Because privileged white women are representative of an exploitive and unjust economic system, they become special targets of Stewart's scorn. What is seemingly a plea for mercy—"Have pity upon us, Have pity upon us, O ye who have hearts to feel for other's woes"—is in actuality a contemptuous taunt. Placed at the end of a string of questions that blatantly underscores the inequity between the two groups, this "plea for mercy" is an expression of anger ironically couched in the guise of a supplicating appeal.[23] Stewart is well aware of the political advantages of expressing anger at white women behind a mask of feminine submission. This ploy not only allows her to attempt to gain white women's sympathy; it also enables her to mask her anger while still expressing it.

Given the deplorable conditions that exist in the "other" America, Stewart insists that the black community pool its resources to claim what is rightfully theirs. This requires creating an alternative historical narrative that records history from a black perspective. It also entails redefining the meaning of the concept "American." Responding to the proposed plan that "free" blacks should be relocated to Liberia provides Stewart with the opportunity to engage in both endeavors. The idea that the black community would want to leave after all the "toils," "labors," "blood," and "tears" they have invested in America particularly enrages her. She conveys her contempt in this bitterly wrought, encapsulated narrative of American "progress":

> The unfriendly whites first drove the native American from his much loved home. Then they stole our fathers from their peaceful and quiet dwellings, and brought them hither, and made bond-men and bond-women of them and their little ones; they have obliged our brethren to labor, kept them in utter ignorance, nourished them in vice, and raised them in degradation; and now that we have enriched their soil, and filled their coffers, they say we are not capable of becoming like white men, and that we can never rise to respectability in this country. They would drive us to a strange land. But before I go, the bayonet shall pierce me through. (71–72)

Depicting whites as malicious, gluttonous thieves, Stewart reverses the conventional race relations paradigm by showing that it is not white Americans who are the rightful inheritors of the nation, but rather the "sons and daughters of Africa." Defiantly standing firm, she resists both psychic and physical displacement, claiming America—"thou land of my birth"—as homeland. No matter how much she "abhor[s] and detest[s] [America's] vices," and "hopes that thy stains will soon be wiped away, and thy cruelties forgotten," she "love[s] and admire[s] thy virtues."[24]

That Stewart perceives herself as "a true born American" (53) and encourages her community to do the same is best illustrated by her proposition that the distinction between races is irrelevant: if whites are Americans so are blacks. "[O]ur souls are fired with the same love of liberty and independence with which your souls are fired," she contends; "too much of your blood flows in our veins, and too much of your color in our skins, for us not to possess your spirits" (19–20). Once again Stewart ironically reverses the conventional race relations paradigm: instead of following the condition of the enslaved black mother, the children of institutionalized rape follow the condition of the "liberty-loving" white father. Born of the same stock, blacks and whites have the same desires. Even if "white blood" does not flow in their veins, their republican ideas "flow" in their consciousness. Because "the whites have so long and so loudly proclaimed the themes of equal rights and privileges, . . . our souls have caught the flame also" (53).

Repeatedly emphasizing that blacks are as American as white Americans, Stewart encourages her community to take the best of a revolutionary tradition and use it for their own advancement. Blacks must make "powerful efforts to raise themselves" in the same way "the Pilgrims" did when they were confronted with British tyranny and difficult living conditions (56). By invoking "the Pilgrims," Stewart implies that the black community is as "American" as the first white European settlers because both share the same pioneering spirit. Indeed, she commands her brethren to "Possess the spirit of independence. The Americans do, and why should not you? Possess the spirit of men, bold and enterprising, fearless and undaunted" (17). She thus transforms her God-given anger into a vision of secular redemption that is as "American" as Benjamin Franklin's thirteen virtues: "Sue for your rights and privileges. Know the reason that you cannot attain them. Weary them with your importunities" (17). Here, then, is Stewart's version of a quintessentially American success ethic, but unlike Franklin's "bold and arduous project of arriving at moral perfection," Stewart's self-help program is articulated in exile, and it is born of collective anger and collective struggle.[25]

Stewart's angry-God self-fashioning enables her to formulate this program and agitate for its implementation. The central paradox for her and other evangelical women, however, is that in order to attain public leadership they have to deny their individuality. And this in effect erases their female subjectivity and invalidates their legitimacy as women in the public sphere. Granted privilege and authority by God, the sacred woman must forfeit her own agency, imagination, and literacy. As a result, the human being, the speaking woman, the writing subject, is literally subsumed in the patriarchal deity.

Stewart's championing of a communal, egalitarian ethic by emphasizing the insignificance of the individual tellingly illustrates this quandary. The ultimate irony is that she argues the point by obsessively referring to her own unimportance. Calling attention to herself concretizes her presence at the same time that it negates it. In her words, she is "a feeble instrument," "one particle of the small dust of the earth" (7), "a drop in the bucket" (70). She relishes the role of martyr: "Many will suffer for pleading the cause of oppressed Africa, and I shall glory in being one of her martyrs" (5). It is not "only for [herself]" that she pleads "but for the whole race of mankind; especially for the benighted sons and daughters of Africa" (37). It is not for herself that she asks for "blessings," "but for all the poor and needy, all widows and fatherless children, and for the stranger in distress" (49). It doesn't matter that she may "sink into oblivion," and that her "name [may] die in forgetfulness" (59). What is important is that God's message reaches a community striving for freedom. Reiterating female unworthiness, disclaiming an individual self, and disavowing historical recognition, Stewart reinforces the gendered ideologies that seek to prevent women from assuming public leadership. Only when she is God's "instrument" can she be a holy warrior against racial injustice.

The Secular Woman Forced to Remove the Angry-God Mask

When Maria Stewart believes she is endowed with patriarchal power, she seizes the opportunity to "arouse" her listeners "to exertion" (3). When she is forced to remove the Godlike mask, however, her ability to feel and speak anger is compromised. Several factors drove Stewart to abandon the posture of masculine authority. Not the least of these were attitudes about women's public activism that pervaded dominant white culture. Mounting a public platform five years before Sarah and Angelina Grimké became lecturers for the American Anti-Slavery Society, Stewart began speaking in front of "promiscuous" audiences when such an activity was considered outside the acceptable norms of female behavior. The specter of women addressing political issues in public, as the Massachusetts Congregationalist clergy's response to Sarah and Angelina Grimké's public speaking demonstrates, threatened the conception of womanhood. In the clergy's view, "the appropriate duties and influence of woman"—and how those "duties and influences" should most effectively be utilized in the newly developing nation—were determined by woman's God-given role in the family.

> The appropriate duties and influence of woman are clearly stated in the New Testament. Those duties and that influence are unobtrusive and private, but the source of mighty power. When the mild, dependent, softening influence of woman upon the sternness of man's opinions is fully exercised, society feels the effects of it in a thousand forms. The power of woman is in her dependence, flowing from the consciousness of

that weakness which God has given her for her protection, and which keeps her in those departments of life that form the character of individuals and of the nation. . . . But when she assumes the place and tone of man as a public reformer, our care and protection of her seem unnecessary; we put ourselves in self-defence against her; she yields the power which God has given her for protection, and her character becomes unnatural.[26]

The clergy articulate a polarized conception of gender in which woman is "mild," "dependent," and "private," and man is "stern," powerful, and public. Their words also betray their anxiety about role displacement, as well as their anger at the threat of eclipsed power. When woman "assumes the place and tone of man as a public reformer," the "natural" distinction between the sexes is treacherously imperiled; when she begins to express opinions outside her divinely ordained sphere of influence, the hegemony of masculine authority is no longer taken for granted. Most revealing, though, is the way in which the clergy see woman's assumption of man's "place" and "tone" as one and the same, for it shows how they equate voice with power and gender them male. A man has the right to speak his opinions "sternly," and when he does, it is woman's duty to "soften" that sternness with her "mild, dependent, [and] softening influence." But if a woman dares to speak "sternly," she fails to perform her national duty and loses her womanhood.

The highly contentious debate about the appropriateness of women's public speaking that the clergy's response to the Grimkés initiates metaphorically encapsulates one of the most pressing problems antebellum women faced in their struggle for cultural articulation: how to claim the authority to participate in, and contribute to, the creation of public culture without forfeiting their gendered sense of authority.[27] Given the commentary of Stewart's contemporaries, as well as internal textual evidence, it is apparent that Stewart confronted this problem. In 1852, for example, when the abolitionist and writer William C. Nell commended William Lloyd Garrison on his early support of "women's equality," he remembered that, "In the perilous years of '33–'35, a colored woman—Mrs. Maria W. Stewart—fired with a holy zeal to speak her sentiments on the improvement of colored Americans, encountered an opposition even from her Boston circle of friends, that would have dampened the ardor of most women."[28]

The opposition Nell refers to is inscribed in Stewart's texts. Indeed, Stewart remarks upon her contested presence so frequently it becomes a repeated refrain. She informs her audience that she is "sensible of exposing [her]self to calumny and reproach" (6); that she "expect[s] to be hated of all men, and persecuted even unto death, for righteousness and the truth's sake" (59); that she is well aware that she makes herself "a hissing and a reproach among the people" (55), and that she has "made [her]self contemptible in the eyes of many, that [she] might win some" (81). She prays that God will "preserve [her] from slanderous tongues" (46); and vows that the "frowns of the world will never discourage [her]" (56). This is the response of a woman painfully aware that she is under attack.

Although the opposition Stewart encountered may have been because of her evangelical message, the fact that she was transgressing gender roles by claiming public leadership was also at issue.[29] Indeed, most scholars believe that Stewart gave up lecturing because of the severity of public censure. According to Dorothy Sterling, for example, "Although Stewart's exhortations did not differ greatly from the sermons of black ministers, the fact that she was a woman made her message unacceptable." Other anthologizers of Stewart's work share Sterling's view. In their interpretations, Stewart was "[d]iscouraged from speaking by unpleasant 'notoriety'"; she was "hurt by criticisms directed against her as a woman for daring to assume the role of public leader"; she was "resented for her religious exhortations and even more for her audacity as a woman." The "high personal cost" of all this discouragement, Marilyn Richardson concludes, engendered in Stewart a painful internal conflict. In order to assume a leadership role, Stewart was required to "[behave] in a manner almost exactly opposite [to] what she had once considered the ideal of black womanhood."[30]

Stewart's contradictory conception of woman's influence as both powerful and limiting reveals her difficulty. On the one hand, she believes that the exercise of woman's pious, moral influence is instrumental to the attainment of African American freedom. On the other hand, however, she interprets "woman's influence" as activism that is effective only within the family. In order to inspire black men to become more committed "advocates of freedom," she reminds them that because woman "can do but little besides using her influence" it is "upon [men] that [she] depends," especially when it comes "to pray[ing] the legislature . . . to grant you all the rights and privileges of free citizens" (55–56). Although Stewart sees the black family's ability to practice traditional gender arrangements as a form of freedom, when she advocates social relations premised on gender role difference, she is unwittingly adopting what Shirley Yee aptly calls "white standards of inequality."[31]

Stewart's difficulty becomes most evident when her conception of female propriety conflicts with her belief that black women should have the right to express anger in public. Because "white standards of inequality" include sanctions against the expression of female anger, Stewart grapples with this problem: Can a woman feel and express anger and still be a true woman who is a respected member of her community? Even though she sees a relationship between female propriety and the attainment of freedom, if she proposes that black women adhere to such standards of behavior, then expressing anger in public breaches decorum. When Stewart dispenses domestic advice, the dilemma emerges into clear view. If women should, as she contends, "possess a delicacy of manners" (7), and be like "mothers in Israel, chaste, keepers at home, not busy bodies, meddlers in other men's matters, whose adorning is of the inward man, possessing a meek and quiet spirit, whose sons were like olive-plants, and whose daughters were as polished corner-stones" (10), how can they also express anger in print and in lecture-halls?

This conundrum raised the question of how Stewart herself could lead a freedom struggle and still be "meek and quiet" and "not [a] busy bod[y]." Repeatedly calling attention to her own speaking belies her discomfort about transgressing middle-class rules of proper feminine behavior, for this recurrence signifies an obsessive need to justify her authority. Moreover, the tension between a visible and ambitious self-assertion—which is gendered male—and a philosophy of Jesus-styled humility and meekness—which is gendered female—reveals Stewart's ambivalence about women's right to claim public authority and anger.

Even though by the end of her speaking career, as Marilyn Richardson observes, Stewart's ideas about women's roles had changed, she was never able to reconcile her public activism with her conception of appropriate middle-class female behavior. Moving from a belief that women should participate in nation-building enterprises through their "influence" to advocating that they should pursue more direct forms of power through intellectual achievement did not resolve the problem.[32] As Carla Peterson notes, Stewart's efforts to maintain her middle-class status reveal how important this self-identification was to her. Besides emphasizing that she perceives herself as a "lady" who possesses a "refined sentiment of delicacy," Stewart also changed her church affiliation from Baptist to Episcopalian. The latter denomination, Carla Peterson explains, "was the religion of choice among upper-class African Americans, promoting an image of social exclusiveness and prompting 'upwardly mobile blacks to transfer their allegiance from Baptist and Methodist denominations.'"[33] Upper-class African Americans did not sanction women's indecorous expression of public anger.

Thus, even behind her angry-God mask, Maria W. Stewart could not avoid the psychic and social obstacles that other women of her era encountered. That she expresses anger in her own right only once—when she publicly resigns her leadership—is highly significant because it is only then that she speaks as a mortal woman protesting gender oppression rather than as God's instrument. Bidding a bitter "farewell" to "Her Friends in the City of Boston," she also bids "farewell" to God as an emotional mediator. After once again justifying her public activism by insisting that it was God's decision to "unloos[e] [her] tongue" "for wise and holy purposes, best known to himself," she can no longer contain her indignation at the opposition that has been directed against her, precisely because she is a woman speaking in God's name (75). In an explosive tirade, she unleashes her pent-up anger by declaring:

> What if I am a woman; is not the God of ancient times the God of these modern days? Did he not raise up Deborah, to be a mother, and a judge in Israel? Did not queen Esther save the lives of Jews? And Mary Magdalene first declare the resurrection of Christ from the dead? . . . St. Paul declared that it was a shame for a woman to speak in public, yet our great High Priest and Advocate did not condemn the woman for a more notorious offence than this; neither will he condemn this worthless worm . . . Did St. Paul but know of our wrongs and deprivations, I presume he would make no objections to our pleading in public for our rights. (75)

Asking and answering her own questions, Stewart argues her case by becoming her own lawyer. Invoking a God who creates strong and accomplished women, and Biblical stories that celebrate their politically important contributions, Stewart justifies the public involvement of black women like herself. Because "holy women ministered unto Christ and the Apostles; and women of refinement in all ages, more or less, have had a voice in moral, religious and political subjects" (75–76), there is ample proof that her public voice is not anomalous. On the contrary, it has a long and distinguished history. The amount of evidence she marshals to prove that women are eminently capable of mastering such a voice is indicative of her angered exasperation with the opposing view. In order to "convince" her audience "of the high opinion that was formed of the capacity and ability of woman" (76), Stewart turns to ancient history, chronicling myriad examples of the ways "women in those days devoted their leisure hours to contemplation and study" (77). "Animated" by a "religious spirit," she shows how they distinguished themselves and their societies by becoming "martyrs, apostles, warriors, . . . divines and scholars" (77).

Stewart uses these historical figures to prove that there is nothing "unnatural" about contemporary women's political impulses. Since "15th century" women "preach[ed] and mix[ed] themselves in controversies" without sacrificing their womanhood (77), surely no dire consequences will result if black women do the same, especially in such an "eventful period" as the early nineteenth century. Thus, Stewart instructs her audiences: "[B]e no longer astonished . . . that God at this eventful period should raise up your own females to strive, by their example both in public and private, to assist those who are endeavoring to stop the strong current of prejudice that flows so profusely against us at present" (76–77). Her anger emboldens her to take this injunction one step further: she warns her "brethren and friends" that if they continue to "ridicule [black women's] efforts, it will be counted as sin" because they will be disobeying God's will (77). Before "return[ing] to [her] subject," Stewart concludes by reiterating the political urgency of black women's intellectual efforts: when they are allowed to become "divines and scholars," their "brilliant wit," "genius," and "talent" will significantly contribute to the race's progress (78).

By summoning female role models from history and the Bible to argue for women's education and moral activism, Stewart engaged in a practice that began in the early republic and became increasingly common as the nineteenth century progressed. As Linda Kerber notes, late-eighteenth-century American writers mined historical sources for examples of women who possessed "ideal" republican qualities. Similarly, in her study of antebellum intellectual women, Susan Conrad finds that "[b]eginning in the 1830s, American intellectual women . . . began to resurrect and place in a historical sequence the memory and deeds of great women."[34] Stewart's angered response to constrictions against women's education, intellectual accomplishment, and public activism is as vehement as white women's. She, like them, is intent on building a nation in which gender does not interfere with woman's access to, and participation in, intellectual endeavors. At the same time, however, both she and white women do not want intellectual endeavors to conflict with their uniquely gendered qualities. Stewart believes, for example, that an intellectual woman "joined the charms and accomplishments of a woman to all the knowledge of a man" (78). A woman can "devote [her] leisure hours to contemplation and study" and still be "refined" and womanly (77).

When Stewart expresses anger at gender injustice in her farewell speech, her public persona assumes a new dimension: it becomes more secular. Indeed, although there is a constant tension between a secular and a religious self that recurs throughout the texts, in this speech, Stewart's secular self takes precedence. Her primary concern is exhorting her community to "follow after godliness" because "[p]ure religion will burst [their] fetters" (80). But in addition to the argument for women's public activism, the speech also contains a vivid account of Stewart's conversion experience, as well as her pained resignation. The speech is remarkable because there are three distinct literary forms embedded within it—a political manifesto, a conversion narrative, and a confessional autobiographical fragment. What provides cohesion among them is the tension between self-willed agency and fated subordination that occurs in each. In the end, the religious exhortation and manifesto propose a vision of progress and celebrate self-willed agency, but the conversion narrative and confessional autobiographical fragment dramatize a pained struggle between will and subordination that tellingly reveals Stewart's secular vulnerability.

The way in which the farewell speech's different literary forms encode not one, but two, will-breaking scenarios underscores Stewart's powerless despair. In her account of a typical conversion experience, Stewart relates how tortuous it was to "renounce all for Christ" because of her "apprehensive fears" that she was not capable of doing so. Once she recognized, however, that it was impossible to "retain the world in one hand, and religion in the other," she was finally able to "bend and kiss the rod" "for [her] Redeemer's sake" (73). Although Stewart ends the narrative by proclaiming that the "heart-cheering promise" of God's love and protection far outweighs her personal sacrifice, the evocative language of rebellion, conquest, and capitulation suggests an erotically charged power struggle between herself and God.[35] This internalized, psychic power struggle—which is conveyed through a personalized literary form—is reenacted once again when it becomes an externalized, social power struggle between Stewart and her community. Surrendering in defeat to her "enemies," her secular will is broken a second time.

Using the language and imagery of military warfare, Stewart makes it clear that she envisions herself as an angered and disillusioned leader who has been forced to leave the "Christian" battlefield. "I am about to leave you," she informs her audience, "For I find it is no use for me as an individual to try to make myself useful among my color in this city" (78). That she makes this announcement immediately following her optimistic prognosis that the community's "prospects are . . . fair and bright" reveals her feelings of anger, disappointment, and rejection at being forced to resign her leadership position (78). Stewart's repeated allusions to warlike encounters confirm that her resignation did not come without a struggle. Perceiving herself as a Christian warrior, she feels as if she is being attacked by "the fiery darts of the devil" (79). Even though God has provided her with armor and weapons for the battle—he "hath clothed [her] face with steel, . . . lined [her] forehead with brass" and engraved "his seal on [her] forehead" (75)—her sense of persecution is so great that "at different periods" she feels "as though the powers of earth and hell had combined against [her]" (79). As a result, she believes "God has tried [her] as by fire" (82). The most poignant illustration of Stewart's defeat, however, is her confession that "Thus far has my life been almost a life of complete disappointment" (82).

The farewell speech's inscription of secular will-breaking ultimately reveals Stewart's vulnerability when she is forced to retreat from the religious realm. Once her Godlike persona no longer masks her gendered powerlessness, the gap between her religious and secular positions becomes strikingly apparent. That this is the moment in which she expresses anger at gender injustice is significant, for it shows that when her patriarchal mask is forcibly removed, she is compelled to speak anger in her own voice, on her own behalf. Although Stewart does not address the tenuousness of her gendered position until this point, her obsessive emphasis on justifying the authority to speak from the very first essay to the concluding "Farewell Address" signals a covert anger at gender constriction. That anger finally erupts into articulation when Stewart's female self is independent of a patriarchal deity's.

Because claiming voice is what enables speaking for God, which in turn fosters the struggle for freedom, it is clear why Stewart is so angered by the deprivation of her leadership. Envisioning heaven as a place where "we shall sing and shout, and shout and sing, and make heaven's high arches ring" (82) evinces how much she longs for an uninhibited space where voice is blissfully unrestrained. Nevertheless, her concluding sentiments in the "Farewell Address" demonstrate that she remains ambivalent about expressing anger at gendered constriction. To understand Stewart's ambivalence it is necessary to consider how she felt about her public speaking. A passage in which she records her conversion from gendered inarticulation to speech provides a clue.

> On my arrival here, not finding scarce an individual who felt interested in these subjects, and but few of the whites, except Mr. Garrison, and his friend Mr. Knapp; and hearing that those gentlemen had observed that female influence was powerful, my soul became fired with a holy zeal for your cause; every nerve and muscle in me was engaged in your behalf. I felt that I had a great work to perform; and was in haste to make a profession of my faith in Christ, that I might be about my Father's business. Soon after I made this profession, the Spirit of God came before me, and I spake before many. When going home, reflecting on what I had said, I felt ashamed, and knew not where I should hide myself. A something said within my breast, "press forward, I will be with thee." And my heart made

this reply, Lord, if thou wilt be with me, then will I speak for thee so long as I live. And thus far I have every reason to believe that it is the divine influence of the Holy Spirit operating upon my heart that could possibly induce me to make the feeble and unworthy efforts that I have. (74)

Stewart's choice of pronouns suggests that in this instance she perceives herself as a leader who stands apart from her community. "My soul became fired with a holy zeal for your cause," she writes. "Every nerve and muscle in me was engaged in your behalf." By establishing distance between herself and her community, she creates a self that is special, powerful, and important. Yet, she expresses anxiety about this self by admitting feelings of "shame" when she speaks in public. Significantly, it is on her way "home"—a female-gendered space—that she begins to feel "ashamed," not knowing where "[she] should hide [her]self." What is particularly revealing is that Stewart admits to having shameful feelings after "the spirit of God came before [her]." Thus, even though she assures her audience that God's command to "press forward" alleviates her misgivings, her recounting of her shameful feelings suggests otherwise.

The "Farewell Address" demonstrates that Stewart was unable to reconcile a militant, antagonistic, angry-God public stance that was gendered male, and a placating, forgiving, Jesus-style humility that was gendered female. In the speech, after all the anger, frustration, anxiety, and disappointment expressed in the conversion narrative, the manifesto, and the resignation, Stewart ends by claiming she has successfully transcended these feelings: "The bitterness of my soul has departed from those who endeavored to discourage and hinder me in my Christian progress; and I can now forgive my enemies, bless those who have hated me, and cheerfully pray for those who have despitefully used and persecuted me. Fare you well, farewell" (82). Like Christ who forgives his crucifiers as he dies in agony nailed to the cross, Stewart, too, forgives, blesses, and "cheerfully pray[s]" for her enemies as she "dies" in her leadership role. By assuming a Christlike persona, Stewart retreats from the stance of a vengeful, punishing god, and replaces it with a forgiving and self-sacrificing posture that makes her reentry into secular womanhood socially acceptable.[36]

That Stewart bids farewell in forgiveness rather than in anger reveals that she internalized the tenets of gendered ideologies of anger. Although she succeeds in making a space for a "a very devout Christian lady" like herself to express divinely inspired wrath, the ending of the "Farewell Address" demonstrates that when she is stripped of her Godlike voice and authority, she is uncomfortable about expressing anger, especially on her own behalf.[37] Like the majority of her black and white female peers, Maria W. Stewart reenters secular culture in bitterness and anger, and she attempts to deny these feelings behind a mask of middle-class Christian propriety.

Lydia Maria Child and Maria W. Stewart: United and Divided

The nation-building impulse that compels Lydia Maria Child and Maria W. Stewart to invent an artistry of anger helps us to understand how "free" black women and white women are simultaneously united and divided in the antebellum period. On the one hand, as gendered subjects in the American republic, they share the same source of anger. Discriminated against politically and economically, they are denied education, citizenship, and the right to become cultural workers and artists. Rendered legally powerless and economically vulnerable, their only recourse is through literary activism, and even there they encounter opposition. In response to these injustices, both women use their anger to imagine a national homeland in which they will not be discriminated against on the basis of gender.

On the other hand, however, as racialized subjects in the American republic, Lydia Maria Child and Maria W. Stewart do not encounter the same obstacles. As a white woman, Lydia Maria Child takes her racial privilege for granted; her humanity is never in question. Thus her response to the failed promises of republicanism is expressed in gendered terms; she uses her anger to envision a reconfiguration of America so that it can accommodate the presence of intellectual white women. Unlike Child's response, Stewart's is expressed in both racial and gendered terms; she uses her anger to envision a radical transformation of America's racial structure that includes rights and freedom for women.

Along with Lydia Maria Child's *Hobomok*, Maria W. Stewart's texts articulate an angered critique at gender and racial exclusion that illuminates a distinctive women's literary tradition of alternative nation-building. As the century progresses, this tradition becomes increasingly more evident in different forms of public discourse. Indeed, by mid-century, women's discontent with the existing political structure is publicly unmasked in domestic novels, slave narratives, and a newly organized white woman's movement. The most telling indication of the public expression of women's discontent at mid-century is the fact that in 1776 Abigal Adams expressed her anger at exclusion from the promises of America in a personal letter to her husband. In 1848, however, the small group of white women who met in Seneca Falls, New York, issued a public proclamation modeled on the Declaration of

Independence.[38] Nevertheless, even though Fanny Fern and Harriet Wilson, two significant mid-century writers who are the subject of the following chapters, write in a dramatically different context of collectively vented anger and discontent, they still encounter the same problem of how to express anger without undermining the primary source of their empowerment—their specifically defined womanly qualities.

SIX

Masking Anger as It Is Spoken

Fanny Fern's *Ruth Hall*

[I]n view of this entire disfranchisement of one-half the people of this country, their social and religious degradation—in view of the unjust laws above mentioned, and because women do feel themselves aggrieved, oppressed, and fraudulently deprived of their most sacred rights, we insist that they have immediate admission to all the rights and privileges which belong to them as citizens of the United States.
—"Declaration of Sentiments" (1848)

[A] few months since a man escaped from bondage and found a temporary shelter almost beneath the shadow of Bunker Hill. Had that man stood upon the deck of an Austrian ship . . . he would have found protection. Had he been wrecked upon an island or colony of Great Britain, the waves of the tempest-lashed ocean would have washed him deliverance. . . . Beside the ancient pyramids of Egypt he would have found liberty. . . . But from Boston harbour, made memorable by the infusion of three-penny taxed tea, Boston in its proximity to the plains of Lexington and Concord, Boston almost beneath the shadow of Bunker Hill and almost in sight of Plymouth Rock, he is thrust back from liberty and manhood and reconverted into a chattel.
—Frances Harper, "Liberty for Slaves" (1857)

"Fourth of July." Well—I don't feel patriotic . . . I'm glad we are all free; but as a woman—I shouldn't know it. . . . Can I go out of an evening without a hat at my side? . . . Can I have the nomination for "Governor of Vermont" . . . ? Can I be a Senator . . . ? Can I *even* be President? Bah—you know I can't. "*Free!*" Humph!
—Fanny Fern, "Independence" (1859)

In 1855, the prime architect of the Declaration of Sentiments, Elizabeth Cady Stanton, responded to criticism leveled against Fanny Fern's best-selling novel *Ruth Hall* in a woman's rights newspaper.[1] Outraged by the negative reception Fern's "tale of sorrow" was receiving in both the mainstream and abolitionist press, Stanton felt compelled to defend the book against its detractors who claimed that Fern had violated standards of propriety by publishing a thinly veiled description of a contentious family feud. In direct opposition to the prevailing view, Stanton applauded the appearance of Fern's novel because it exploded the notion that women can rely on men for economic, legal, and social protection.

To Stanton, Fern's writing of *Ruth Hall* is an inspiring act of resistance against the "romance" of dependency. As the story of one woman's self-willed triumph over economic adversity, it teaches the "great lesson" "that God has given to woman sufficient brain and muscle to work out her own destiny unaided and alone." That Fern exposes the cruelties of her own family is irrelevant, because whether "selfish male monsters" are "a father, a brother, a husband, or a Southern slave-holder," when a man "robs" a woman of her "God-given rights," he is a tyrant and should be named as such.

Because Fern has made the heretofore unwritten story of "petty tyrannies in the isolated household" public, Stanton regards the publication of *Ruth Hall* as a major triumph, for now other women will be able to recognize their own oppression and respond appropriately. For her, *Ruth Hall*, as a specifically gendered example of American resistance to "tyrants," provides a useful model of fearless expression. She encourages women to relinquish "false notions of justice and delicacy" and claim their "right . . . to condemn what is false and cruel wherever we find it" just as Fern does. She wants women to associate their own experiences with Fern's and recognize that anger at male members of their own household is justified. For when a woman "awakes to the consciousness" that her own father, brother, or husband is a "tyrant," "her honest indignation will ever and anon boil up and burst forth in defiance of all ties of blood and kindred." Stanton especially wants to impress upon her readers that, as Fern's example demonstrates, woman's public expression of anger is a strategic political tool. "If all tyrannical parents, husbands and brothers knew that the fantastic tricks they play at the hearth-stone, would in time be judged by a discerning public," Stanton warns, "no one can estimate the restraining influence of such a fear." Because *Ruth Hall* reveals an intimate portrait of "tyrannical parents, husbands and brothers" in the patriarchal house of woe, Stanton commends Fern for helping women recognize that their own anger at men is both justified and politically powerful.

Stanton's emotionally charged, partisan response was far from anomalous. On the contrary, her voice was one among many taking part in a debate shaped by the increasing commercialization of the publishing industry. For Fern's novel was a locus of attention not only because she was a popular newspaper columnist known for her biting wit and daring satire, but also because her enterprising publishers had decided to use "extraordinary exer-tions to promote [its] sale."[2] Launching a publicity campaign devised "to titillate the sensibilities of the public" through a barrage of advertising, mystery, and allure, one of their tactics was to introduce the idea that *Ruth Hall* was autobiographical. Indeed, they went so far as to suggest that the vengeful portrait of the protagonist's brother was based on Nathaniel Parker Willis, an editor and poet well known in New York publishing circles. Willis was in fact Fanny Fern's brother.[3]

Providing this information was a particularly enticing ploy since Fern had been writing pseudonymously until that point. Confident that her pseudo-nym would protect her from slander, she based her first novel on her own harrowing experiences as a genteel mother who struggled to support herself and her children after she could no longer depend on male support. Essen-tially a Franklinian story of success recast in gendered terms, *Ruth Hall* celebrates a heroic protagonist's triumph over selfish and hypocritical fa-thers, brothers, businessmen, and lawyers in her quest for professional and economic independence. But once the novel is regarded as autobiographical, a pseudonym can no longer protect Fanny Fern from public censure. Indeed, within a few weeks, her situation worsened considerably when one of the newspaper editors she had previously worked for completed her unmasking with a vengeance. Because he was so incensed that she had left his employ for a more lucrative position, and then portrayed him as a greedy scoundrel in *Ruth Hall*, he retaliated by publishing a book that contained a slanderous version of her biography, as well as unfavorable criticism of her work.[4] Since the very first line of the first chapter, entitled "Genius in Pantalettes," identi-fies Fanny Fern as Sarah Payson Willis, "daughter of Mr. Nathaniel Willis, one of the most industrious and respected citizens of Boston" and "sister to Mr. N. P. Willis, the brilliant essayist and poet," there was no longer any question as to who was the author of *Ruth Hall*. Vulnerable and exposed, Fern was lambasted for expressing "unfemininely bitter wrath and spite" against the male members of her family. Accused of "demean[ing] herself as no right minded woman should have done," her most heinous crime was engaging in unfilial behavior.[5]

The fact that so many people seized the opportunity to pronounce whether Fern's vitriolic depiction of undemocratic men was a criminal breach of moral ethics indicates just how contested the ideal of "womanly" behavior had become by the mid-nineteenth century. For what was ultimately at stake in the debate over *Ruth Hall* was whether a woman had the right to express anger publicly at men and still be deemed "womanly," respectable, and capable of rational authorship. The effort both male and female reviewers made to enforce the disjunction between anger and womanhood betrays a lurking fear that emotional boundaries were being redrawn. Indeed, it is clear from the reviewers' anxious responses that the expression of women's anger in public signified a direct challenge to the maintenance of unequal gender roles and privileges. As one reviewer of *Ruth Hall* candidly admitted, "As we wish no sister of ours, nor no female relative to show toward us, the ferocity [Fern] has displayed toward her nearest relatives we take occasion to censure this book that might initiate such a possibility."[6]

The fact of the matter is, however, that "such a possibility" had already been "initiated" by the institutionalization of the woman's rights movement, and *Ruth Hall* is one of its popular manifestations. Like much woman's rights literature, *Ruth Hall* expresses anger at exclusion by castigating the hypocrisy of a patriarchal version of democracy. Also like much woman's rights literature, Fern delineates an angered confrontation between the sexes that was considered unavoidable. As the remarks of one woman's rights activist suggest, there was an implicit understanding among some of the movement's most vocal members that the public expression of anger was a necessary part of the woman's rights enterprise. In an essay addressing the issue of separatism, for example, Paulina Wright Davis assures her readers that engendering "antagonisms" and "competition" between "one class or sex" and the other is not the movement's primary goal. At the same time, however, she acknowledges that "in the transition state through which women must pass from the drudge, the frivolous toy, up to the ideal woman, we see not how she is to escape this evil; she must e'en pass through the fiery furnace, and we can only pray that she may come forth unscathed, with not even the smell of fire upon her garments."[7] Participants in the woman's rights movement thus recognized that passing through the "fiery furnace" of anger is an essential part of women's conversion from patriarchal appendage to independent nation-builder.

Davis's notion that women cannot "escape" the "evil" of "antagonisms" in their quest for rights and freedom indicates how attitudes about anger were changing by the mid-nineteenth century. Two factors contributed to this change. To begin with, women such as Lydia Maria Child, Maria W. Stewart, Sarah Grimké, Angelina Grimké, Margaret Fuller, and other writers and reformers who became publicly visible in the 1820s, 30s, and 40s, created a discursive space for articulations of discontent that an organized woman's movement could fruitfully exploit. Most important, however, was the cumulative effect of abolitionist agitation that profoundly affected the change in attitudes. The movement created a public discourse of exclusion and moral outrage that woman's rights activists used to challenge the assumption that womanhood and anger were mutually exclusive.[8]

Nowhere is this more apparent than in the way in which Elizabeth Cady Stanton relies on abolitionist rhetoric to justify the validity of white women's anger in her essay on *Ruth Hall*. As Fern's case demonstrates, it was not possible for women to "come forth unscathed" when they criticized men in public. Because Stanton was acutely aware of this, she knew that the accusations against Fern offered a useful opportunity to argue that fighting for the right to equal expression was an essential part of the woman's rights enterprise. Using Fern's experience as an example, she shows how women are oppressed by a double standard of expression. While men can "ridicule" "mothers, wives and sisters" with impunity "since [they] first began to put pen to paper," when a woman exposes "a few specimens of dwarfed and meager manhood," a "furor" erupts.

Most significant, however, is that in order to argue her point convincingly, Stanton draws a direct relationship between Fern's experience as an oppressed white woman and that of a slave's. Distressed that *Ruth Hall* received a "severe" review in the *Anti-Slavery Standard*, Stanton contends that Fern's story should be read as if it were a slave narrative. "Read 'Ruth Hall,' as you would read the life of 'Solomon Northrup,' a Frederick Douglass," she commands, "as you would listen to the poor slaves in our anti-slavery meetings." By employing this strategy, Stanton argues that in the same way abolitionists are outraged by the oppressed slave, they should also be outraged by the story of the oppressed woman. Like slaves struggling valiantly for their freedom, Fanny Fern is also a quintessential American crusader of justice. Moreover, by equating gender oppression with racial oppression, Stanton establishes a direct correlation between the validity of the slave's anger and that of the white woman's. In the same way the slave has the right to express anger at his deprivation of freedom, so does the white woman who finds herself in a similar situation. This tactic allows Stanton to show that woman's anger is not only an appropriate response to injustice; it is also socially transformative and heroic.

Stanton thus shrewdly attempts to sever anger from its specifically gendered significations. Concluding the essay with the provocative question, "What are the strokes, the paddle or the lash, to the refined insults, with which man seeks to please or punish woman?" Stanton equates the white woman's position with that of the slave to show that "the cruelty . . . of father and brethren" is the same for white women in domesticity as it is for blacks in slavery, and therefore they have the same right to be angry. Vehemently rejecting a Jesus-like, feminine-styled doctrine of "Love your enemies," Stanton makes the point that women, like slaves, should not be expected to love their tyrannical fathers. "Because a villain for his own pleasure, has conferred on me the boon of existence, by what law, other than the Christian one— 'Love your enemies'—am I bound to love and reverence him who has made my life a curse and a weariness, and who possesses in himself none of the Godlike qualities which command my veneration?" By using the logic and language of abolitionism, Stanton vindicates white women's "cruel wrongs" and urges their unrestrained expression, regardless of the costs.[9]

We get some sense of how radical Stanton's ideas about women and anger are when we consider how another influential woman's rights activist, Caroline Dall, responds to Stanton's comments in the newspaper's very next issue.[10] While Dall begins by commending Stanton for expressing her "moral indignation" with such "fearlessness," she feels compelled to offer a different view of Fern's "slanderous autobiography." Like many of Fern's detractors, Dall finds Fern's depiction of her relatives an inexcusable offense. Personally acquainted with "those readers in the city of Boston and its vicinity who have known its authoress and her family connections on all sides for years," she suspects that Fern is as "imprudent and heartless" as they say she is. According to Dall, not only is Fern devoid of good character and sound morals; she also lacks talent. In order to discredit Fern's authority to speak anger in public, Dall judges the novel on aesthetic grounds and pronounces it wanting. She agrees with other "competent judges" that *Ruth Hall* is a "slovenly performance," "by no means the work of a ripe and well-trained woman." Because Fern was incapable of transcending her "peculiar irritations," she had no right to "hold [them] up for the benefit of [her] fellow-men." Only authors who "outlive" anger-provoking experiences are worthy of creating art.[11] Dall uses aesthetic standards to invalidate an author whose vision threatens her own value system.

What clearly offends Dall is Fern's "bitter views of men and things" as well as her "lack of nobleness and generosity." But Fern's cynical world view and obstinate self-centeredness are not the only things that bother Dall. The fact that Fern flaunts a male-styled confrontational approach to sexual warfare upsets her the most. Indeed, what her disagreement with Stanton ultimately reveals is that Dall is terribly uncomfortable about women using "'manly' wit and the sarcasm of a soured soul" in their emancipation struggles. Whereas Stanton asserts that confrontational "resistance to tyrants is obedience to God," Dall counters that "Resistance may be a duty, but not that which consists in warlike defence—only that which abides in noble self-restraint." Whereas Stanton believes that public exposure is a deterrent, Dall insists that "holding [a father] up to public scorn in his old age will never . . . lead him to the God whom he has outraged." Whereas Stanton wants the oppressed daughter to tell her story without restraint, Dall believes that "if the child owes the father . . . no respect," she nevertheless "owes him—her silence." Given these views, it is not surprising that while Stanton takes pains to draw a relationship between "domestic" novels and slave narratives, Dall vehemently denies the association. "When Fanny Fern offers us Ruth Hall as a true narrative, and proves it, we will read it as we would the story of a fugitive; until then we can only read it as a fiction, and denounce it for want of 'literary merit.'" Thus Dall seeks to disengage the relationship between gender oppression and racial oppression that Stanton works so hard to establish. Because in her view Fern's crude tactics foster a "great depravity in the public taste," she is horrified at the idea that Fern should be associated with "the cause."

Dall's class-conscious analysis makes it impossible for her to regard woman's public expression of anger as a socially acceptable political tool. To her, anger is inappropriate and crass; thus she advocates a traditional female-styled model of forgiveness and stoical self-restraint that preserves class boundaries by keeping unruly emotional expression in check. Dall's position helps us to appreciate the brilliance of Stanton's tactics. By suggesting that good, moral citizens respond to gender oppression in the same way they respond to racial oppression, Stanton argues that gendered anger is worthy of the same respect, approval, and sympathy as racial anger. In other words, Stanton attempts to prove that woman's anger is not "unwomanly" or indecorous because it, too, is sanctioned by a natural rights philosophy as well as God's laws. When we see how Dall perceives Fern's angered expressions once they are severed from an acceptably moral context, we understand why Stanton makes the argument that she does.

The different positions on anger and womanhood that the controversy over *Ruth Hall* generated reveal not only a debate about whether anger could be regarded as a proper female response, but also whether it posed a threat to a rapidly industrializing nation that was reliant upon an ideology of rational self-restraint.[12] By the mid-nineteenth century, the notion that anger signified danger was deeply entrenched. In their study of marriage and child-rearing manuals as well as women's magazine fiction, Carol Zisowitz Stearns and Peter N. Stearns found that, "Victorians often chose metaphors for anger implying that the feelings came from an evil source outside the self. The essential self was the rational self, while the angry feelings were intrusions."[13] They also concluded that while in theory prescriptions against anger were supposed to apply to both men and women, there was clearly a gendered double-standard. In their assessment:

> The bottom line was . . . that angry women were worse than angry men. . . . [A]t least there were some discussions of the anger felt by decent men, who must, of course, struggle with their anger and overcome it. No such struggle was allowed a woman, for even in feeling anger she proved her bad character. . . . Anger in women made the Victorians more uncomfortable than did anger in men. If the advice books could mention the subject in passing, it was almost impossible to write a story with a good but angry woman, for the Victorians had a failure of imagination in actually conceiving of a woman who could be both.[14]

Clearly, however, the proliferation of slave narratives, domestic novels, and woman's rights literature made the public expression of anger in and at the familial, marital, and national house much more imaginable than it had been earlier in the century. Indeed, scholars who have studied these genres note that the expression of anger shapes content as well as themes. In her study of slave narratives, for example, Frances Smith Foster points out that after the Compromise of 1850 sanctioned the expansion of slavery and the fugitive slave law that permitted agents to track down runaway slaves who had found a haven in northern "free" states and return them to slavery, "slave narratives began to display anti-American tendencies. . . . [T]he writers' displeasure is directed not only against slaveholders but against the U.S. government as well." She cites the tone and sentiment of Ellen and William Craft's realization that they "thought it best . . . to leave the mock-free Republic, and come to a country where we and our dear little ones can be truly free" as a representative example.[15] Marion Wilson Starling also comments on the heightened antagonism of the mid-nineteenth-century narratives. "The slave narratives of this period," she writes, "are generally distinguishable . . . from those of other years by virtue of [a] vogue for rhetorical vindictiveness."[16] In a similar finding, students of women's literature also note an angry undercurrent in the stories, novels, and essays written primarily for white women by white women. In her study of white women's domestic fiction, for example, Nina Baym matter-of-factly states that "the presence of anger is understood as a basic fact of the [domestic] heroine's emotional makeup."[17] And not surprisingly, the editors of a collection of woman's rights literature conclude that the selections "represent some of the lively, important debates of the nineteenth century, as the women expressed anger, hope and disagreement about the obstacles and possibilities for change in the conditions of women's lives."[18]

The presence of these interrelated discourses did not mean, however, that women could express anger straightforwardly or without consequences. Indeed, as the response to *Ruth Hall* demonstrates, it was far from acceptable for white middle-class women to express anger directly at men. Nor was it possible for authors of slave narratives to express anger overtly at whites and their racist institutions. African-American writers and their northern abolitionist sponsors had to be acutely sensitive to their white readers' expectations, prejudices, and value systems, and thus shape their stories accordingly. Since the main function of the slave narrative was to provoke action by generating sympathy, narrators had to be particularly careful about how they represented characters, events, and the sources of blame and misery. Because they did not want to alienate the audience they hoped to politicize, they had to be especially inventive when it came to expressing anger at whites and their dehumanizing institutions. Moreover, in order to appeal to middle-class values that included the repression of anger and the triumph of self-control, it was not in the narrators' best interests to depict a protagonist who did not share these traits and values.[19]

Large-scale religious changes also contributed to the repression of anger in mid-nineteenth-century literature. The shift from a harsh Calvinism to a more optimistic, humanitarian religious culture that many scholars attribute to the growth of capitalism involved a highly gendered imaginative reconstruction of, and relationship to, religious icons. During a period in which, as Barbara Welter evocatively puts it, the "skyscraper . . . replace[s] the steeple as a symbol of the American dream," religion became relegated to the feminine realm. As the repository of culturally sanctioned, female-gendered values such as meekness, humility, and lack of greed, it is not surprising that by the mid-nineteenth century a humane, forgiving, socially aware Christ gradually replaced the earlier Calvinist-styled angry and punitive God.[20]

This theological shift profoundly affected women's literary imaginings. Not only did the model of a sacrificed Christ allow women writers to elevate their protagonists' stories of pain and suffering to a sacred level; it also suggested that their experiences, like those of the martyred Christ, were worthy of recognition and respect. The problem, however, is that when a forgiving, turn-the-other-cheek, Christlike model becomes the only justifiable "womanly" response to injustice, women are left without a way to express anger that does not automatically threaten their gendered source of power. Because the shift to a "more domesticated, more emotional, more soft and accommodating" religious worldview provided a cultural model that encouraged the repression of female anger, it is evident why woman's rights activists found abolitionist rhetoric so compelling.[21] Rooted in Old Testament vengeful-God logic, it preserved the right to respond to injustice with anger.

Women's and African Americans' pursuit of rights and liberty created a new context for the expression, reception, and contestation of female anger by the mid-nineteenth century. Indeed, the struggle black and white women engaged in to claim an equal right to feel and express moral outrage in the century's earlier decades made the collective expression of a specially gendered moral outrage by the mid-nineteenth century possible. It is this context in which Fanny Fern wrote and published *Ruth Hall*.

Putting It on Paper: The Text as Witness

"Never put anything on paper, never put anything on paper," said Mr. Ellet, in a solemn tone, with a ludicrously frightened air; "parchments, lawyers, witnesses, and things, make me nervous."—A conversation between Ruth Hall's father and father-in-law regarding economic support for Ruth and her children

By writing *Ruth Hall*, Fanny Fern provided a way for her female readers to experience their anger at the failed promises of democratic America while denying that they were doing so. Creating male, working-class, and child characters who speak the anger her autobiographical protagonist and readers feel, but are prohibited from articulating, Fern vindicates white, middle-class women's anger at the same time that she masks its expression. Equally significant, her purported embrace of an ethic of forgiveness in a novel that celebrates vindictiveness enables her female readers to experience the vicarious thrill of revenge while simultaneously adhering to conventional codes of Christian humility.

Based on Fanny Fern's own experiences of humiliation, betrayal, and poverty, *Ruth Hall* tells the story of a woman who overcomes these obstacles by using her anger as artistic inspiration: Ruth Hall, like Fanny Fern, becomes a writer. Many of the events Fern dramatizes in *Ruth Hall* were literally true: Fanny Fern, born Sarah Payson Willis, was happily married to a man who died, leaving her financially and economically vulnerable with two children to support. These circumstances led to nasty disagreements about financial matters with her father and her husband's parents, and both used the withholding of money as a weapon against her.[22] In addition, Fanny Fern's influential brother, the editor and writer Nathaniel Parker Willis—Hyacinth in the novel—did actually belittle her literary aspirations when she appealed to him for help. The note Hyacinth writes to Ruth Hall in the novel closely resembles the one Willis actually penned. "You overstrain the pathetic, and your humor runs into dreadful vulgarity sometimes," Willis concluded after reading Fern's sample articles. "I am sorry that any editor knows that a sister of mine wrote some of these which you sent me. In one or two cases they trench very close on indecency. For God's sake, keep clear of that."[23]

Fanny Fern was too enraged at her gendered powerlessness and exclusion to "keep clear" of "indecency." Denied access to financial resources and courts of law, she uses writing to inscribe an interpretation of history that challenges that of the powerful men who abuse and malign her. In this sense, Fanny Fern's autobiographical novel is a form of history-writing because it provides an interpretation of facts based on a female view of the truth. As a record of one woman's everyday triumphs and defeats, *Ruth Hall* chronicles a different kind of war and a different kind of treaty than those that occur on the male battlefield. Words are the weapons that secure the victory of retribution.

It is significant, however, that Fern can not record Ruth's history using the standard "woman's fiction" plot because the orphan-to-marriage story will not accommodate the one she wants to tell. Instead, she utilizes a journey plot like the one used in slave narratives, thereby associating Ruth Hall's metamorphosis with that of a liberated slave's, and her story with the abolitionism that partly justifies her telling it. Fern has Ruth Hall move through different stages of awareness in much the same way a slave does as he or she travels to freedom. First Ruth loses her innocence when she can no longer rely on male support; then she resolves to seek emotional and economic autonomy in an effort to achieve freedom. Her discovery of writing is both the means of escape from powerlessness and the assurance that permanent freedom has been attained.[24] By invoking the slave's journey from enslavement to freedom, Fern implies that the white, genteel woman's journey from dependency to independence constitutes the same form of liberation. She appropriates abolitionist rhetoric and slave narrative plot features to serve her own nation-building purposes.

Fanny Fern transforms her private, anger-provoking experiences into a gendered form of history-writing that inspires white, middle-class women to fight for their rightful privileges. In the preface to *Ruth Hall*, Fern uses images of heat to convey a dual message about anger and the act of writing. "Cherish[ing] the hope that . . . [the text] may fan into a flame, in some tried heart, the fading embers of hope, well-nigh extinguished by wintry fortune and summer friends," she suggests that the written text comforts as well as disrupts (3). Fern recognizes that "fan[ning] into flame . . . the fading embers of hope," necessitates arousing women's anger, because it is only then that they will act to change anger-provoking situations. She also realizes that this process requires transgressing the boundaries of mid-nineteenth century novel writing conventions: a different history needs a different form. "[A]ware that [her text] is entirely at variance with all set rules for novel-writing," Fern informs her readers that she is entering male bastions of power without permission (3). "I have avoided long introductions and descriptions, and have entered unceremoniously and unannounced, into people's houses, without stopping to ring the bell" (3). Once inside, Fern, the accomplished author, demonstrates that in order to become a competent historian, her readers—like Ruth Hall and herself—must reconsider what it means to be a woman. An essential part of that reconsideration is acquiring the freedom to feel and express anger, because it is this anger that ultimately preserves the very essence of democracy.[25]

In *Ruth Hall*, Fanny Fern takes the politics of moral emotionalism to its utmost extreme. Arguing that white, middle-class women should have equal access to anger as well as to ambition, Fern invests the ideology of female superiority with a democratic, capitalist ethos. Because intelligent and industrious women like Ruth Hall have not been corrupted by the profit motive, it is they who are closer to truly democratic values. Thus they have every right to express anger when those values are trampled upon. Unlike cruel, unfeeling, avaricious men—typified by Mr. Ellet, Ruth's father—who have abused democratic principles in their quest for monetary success, Fern contends that women like Ruth Hall are the true custodians of democratic principles. Their ability to feel and express anger is essential to preserving the nation's ideals.

Fern dramatizes this point when she shows how "prosperous" men like Mr. Ellet make a mockery of America's most cherished values. In two scenes that underscore the injustice of an economic system that rewards men only, Fern depicts the sickly, poverty-stricken Ruth sitting destitute "in her little, close attic" (122), while Mr. Ellet smugly boasts about his success:

> "Fine day, Mr. Ellet," said a country clergymen to Ruth's father, as he sat comfortably ensconced in his counting-room. "I don't see but you look as young as you did when I saw you five years ago. Life has gone smoothly with you; you have been remarkably prospered in business, Mr. Ellet."
>
> "Yes, Yes," said the old gentleman, who was inordinately fond of talking of himself; "yes, yes, I may say that, though I came into Massachusetts a-foot, with a loaf of bread and a sixpence, and now—well, not to boast, I own this house, and the land attached, beside my countryseat, and have a nice little sum stowed away in the bank for a rainy day; yes, Providence has smiled on my enterprise; my affairs are, as you say, in a *very* prosperous condition." (Fern's emphasis, 123)

That Fern refers to Benjamin Franklin's success story at this juncture is especially significant. Coming into Massachusetts "a-foot, with a loaf of bread and a sixpence," Mr. Ellet begins his path to prosperity much like Franklin does when he arrives hungry and short of cash in Philadelphia. Yet, Mr. Ellet's values and behavior shamefully betray everything Franklin represents. As a selfish tightwad deaf to his daughter's needs because of his own greed, he is a perversion of Franklin's virtuous, self-made man for whom sincerity and justice are supposed to be guiding precepts.[26] Ruth Hall's behavior, on the other hand, demonstrates how Franklin's original vision of a virtuous citizen can be restored. Although she, too, starts her "climb" to success "at the lowest round of the ladder" (121), "eating a "loaf of bread . . . for every day's three meals" (113), she never loses sight of others; her new-found power is never abused. Indeed, the pinnacle of her success is when "the family circle [can become] complete" in a home she can afford to own (198).

Ruth Hall is an expression of rage at a patriarchal system that denies white, middle-class women independence, power, and economic solvency. Women's dependency on men, Fern argues, conflicts with the fundamental tenets of republicanism. Using Ruth Hall's transformation from a dependent wife and daughter to a self-sufficient writing mother, Fern demonstrates how democracy, individualism, and independence assume new meaning when they are interpreted by a white, middle-class woman, based on her own experiences. This perspective does not, however, lead Fern to question the basic structure of a racialized, class-stratified America. On the contrary, *Ruth Hall* is a fantasy of white, middle-class women's equality in the capitalist marketplace, and it is the function of "others"—benevolent white men, as well as white and black working-class women—to help Ruth Hall reach her ultimate destination.

Ruth Hall's obsessive desire to secure economic independence signals Fanny Fern's profound anger at the ways in which white, middle-class women like herself are denied economic solvency. In one of the novel's most dramatic moments, Fern uses the metaphor of a lone traveler negotiating rough waters in an insecure vehicle to dramatize her autobiographical heroine's tenacious struggle to make a living. After Ruth's husband dies and she has no other means of support, she looks for work as a seamstress and teacher, the quintessential female employments for mid-nineteenth-century middle-class white women who found themselves in unfortunate circumstances.[27] When these jobs don't work out, Ruth next decides to try a profession newly available to genteel women: writing for "the papers." Thrilled that "[t]his means of support would be so congenial, so absorbing," so unlike the monotony of sewing, which precluded any kind of intellectual engagement, she contacts her brother, Hyacinth, a "prosperous editor of the Irving Magazine" (115), hoping he will give her work. Not surprisingly, he is as malicious as all the other men Ruth has thus far asked for help. Responding to her request by pronouncing that she has "no talent," he admonishes her to "seek some *unobtrusive* employment" (Fern's emphasis, 116).[28]

Underlying Hyacinth's crude dismissal is the belief that Ruth should perform domestic tasks so that a gendered separation of labor remains intact. But Ruth is determined; she angrily declares that she has already "tried the unobtrusive employment [and] the wages are six cents a day" (116). She dismisses Hyacinth's comments with a "bitter smile," and in one of the text's most spirited soliloquies, she vows that she will prove him wrong no matter what it takes to do so.

> "I *can* do it, I *feel* it, I *will* do it," and [Ruth] closed her lips firmly; "but there will be a desperate struggle first," and she clasped her hands over her heart as if it had already commenced; "there will be scant meals, and sleepless nights, and weary days, and a throbbing brow, and an aching heart; there will be the chilling tone, the rude repulse; there will be ten backward steps to one forward. *Pride* must sleep! But—" and Ruth glanced at her children—"it shall be *done*. They shall be proud of their mother. *Hyacinth shall yet be proud to claim his sister.*" (Fern's emphasis, 116)

Fern's emphasis on the action verbs can, feel, will, and shall, spoken by an authoritative female character, signals a profound self-assertion that is anomalous in women's domestic fiction in this period. *Ruth Hall* "contain[s] the fiercest repudiation of kin and blood ties in women's writing of the time," Nina Baym proclaims. Because the text envisions a triumphant heroine who is "satisfied with an independent career and has no wish to enter any domestic situation," Baym argues, it differs from other "woman's fictions" which conclude with marriage and the idealization of domesticity.[29] In a similar interpretation, Joyce Warren characterizes *Ruth Hall* as "revolutionary" because it advocates women's economic independence and privileges self-assertion over self-sacrifice as a female virtue.[30]

There is another reason why Fern's conception of female independence is "revolutionary." In her vision, women's ability to feel uninhibitedly a wide range of emotions is as important as achieving economic self-determination. Allowing Ruth to *feel* power as well as pride, Fern creates a female protagonist who not only *feels* in true womanly fashion, but also one who *acts* on those feelings in both a masculine and feminine manner. Even though Ruth claims her "pride must sleep" for her children's sake, she does not react to her brother's rebukes based on the dictates of a feminine-styled "heart" that requires "the discipline of the passions, [and] the regulation of the feelings and affections."[31] On the contrary, Ruth unabashedly acknowledges her wounded pride and defiant anger. She does so, however, in the privacy of her own apartment, not in public.

Fern thus enlarges the realm of acceptable *private* feelings for women, promoting a version of female independence that exceeds economic self-sufficiency and business savvy. Portraying a heroic protagonist who nurtures children, the public, and her own ambitions, Fern demands that women have the right to feel, express, and act on anger *privately* and still be deemed "womanly" by the larger culture. She does so by creating a genteel feminine-styled heroine who utilizes a masculine-styled anger to claim the promises of America that white middle-class women are denied.

Fern achieves this feat by combining easily discernible masculine and feminine codes to depict Ruth Hall's feelings, reactions, and motivations as she struggles to achieve economic and psychic freedom. After Ruth reads her brother's dismissive letter in the scene noted above, "a bitter smile struggled with the hot tear that fell upon [her] cheek" and it "disfigured her gentle lip" (116). Her brother's arrogant assumption that she has "no talent" thwarts her plans, wounds her pride, and arouses her ire. But as a woman, Ruth is not supposed to feel pride, let alone anger, on her own behalf. Fern resolves this problem by linking pride to motherhood and anger to womanhood. When Ruth delivers her soliloquy, her masculine-style resolve is fortified by an accompanying masculine-style physical response: she "leap[s] to her feet" as soon as she begins to speak. This seemingly simple gesture connotes action, mobility, and the assumption of a fully erect, versatile posture. It also evokes Sarah M. Grimké's militant rhetoric from the 1830s: "I ask no favors for my sex. I surrender not our claim to equality. All I ask of our brethren is, that they will take their feet from our necks and permit us to stand upright on that ground which God designed us to occupy."[32]

Two lines later, however, Fern renders the sure-footed, self-assertive Ruth in an archetypal female posture, "clasp[ing] her hands over her heart as if [the struggle] had already commenced" (116). Calling attention to the "heart"— the sanctified feminine symbol of domesticity, emotion, and higher moral virtue—Ruth's hands are clasped in feminine-style prayerful entreaty. Fern uses the same technique to convey Ruth's anger. She modifies stereotypical images of womanhood with adjectives that connote discontent: the ubiquitous female tear is "hot," the smile "bitter," the "gentle lip" "disfigured." When Ruth "close[s] her lips firmly," it is not in silence but in stubborn resolve. By yoking suggestive masculine-style gestures and images to feminine-style stereotypes, Fern creates a heroine who is both angry and womanly at the same time.

Given Fern's view that a patriarchal system keeps women emotionally stunted, it is significant that expressing anger is Ruth Hall's first act of independence. Only when women are rudely forced to confront the inadequacies of female dependency, Fern implies, do they discover an independent self capable of expressing an unlimited range of feelings. By linking Ruth Hall's self-assertion, her decision to become a writer, and her expression of anger, Fern creates a woman writer who uses unbounded emotional expressiveness to tell stories about personal injustices that have public implications. For Fern, equal access to anger is essential to female independence as well as female liberation.

Fern conveys this conviction by showing that Ruth's conversion experience and her ability to express anger are integrally related. Precisely at the moment in which Ruth recognizes and expresses anger for the first time, her transformation from a weak and dependent silenced victim to a capable and independent-speaking celebrity begins.[33] Shedding that first "hot tear," Ruth embarks on a dangerous journey in search of a new kind of gendered identity.[34] Her commitment to writing marks the beginning of her sojourn, and the motivation behind it is her anger at gendered constrictions. The seemingly "placid Ruth" is in actuality "a smouldering volcano" (70).[35]

While the quest for emotional and economic freedom is Ruth's ultimate journey, she takes numerous side trips en route. Indeed, one of the most important excursions Ruth and her readers take is a journey to consciousness about the instability of the white, middle-class woman's position under a patriarchal economic system. From the opening scene in which Ruth meditates on her impending marriage, to the closing scene in which she hears a bird sing as she passes "from under the old stone gateway" of the cemetery in which her husband's body is buried, Fern depicts Ruth Hall's emerging awareness of her own vulnerability (211).

When we first meet Ruth, she is a naive and inexperienced young woman whose understanding of independence and freedom is based on a male model of interpretation. As a new bride she "moved about her apartments in a sort of blissful dream. How odd it seemed, this new freedom, this being one's own mistress" (18). Ruth mistakenly believes that having a husband and her own apartments in her in-laws' house is a form of freedom. Emphasizing that Ruth's belief in the "blissful dream" persists as long as she remains married, Fern shows that dependency in marriage keeps women like Ruth Hall in a perpetual childlike state. After her husband can afford to buy them a house of their own, "Ruth danced about, from room to room, with the careless glee of a happy child, quite forgetful that she was a wife and mother; quite unable to repress the flow of spirits consequent upon her new-found freedom" (28).

Fern's depiction of Ruth as a naive and dreaming child underscores her point that women can never attain freedom when they are reliant upon male support. To believe, as Ruth Hall does in her uneducated state, that a woman can experience freedom in her traditional domestic role is to be deceived by patriarchy's "blissful dream." Before Ruth falls into a gendered loss of grace, her conception of freedom is as misguided as her sense of security. Only when Ruth relies on no one but herself can she know the true meaning of independence and freedom.[36]

Fern's depiction of Ruth's painful journey from ignorant inarticulation "into self-definition and verbal power" makes clear that, in her view, to become a writer is to gain access to a full range of emotional expression not limited by gender.[37] Yet, she also shows that before Ruth can take advantage of her newfound privilege, she must be completely purged of her former identity as dependent wife and mother. In a series of dramatic episodes that punctuate the first half of the narrative, Ruth is gradually divested of all trappings of traditional womanhood. The process begins when her first-born child dies from the croup, for it is then that Ruth confronts the precariousness of the "blissful dream" of domesticity; it is accelerated when she is left penniless after her husband's death. As a "mourning mother" and an impoverished widow, Ruth is completely severed from her primary source of gendered status and power (46).

Without male protection and her wifely role, Ruth becomes increasingly helpless and vulnerable. Regarded as sexual prey by a "low-browed, pig-faced, thick-lipped" boarder (73); an easy target of deception by a money-hungry lawyer; and unworthy of financial support by her father and in-laws, Ruth is the ultimate victim of deception and abuse. In one harrowing scene after another, she is literally dispossessed of all material and psychic connections to her former role. Her husband's clothes are illegally confiscated by an unscrupulous lawyer; she is forced to sell a "coral pin" that was a cherished gift from her husband (97); and the child that resembles her husband is the one who her in-laws "kidnap" when she is most destitute. Ruth is thus forced to relinquish all traces of her married life. Through this plotting, Fern expresses rage at white women's lack of rights in a capitalist system that fosters female dependency yet makes no provisions when women are deprived of male support. Without a husband, Ruth can own nothing: neither clothes, jewelry, children, nor her own identity. Only *after* Ruth has been forced to part with her husband and everything he symbolizes can she become an emotionally and economically independent writer.

The culmination of Ruth's disinheritance is a mythic death journey into a highly gendered version of hell. In a scene strikingly similar to the one in Dante's *Inferno* when the pilgrim and Virgil descend into "the doleful city" of hell, Ruth and her daughter, Katy, "descend" into a "hell" in which "fragile wives" and "chained" mothers are left "forgotten by the world and him in whose service [their] bloom had withered" (109). Accused of being insane by husbands who tire of them, and then run off with their children, these women have no law to protect them because "the law, you see, as it generally is, was on the man's side" (111). Like the scene in the *Inferno* in which the pilgrim reads "in somber colors inscribed along the ledge above a gate," "Abandon Hope, Forever, You who Enter," the scene in *Ruth Hall* begins with Katy asking her mother: "What is it on the gate? Spell it, mother." When Ruth replies, " 'Insane Hospital,' dear; a place for crazy people," and the mother and child pass through the gate, we know that like Dante's pilgrim, they, too, will learn about the mysteries of eternal suffering. The difference, however, is that in Fanny Fern's mid-nineteenth-century imaginative universe, the mysteries Ruth and Katy encounter concern womanhood in a patriarchal hell.[38]

After the "gate-keeper" invites them in, Ruth inadvertently learns that one of her beloved friends, Mrs. Leon, has just died there the day before. Placed in the institution by her foppish husband who "left her . . . for her health, while he went to Europe" (109), Mary Leon perishes alone and friendless, a shadow of her former beautiful self. When Ruth learns that her friend's "corpse" is "in the house," she insists on "see[ing] the body" (109, 110). Granted permission by the male superintendent who believes Mr. Leon is "a very fine man," Ruth is led by the "matron of the establishment," a "gaunt, sallow, . . . bony" woman "with restless, yellowish, glaring black eyes, very much resembling those of a cat in the dark" (110), through "massive doors" and dark corridors full of chained and screaming women (111). After they "[descend] a flight of stone steps, into a dark passage-way," they arrive in the "cellar" where Mrs. Leon's emaciated body lies in "a rough deal box" (111). As "the gibbering screams of the maniacs over head echoed through the stillness of that cold, gloomy vault," Ruth "hurried[ly] glance[s] at the corpse" and then bursts into tears (111). Upon questioning the matron whether Mary asked for anyone before she died, Ruth learns that some "scribbling" "on a bit of paper" had been found "under [Mary's] pillow," and that the matron happens to have it in her pocket. Standing next to Mary Leon's body, which is visible by the light of a "small lamp" (111), Ruth reads these words: "I am not crazy, Ruth, no, no—but I shall be; the air of this place stifles me; I grow weaker—weaker. I cannot die here; for the love of heaven, dear Ruth, come and take me away" (112).

Fern uses this scene to convey two crucial messages about female emancipation: in order to achieve liberation, women must shed their dependent identities and learn the mysteries of survival from those who have left a permanent record of their sufferings. Women's writing transmits knowledge as well as truth; it teaches other women how to remain sane in a misogynistic world. Learning this lesson, Ruth completes the final stage of her conversion experience. Because the murdered body of Mary Leon symbolically represents the deadly consequences of female dependency, when Ruth insists on "seeing" it, she acts out a ritual of departure from traditional womanhood and all its pernicious associations. Indeed, her tears are a sign that she has not yet achieved emotional independence because she is still responding to gender injustice based on a feminine model of noble self-restraint. But as soon as Mary Leon is "buried," so, too, is Ruth's inability to recognize and express anger at men.

Ruth's urgent desire to see Mary Leon's body reveals her need to acknowledge the passing of her own dependent state. "Glanc[ing] at the corpse" of her dead friend, she views female dependency for the last time. Thus Mary Leon's death marks Ruth Hall's birth into a new state of being. She leaves hell strong enough to make the slow ascent into purgatory because she now possesses the knowledge of survival gained from Mary Leon's martyrdom: that writing is a way to express rage and still remain sane.

This lesson is especially important to Ruth Hall when she becomes a successful writer. In another key passage that uses a traveling metaphor, Fern makes it clear that fashioning an emotionally independent female identity is fraught with difficulties. Yet, like so many other women writers of the period, she masks her anger at the tenuousness of the woman writer's status by depicting her autobiographical protagonist as a struggling mother who "scribbles" only because it provides sustenance for her children.[39] In the narrator's words: " 'Floy' scribbled on, thinking only of bread for her children, laughing and crying behind her mask. . . . [H]er little bark breasted the billows, now rising high on the topmost wave, now merged in the shadows, but still steering with straining sides, and a heart of oak, for the nearing port of Independence" (133).[40]

Writing newspaper articles from behind the mask of a pseudonym, Ruth is becoming increasingly popular. The recognition, however, has its toll. As an object of public scrutiny, her identity is continually threatened. No longer an inconsequential domestic woman, her self-created mask is always at risk of being redesigned, replaced, or removed by "conjecturing" readers. Not only do these readers prod Ruth Hall's publisher to "divulge her real name," they construct her identity based on the language, style, and opinions of her prose. "[B]ecause she had the courage to call things by their right names, and the independence to express herself boldly on subjects which to the timid and clique-serving, were tabooed," some think she is a man; others believe she is "a disappointed old maid," "a designing widow," or "a moonstruck girl" (133). Along with constructing her identity, the public also subjects her to judgment and ridicule: "Some tried to imitate her, and failing in this, abused and maligned her; the outwardly strait-laced and inwardly corrupt, puckered up their mouths and 'blushed for her;' the hypocritical denounced the sacrilegious fingers which had dared to touch the Ark; the fashionist voted her a vulgar, plebeian thing; and the earnest and sorrowing, to whose burdened hearts she had given voice, cried God speed her" (133).

When a woman writes her way to success by "steering" her own "little bark" to a "port of Independence," Fern shows, her newfound identity is continually under siege. Yet Ruth Hall has no trouble safeguarding her hard-won achievement as long as she pursues her goal with self-sacrificing determination. Dismissing the abuse by "laughing and crying behind her mask," her mighty resolve remains unshaken. Clearly, however, Fanny Fern's anger about the assault on the writing woman's identity inspires this fantasy of the stalwart woman writer. She cloaks her rage behind the mask of satire.

Sending Ruth on a journey into a new kind of womanhood, Fern charts a path to social change via authorship that her readers can also follow. Thus they, traveling along with Ruth, experience emotional catharsis in the same way Ruth does: they vent anger at a system that fails to deliver the promises of liberty, independence, and economic security to women. In the end, however, the reader, like Ruth Hall, must deny anger's existence. For although Fanny Fern creates a heroic protagonist who can feel anger and still be a womanly woman in private, she does not allow Ruth Hall to express that anger publicly. Nor does she allow her own vengeful feelings to be openly acknowledged. On the contrary, she has other characters speak Ruth's anger for her, and she uses the act of writing itself to vindicate her rage. Such displacement is essential for Fern because if she transgresses emotional boundaries completely, she will end up in cultural exile, bereft of the intellectual and financial resources of her newly reconstituted middle-class status.

Fern masks anger as she speaks it by obscuring its expression in textual strategies that conceal their underlying intentions. One such strategy is her creation of an uneducated, working-class woman whose approach to men and anger is radically different from that of her genteel protagonist's. In contrast to the demure Ruth Hall, Mrs. Skiddy believes that "when a woman is married, . . . she must make up her mind either to manage, or to be managed" (107). As a woman who "prefer[s] to manage," Mrs. Skiddy is shrewd, vengeful, and strong. She has no qualms about expressing anger directly, nor does she hesitate to act on it when her husband takes her for granted. Yet Mrs. Skiddy is overworked and poor, and the implication is that she is going to stay that way (107).[41] Her main function is to be Fanny Fern's ventriloquist. Mrs. Skiddy expresses the kind of anger at men that only a working-class woman who never hopes to attain middle-class status can utter.

Fern has black women servants perform the same function: they speak Ruth Hall's anger and misery for her, thus reinforcing her genteel status. Reduced to washing her own clothes in her "stony-hearted" rich cousin's house, Ruth's unjust drudgery is bemoaned by the servants who note that after "she shoulder[ed] that great big basket of damp clothes and climb[ed] up one, two, three, four flights of stairs to hang them to dry in the garret," she "look[ed] so pale about the mouth, and [was] holding on to her side, as if she would never move again" (83). That Fern has black women sympathetically comment on the injustice of Ruth's situation betrays her racialized vision of work, womanhood, and a democratic America. Clearly it is only Ruth Hall's freedom, independence, and economic solvency that concerns her. When black women perform back-breaking labor it is not a problem; but when genteel white women do the same tasks they are deprived of their racialized rights. Using black women to elicit sympathy from white readers because Ruth Hall has been forced to assume their degraded position is a particularly pernicious form of racialized nation-building that becomes increasingly prevalent after the Civil War.[42]

Revising captivity motifs is another textual strategy Fern employs to express anger as she simultaneously obscures it. Like Lydia Maria Child, she, too, uses captivity motifs to make a specifically gendered point about community, enslavement, and freedom. When Ruth is financially insolvent, her in-laws steal one of her children and place her in captivity. The child's capture by the hostile Calvinists and her rescue by the brave, crusading mother is yet another example of a subversive inversion of a captivity narrative by an antebellum woman writer.[43] Yet unlike Child's Calvinists, Fern's do not hold intellectual women captive; on the contrary, they hold the whole culture captive by endangering America's potential for prosperity. Because Ruth's in-laws stubbornly cling to outmoded values and practices, they threaten individualism and capitalist enterprise.

Over and over again throughout the text, Ruth's anti-progressive in-laws are depicted in stark contrast to Ruth and her husband, the archetypical democratic individualists (137). Unlike the enterprising and loving young couple who value privacy and refuse "to stand and take" death because that is "what the Lord sends" (47), the in-laws are miserly, tyrannical, and intrusive, "like two scathed trees, dry, harsh, and uninviting" (24). The "doctor's sitting room" symbolically represents an antiquated and lifeless Calvinism that asphyxiates a younger, more vital culture (128). "[C]lose and stifled," with "the windows hermetically sealed," it is a mausoleum of mid-nineteenth-century artifacts frozen in a seventeenth-century mentality (127–28). Informing us that "The remarkable Escape of Eliza Cook, who was partially scalped by Indians" is among the books on a "centre table," Fern craftily inserts a clue to help the reader interpret the in-laws' cruel behavior toward their grandchild (128). In the same way Eliza Cook was held captive by Indians, so, too, is Ruth's daughter, Katy, held captive by Calvinists.

Imprisoned in the emotionally vacant and airless house, Katy is not only deprived of amusement and affection; she is also physically and psychologically tortured. Forced to perform unpleasant domestic tasks, Katy is treated like a slave. At one point her demonic grandmother even cuts off her "foolish dangling curls" in an attempt to literally "cut off" the mother's influence and value system (138). In Fern's rendering of the captivity narrative, unfeeling, dictatorial Calvinists replace the "bloodthirsty" Indians, and the savior is a mother, not male soldiers. One feature of the original plot she doesn't change, however, is that money remains the most important barter of exchange. In the same way the "twenty pounds" that was Mary Rowlandson's "price of . . . redemption" "was raised by some Boston gentleman," in Fern's mid-nineteenth-century interpretation, Katy's "price of redemption" is her mother's economic success.[44] For once Ruth Hall has steered "her little bark" to "the nearing port of Independence" by becoming a well-paid and popular writer, she then has the financial resources to support both her children in style.

Fern's masking of anger is most deliberate, however, in the way she seemingly resolves the issue of anger and forgiveness in the text's conclusion. In an important scene, Ruth, her two daughters Nettie and Katy, and Mr. Walter, the benevolent male editor who mentors, protects, and mediates for Ruth in the public arena, are reunited for a triumphant meal. With the assistance of Mr. Walter, Ruth has just rescued her daughter Nettie from the clutches of her tyrannical in-laws, Mr. and Mrs. Hall.

The function of the triumphant meal is to celebrate the success of Ruth Hall's democratic values over the tyranny of an outmoded, patriarchal system that no longer has the power to hold America's economic prosperity in captivity. Symbolizing Ruth Hall's ability to feed herself, her children, and her culture, the meal also implicitly makes a case for the moral justification of the writing woman's righteous rage against those individuals and institutions who have deprived her and her children of their rightful privileges. For the "plentifully-furnished table" can't help but remind readers of the pitiful loaves of bread and quarts of milk that Ruth and her daughter Nettie are forced to consume just a hundred pages earlier; and the "fine-looking hotel" the splendid meal is served in is a far cry from the ugly and cheerless boarding house that she and Nettie are forced to tenant when they can't afford to live anywhere else (186).

At the same time the symbolic meal celebrates Ruth Hall's triumph, however, it also reinforces traditional gender arrangements with a subversive twist. Bringing together an economically solvent mother, a benevolent paternal figure, and two healthy and resilient children, the meal epitomizes the restoration of the stable middle-class family, with one important exception: the domineering husband is replaced by the reverent editor and businessman who defends the "motherly" writing woman's reputation by articulating the anger she is not allowed to express in public. Mr. Walter not only "speak[s] for" the meal; he also "speaks for" Ruth when she feels anger at her oppressors (186).

In one of the novel's most satisfying moments, Mr. Walter exposes the duplicity of the man who, acting on Ruth's father-in-law's behalf, lies to Ruth about her rights to her husband's property, and, later, refuses to use his influence to help her secure a teaching position. When Mr. Walter asks the suggestively named Mr. Develin, who is a bookseller, who his "most successful lady authors" are, Mr. Develin names a number of writers without mentioning Floy, Ruth Hall's pseudonym. Incensed by the omission, Mr. Walter informs Mr. Develin that he "[has] been told" "that 'Life Sketches,' by 'Floy' has had an immense sale—a larger one, in fact, than any of the [other titles]" Mr. Develin has mentioned (206). Mr. Develin testily responds that the only reason why Floy is popular is because of the influence of her brother, "Hyacinth Ellet, the Editor of 'The Irving Magazine'" (206). This comment allows Mr. Walter to "set [him] right" by providing the "correct" "version" of Floy's story: not only were Floy's articles *never* published in the Irving Magazine, he knows for a fact that Hyacinth Ellet "never recognized 'Floy' as his sister, till the universal popular voice had pronounced its verdict in her favor. Then, when the steam was up, and the locomotive whizzing past, he jumps on, and says, 'how fast *we* go!'" (Fern's emphasis, 207). Leaving the shop, Mr. Walter indignantly exclaims: "[O]f all mean meanness of which a man can be guilty, the meanest, in my estimation, is to rob a woman of her justly-earned literary fame, and I wish, for the credit of human nature, it were confined to persons of as limited mental endowments and influence as the one I have just left" (207).

Fern expresses anger about Floy's artistic devaluation by having an upstanding male character—"the impersonation of all that was manly and chivalrous"—fight her battles for her (194). This strategy enables her to vindicate the righteousness of her protagonist's anger, at the same time that she constructs a new image of a male protector. Mr. Walter is not only a man whose "eyes . . . [glisten] with tears" when he sees Ruth living in abject poverty (162); he is also a man who never fails to pay tribute to Ruth's talents, achievements, and bravery. Most important, he is a man who uses his power to foster Ruth Hall's independence, not impede it.

In addition to silencing Ruth's anger as it is spoken through the creation of an authoritative male medium, Fern also uses a dialogue between Ruth and her daughters to resolve the issue of anger and forgiveness in a socially acceptable fashion. At one point during the celebratory meal, Nettie and Katy have "an animated conversation" in which Katy details the horrors of what it was like to live with her grandparents. She has "a great, big mark on [her] arm," she explains, because her grandmother beat her when she refused to listen to her "[talk] very bad about mamma" (191). Getting angrier and angrier as she listens, Nettie "plant[s] her tiny foot firmly upon the floor" and exclaims, "Katy, I *must* do something to her," . . . "she *shan't* talk so about mamma. Oh, if I was only a big woman!" (Fern's emphasis, 191).

The ensuing exchange between the two girls and their mother encapsulates mid-nineteenth-century attitudes about anger, and subversively encodes Fern's radical position:

"I suppose we must *forgive* her," said Katy thoughtfully.

"I won't," said the impulsive little Nettie, "never—never—never."

"Then you cannot say your prayers," said the wise little Katy; "forgive us, as we forgive those who have trespassed against us."

"What a pity!" exclaimed the orthodox Nettie; "don't you wish that hadn't been put in? What *shall* we do, Katy?"

"Nettie," said her mother, who had approached unnoticed, "what did you mean when you said just now, that you wished you were a big woman?"

Nettie hung her head for a minute, and twisted the corner of her apron irresolutely; at last she replied with a sudden effort, "you won't love me, mamma, but I will tell you; I wanted to cut grandma's head off." (Fern's emphasis, 191–92)

Upon hearing Nettie's reply, Ruth responds in a way that would make Caroline Dall proud. She chastises the child, reminding her such feelings are "not right," and she uses the episode to teach important moral lessons. Because their "grandmother is an unhappy, miserable old woman," doomed to live out a "dreadful old age," they should have pity for her, not contempt. Furthermore, unlike their grandmother, who "unless she repents, . . . will live miserably, and die forsaken, [because] nobody can love her with such a temper," the children should practice Christian principles and conquer their vengeful feelings, for then they will be assured of prosperity and love (192).

In this magnificent ploy, Fern encodes two responses to anger and humiliation that her readers were sure to recognize. Ruth's and Katy's is the Caroline Dall, turn-the-other-cheek, Jesus-style, feminine response, while Nettie's is the Elizabeth Cady Stanton, confront-the-oppressor, angry-God, masculine response. By adopting this strategy, Fern speaks to readers who embrace either persuasion, even though on the textual level the feminine-style is privileged over the masculine-style. At the same time, however, there is nothing more ironic than Fern having Ruth tell the child who "is Ruth 2nd, in face, form and feature" that her vengeful impulses are "not right," when the text itself is an act of revenge against those who have abused and maligned Fern the author (186).

By supplying ample proof through characterization and plot development that her vengeance is justified, Fern ironically undercuts the forgiveness resolution throughout the course of the text. Making Mr. Hall incessantly repeat, "That tells the whole story," for example, she calls attention to the issue of truth, storytelling, and maliciously biased points of view.[45] By having Ruth's father proclaim, "Never put anything on paper, never put anything on paper . . . parchments, lawyers, witnesses, and things make me nervous," she underscores the power of the word against the patriarchal institutions and practices that deny women the right to be witnesses to male crimes (72). When Fern's version of the story is put "on paper," the text becomes both witness and judge, and as such it rules that her persecutors serve harsh sentences. Thus, even though on one level the text pays lip service to a feminine-style mode of forgiveness, on another level, the act of writing itself advocates a masculine-style mode of revenge achieved not through violent maiming, but through the written text. In this way writing combines both a masculine and feminine style of anger while denying that it does so.

Fanny Fern's "Practical and Democratic" Genius

You are strongly attached to place, and are intensely patriotic. You believe in Plymouth Rock and Bunker Hill. You are not content without a home of your own.—A male phrenologist's determination when he examines Ruth Hall's head

An enormously popular writer who reached hundreds of thousands of readers, Fanny Fern was instrumental in creating a space for the expression of white, middle-class women's anger at the failed promises of democratic America.[46] When seen as part of a specifically gendered tradition of literary nation-building, Fern's artistry of anger is not as anomalous as many scholars have posited.[47] What is unique, however, is the way she uses democratic rhetoric to make white women's anger an acceptably American response to inequality. Adapting abolitionist language and logic, she underscores the hypocrisy of a nation that refuses equal rights and privileges to its white republican daughters. Given Fern's popularity, it is clear her message struck a chord. As one fellow woman writer, Grace Greenwood, observed at the end of Fern's career, "Her genius is practical and democratic, and so has served the people well, and received a generous reward in hearty popular favor." Because Fern champions the "poor unfortunate in the utmost extremity of shame and . . . abandonment" and "never fails" to "chastise the [snob] with the valor of her tongue," she upholds the very essence of democratic values. Her "honest American blood" has every right to "boil" when confronted with inequality.[48] Grace Greenwood justifies Fern's anger in the same way Elizabeth Cady Stanton does: both claim that Fern's response to injustice is archetypally American.

Fanny Fern's ability to fashion herself and her autobiographical protagonist as model republican mothers who use their anger to preserve democratic values explains why her work was so well received. Fellow women writers such as Grace Greenwood helped to circulate and reinforce Fern's patriotic self-creation. Throughout an essay on Fern, she stresses the masked writer's maternal qualities. Not only does she recount a story in which Fern stops on the street to admire a baby; she also quotes Fern's contention that raising her grandchild without the benefit of servants was more important than creating literature: "Our little Effie has never been left with a servant, and, although to carry out such a plan has involved a sacrifice of much literary work, or its unsatisfactory incompleteness, I am not and never shall be sorry. *She* is my poem" (Fern's emphasis). Fern's "maternal tenderness," according to Greenwood, "melt[s] through" her "mask of belligerent pride and harshness." It is Fern's adherence to republican motherhood that makes her a model woman. Greenwood underscores this point by assuring her readers that "[W]hatever masks of manly independence, pride, or mocking mischief Fanny Fern may put on, she is, at the core of her nature 'pure womanly.'"[49]

Greenwood's vindication of Fern's "pure womanliness" helps us to understand that Fern's "practical and democratic" genius was her ability to criticize patriarchal institutions and practices without undermining women's traditional source of empowerment. By satirically exposing the obstacles that prevented white women like herself from becoming ideal republican wives and mothers, she appealed to commonly held nationalist values. Thus when she has "the spirit of '76" flash from Ruth Hall's eyes, she creates a protagonist whose emotions and worldview are as American as those of the founding fathers (190).

At the same time, however, Fern's quintessential American protagonist is so womanly, maternal, and self-sacrificing, that men cannot help but marvel at these qualities. The phrenologist who "examines" Ruth's character finds that her "maternal feelings are very strong. . . . [She has] more than ordinary fortitude, but [is] lacking in the influences of combativeness. [Her] temper comes to a crisis too soon; [but she] cannot keep angry long enough to scold. [She] dislike[s] contention" (169–70). And in one of the text's most ironic concluding scenes, Mr. Walter launches into an impassioned tribute to Ruth Hall's strength of character, noting that although "thorns have pierced her tender feet," and "storms have beat pitilessly on her defenceless head," Ruth remains meek, dignified, and unaffected by worldly success (192–93).

Writing during a time in which African American and woman's rights freedom struggles provided a new language for the expression of righteous rage, Fanny Fern appropriated both discourses to advance white middle-class women's nation-building. Simply put, she wanted her constituency to have an equal share of the power and resources white men had allocated to themselves. Elizabeth Cady Stanton discerned a relationship between *Ruth Hall* and a slave narrative because she knew that Fern's text, like a slave narrative, was testifying against political and social injustice. Stanton also believed that *Ruth Hall* challenged white male systems of oppression in the same way abolitionist rhetoric did. An analysis of Harriet Wilson's *Our Nig* reveals how perceptive Elizabeth Cady Stanton was when she sensed that a domestic novel like *Ruth Hall* had much in common with an African American slave narrative.

SEVEN

The Text as Courtroom

Judgment, Vengeance, and Punishment in Harriet Wilson's *Our Nig*

Nothing turns her from her steadfast purpose of elevating herself. Reposing on God, she has thus journeyed securely. Still an invalid, she asks your sympathy, gentle reader. Refuse not, because some part of her history is unknown, save by the Omniscient God. Enough has been unrolled to demand your sympathy and aid. . . . Frado has passed from [her tormentors'] memories, as Joseph from the butler's, but she will never cease to track them till beyond mortal vision.
—Harriet Wilson, *Our Nig* (1859)

In many ways Harriet Wilson's *Our Nig; or, Sketches From the Life of a Free Black, In a Two-Story White House, North. Showing That Slavery's Shadows Fall Even There* (1859) can be read as a novelization of Maria W. Stewart's life and concerns. As the story of a young black woman's struggle to achieve physical, emotional, and economic independence in the "free" North, Wilson's autobiographical novel provides a personalized view of the problems Stewart eloquently identified. For *Our Nig* not only dramatically illustrates that slavery is a national "plague" whose lethal power knows no regional boundaries; the text also addresses the ways in which "free" blacks are systematically denied humanity, economic solvency, educational opportunities, and a home of their own in what is supposed to be a model republic.[1]

Wilson's novelization of these issues is as gender conscious as Maria W. Stewart's political philosophy. In her imaginative vision, when a "free" black woman encounters racism and discrimination, issues of motherhood, womanhood, and the degendering of work become central. Thus, Wilson and Stewart share a concern for the specifically gendered experience of enslavement as well as its enraging repercussions. Yet their different relationship to Christianity significantly affects how their rage at the failed promises of American democracy is figured and expressed. While Maria W. Stewart stands behind the mask of a patriarchal God in order to assume voice, visibility, and leadership, Harriet Wilson stands behind the mask of secular vulnerability in order to assume God's prerogative of pronouncing judgment on her oppressors and their racist culture. Her tale of a brutalized child who grows into womanhood and finds salvation in literacy both disguises and reveals her enraged contempt for a nation that exiles black women.

Assuring readers that she and her autobiographical protagonist are upstanding, trustworthy witnesses is essential to Wilson's enterprise. The challenge of this task is self-reflexively addressed in the text. Halfway through the novel, one of the newly arrived Bellmont sons, James, counsels the "frail child [who has been] driven from shelter by the cruelty of his mother" that she "must try to be a good girl" (50). "If I do, I get whipped," Frado sobs in reply, "They won't believe what I say" (51). Here Wilson makes clear that being "a good girl" does not guarantee protection and trust; on the contrary, being a "good girl" in a diseased white house results in dehumanization and violent maiming. Frado must find other ways to gain credibility.

The same is true for Wilson the author: she must devise strategies so that her audience will "believe what she says" without getting "whipped" for gender insurrection. Indeed, the question of how to create a vengeful female protagonist who is also a true woman deserving of her "colored brethren's" sympathy is an especially pressing issue (Preface). Because Wilson is reliant upon the black community to buy her life story, she is faced with the problem of how to construct her autobiographical protagonist as a respectable woman whose values and behavior do not conflict with those of her "faithful band of supporters and defenders" (Preface). Complicating the matter is that Wilson has to create a heroine who experiences monstrous cruelty and brutality without becoming monstrously cruel and brutal herself.

One of Wilson's advocates, Margaretta Thorn, raises this issue explicitly in the text's appendix. In a letter addressed "To the Friends of Our Dark-Complexioned Brethren and Sisters," Thorn writes:

> Early in life [Wilson] was deprived of her parents, and all those endearing associations to which childhood clings. Indeed, she may be said not to have had that happy period; for, being taken from home so young, and placed where she had nothing to love or cling to, I often wonder she had not grown up a *monster*; and those very people calling themselves Christians, (the good Lord deliver me from such,) and they likewise ruined her health by hard work, both in the field and house. She was indeed a slave, in every sense of the word; and a lonely one, too. (Thorn's emphasis, 138–39)

Thorn's central point is that Wilson's ability to withstand dehumanizing experiences without losing her humanity makes her an extraordinary woman worthy of patronage. Compared to "those very people calling themselves Christians," Wilson is a paragon of virtue, womanliness, and citizenship.

In order to preserve her credibility as an aggrieved mother appealing for readers' "sympathy and aid" (130), Harriet Wilson must distinguish her autobiographical protagonist's anger from that of her oppressors. The mother and daughter "she-devil[s]" who torture Frado are "haughty, un-disciplined, arbitrary and severe" "tyrants" who are frequently enraged (17, 22, 25, 107). Heinous and unjustified, their anger is a poisonous weapon in the war against black women. If these white women, who are a parody of Christian womanhood, feel and act on anger without restraint, how can an "afflicted mother" who, beyond all else, wants to care for her child in a home of her own, have the same feelings (137)?

Wilson resolves this problem by using her text as a courtroom in which she propounds the moral efficacy of righteous anger and the quest for vengeance. Because these responses enable the possibility of personal and civic reparation, they are fundamental to the attainment of justice. In her courtroom, Harriet Wilson is an outraged witness who also assumes the power to judge the behavior of her oppressors. Instructing readers not only "to listen but also to *do something* about the wrongs that have been enumer-ated" is her verdict.[2]

Harriet Wilson's Many Masks

Harriet Wilson successfully masks her political project because she is an "erudite" "sister" who is the ultimate trickster (Preface). Like Frado, her autobiographical protagonist who was "ever at some sly prank" and "shielded" from punishment by an audience appreciative of her "antics," Wilson is also "ever at some sly prank" "shielded" by the adoption of different personas (38): destitute mother, diffident author, domestic fictionalist, abused victim, social critic, and enraged male abolitionist. Merging elements from seduction novels, domestic fiction, gothic fiction, trickster tales, evangelical conversion narratives, and slave narratives, Wilson speaks to different reading communities, tricking each into believing they will be hearing a familiar story.[3] Whether readers are the "colored brethren" to whom she appeals for "patronage," or white, middle-class consumers eager to prove their altruistic sentiments by supporting a poverty-stricken mother, Wilson plays upon their values, sympathies, and expectations behind the mask of multiple, shifting identities. Assuming these identities allows her, like Frado, to "venture far beyond propriety . . . shielded and countenanced" (38).

The author's various names are evidence of the care with which she constructed her personas. The name in which the book is copyrighted, "Mrs. H. E. Wilson," signifies middle-class respectability, and the Preface, ostensibly authored by the same person, reinforces this impression. In her introductory remarks, H.E.W. underscores her adherence to the tenets of antebellum female literary and emotional culture by presenting herself as a desperate mother in dire need of support and protection. Powerlessness, vulnerability, and forbearance are key themes: "In offering to the public the following pages, the writer confesses her inability to minister to the refined and cultivated, the pleasure supplied by abler pens. It is not for such these crude narrations appear. Deserted by kindred, disabled by failing health, I am forced to some experiment which shall aid me in maintaining myself and child without extinguishing this feeble life."

By disavowing literary capability, H.E.W. situates herself in female-gendered terrain. The explanation of why she is "offering" her writing to "the public" implies that such an event needs justification. Well aware that her "crude narrations" lack skill, H.E.W. attempts them only because economic need forces her to; she has no intention of competing with those who "minister to the refined and cultivated" using "abler pens." Suggesting that the only reason she is writing is because it will enable her to perform her most sanctified womanly role—mothering her own child—Wilson presents herself as a loving and responsible maternal figure who is "forced" to "experiment" with writing as a last resort. Emphasizing her human, womanly, and racialized weakness, Wilson uses secular vulnerability as an authorizing strategy. Unlike, for example, Lydia Maria Child's assertion that her *Appeal in Favor of Americans Called Africans* should be read because it contained "the truth" spoken by a reputable white woman writer, Wilson asks that her text gain a hearing because it is her last hope for survival.[4] Moreover, by reporting that she will not "divulge every transaction in [her] own life," she assures "the public" that she knows how to practice the cherished Christian virtue of self-restraint. Although her story will reveal "disclosures of [slavery's] appurtenances North," she has "purposely omitted what would most provoke shame in our good anti-slavery friends at home."

Behind the mask of Mrs. H. E. Wilson, "the writer" depicts herself as a vulnerable motherly woman who exercises Christian self-governance. In this gendered self-construction, there is no place for anger. As a "humble" woman who frankly confesses her "errors" and fears "severe criticism," Wilson implies that her only relationship to anger is as a victim. Instead of expressing anger at those who attempt to silence her, she dreads becoming a target of the anger of others. "My humble position and frank confession of errors will, I hope, shield me from severe criticism." Humility and honesty—not anger and duplicity—are her "shields" against rebuke.

H.E.W.'s virtuous self-portrait is reinforced by the testimonials of those "who speak a few words in her behalf," which are contained in the appendix (133). Whether these testimonials are written by Wilson or her friends, what is most significant is that they employ the language and codes of antebellum female literary culture to promote the author's "interesting work" (137) and vouch for her upstanding character.[5] In the longest and most detailed letter, Allida depicts Alfrado—yet another of the author's names—as a seduced and abandoned "afflicted mother," a "sorrowful, homeless" (137) Christian woman who is the victim of "former hard treatment" (133) and a "faithless husband" (136). Allida's Alfrado participates in a female literary culture in which women give each other "portable inkstand, pens and paper" as "little memento[es] of affection" (134); read the Bible to each other (135); and share their poetic inspirations (135, 137). Repeated allusions to God's "lowly lot" (136) and "tenderness and love" (137) make clear that this literary culture is grounded in the New Testament rhetoric of a gentle, loving Christ who protects the impoverished, humble, and homeless. This selective Biblical interpretation precludes anger—God's as well as that of the "weary saint[s]" (137). Because the "High Priest above" (137) will not forsake the "poor and needy" (135) in his or her "dark, trying hour" (135), comfort, relief and reassurance are the believer's proper emotional responses. And it is precisely these feelings—not frustration, anger, or bitterness—that inspire Alfrado to write poetry.

Embedded in Allida's testimonial is the notion that women's literary culture is an extension of their familial roles and religious fervor; thus it is socially acceptable. Women read and write to maintain intimate relationships, affirm faith in God, and "comfort and strengthen" those in need. Alfrado's reading and writing practices conform to these expectations. In the "part of a letter [Alfrado] wrote" to a dear friend whom she calls her "mother," which Allida "trust[s] it will be no breach of confidence" (134) to include in her testimonial, Alfrado describes how she felt when she arrived "at the institution, prepared for the *homeless*." After flinging herself on the bed and crying, "until [she] could cry no longer," she "rose up and tried to pray; the Saviour seemed near. I opened my precious little Bible, and the first verse that caught my eye was—'I am poor and needy, yet the Lord thinketh upon me.' O, my mother, could I tell you the comfort this was to me. I sat down, calm, almost happy, took my pen and wrote on the inspiration of the moment" (135).

The poem Alfrado writes "on the inspiration of the moment" seeks solace in the idea that the desperation she is enduring has also been endured by God. When he "dwelt below," her Redeemer was rejected by "his own," and forced to make "[t]he cold, cold earth his bed." The implication is not only that Alfrado's feelings are sacred; it is also that she sees herself as God's equal. Indeed, after she concludes the poem with an allusion to God's "unsheltered head," she comments in her letter, "But *my* head *was sheltered*, and I tried to feel thankful" (Alfrado's emphasis).

"Trying to feel thankful" in the midst of deprivation suggests that Alfrado is valiantly attempting to displace other feelings—most notably anger and bitterness—into the Christian framework of humble forbearance. Such an effort arouses readers' sympathy and admiration, for Alfrado's struggle is a recognizable experience. Although signs of suppressed anger are glaringly present in "blinding tears" and the violence of bodily movement—"I flung myself on the bed and cried"—there is no overt acknowledgment of these feelings; it is as if they are literally excised from her emotional life. Alfrado's suppression of anger not only aids that of the reader; it also reinforces the commonly held belief that anger is not a socially acceptable emotion for a respectable Christian woman.

That the author of *Our Nig* is a respectable, Christian woman is precisely what the three writers included in the appendix want to prove. Each vouches for the author's credibility by emphasizing her virtue, honorable character, and undeserved hardship; and each uses gendered language and allusions to do so. Like Allida, Margaretta Thorn stresses Wilson's victimization, attesting to "the truth of her assertions" about "the many privations and mortifications she has had to pass through" (138). Characterizing her as "a child of misfortune" (138), Thorn assures readers that "[s]he was indeed a slave, in every sense of the word; and a lonely one, too" (139). Yet, she also makes it clear that Alfrado's respectability is never imperiled by this condition. When she refers to Wilson's urgent maternal responsibilities, she is quick to add in a parenthetical aside, "by the way, she has been married" (139). Thorn, like Allida and C.D.S., the writer of the briefest testimonial, insists that Wilson warrants patronage because of her virtuous character. The author is a "worthy woman" (139) "deserving of affection and kindness" (139) as well as "the sympathy of all Christians, and those who have a spark of humanity in their breasts" (140). Although the "worthy woman's" face is "black" (133) and "[s]he is one of that class, who by some are considered not only as little lower than the angels, but far beneath them" (138), she possesses all the attributes of respectable, middle-class womanhood. Vulnerable, pious, and pure, she cherishes home and motherhood; "writing an Autobiography" is just "another method of procuring her bread" when she can not rely on traditional means of support (137).

When Mrs. H. E. Wilson stands behind the mask of "Our Nig," however, this portrait is ironically reversed. No longer is the author a pious, demure, "worthy" woman writing for economic survival; instead, she is a bitter iconoclast writing for revenge. As many critics have noted, Wilson's use of the racist appellation "Our Nig" as a pseudonym on the text's title page is a masterful subversive ploy. By juxtaposing the "Our Nig" of the title—the "free black" who is degraded and possessed by others—to that of the "Our Nig" who claims authorship, Wilson triumphantly resists a dehumanizing tyranny that attempts to strip black people of subjectivity. Claiming the vile diminutive epithet only to satirize it, Wilson proves that not only does "Our Nig" possess herself, she also possesses her own story.[6] Yet, she does so, as Joanne Melish astutely observes, by underscoring her objectified, enslaved status. Her claim to authorship is not as a "free black" but as the enslaved "Our Nig." The supreme irony, however, is that even within the confines of a debilitating racist power structure, "Our Nig" has the power to transform herself.[7] That "Our Nig's" self-invention mimics one of America's most hallowed traditions—the national and personal mythology of regeneration—is equally transgressive.

As "Our Nig," Harriet Wilson expresses the rage that Mrs. H. E. Wilson so skillfully masks, for when Mrs. H. E. Wilson becomes "Our Nig," she adopts the tone, perspective, and sensibility of a publicly enraged male abolitionist. In this posture, all the cherished precepts of middle-class female culture that are inscribed in the preface and testimonials are radically overturned: sacrilege replaces piety; cunning replaces virtue; retaliation replaces forbearance. Wilson's entry into this reconstructed universe is predicated upon her appropriation of a male-gendered emotional and political repertoire.

Contemporary responses to the public activity of female abolitionists Frances Ellen Watkins Harper and Mary Ann Shadd Cary illustrate why such an appropriation was necessary: in the public imagination, femininity and righteous rage were antithetical. Repeated allusions to Harper's and Shadd Cary's feminine bearing and dignified speech assured readers that these women had not stepped into the masculine realm of militant agitation. "William Still once described Frances Harper as 'gentle,' as well as an 'earnest, eloquent, and talented heroine,'" Shirely Yee reports.[8] Other commentators praised Harper's talents by employing similar female-gendered words and associations. "Mrs. Harper . . . uses chaste, pure language." She has a "femininely sensitive" "nature." "Her manner is marked by dignity and composure. She is never assuming, never theatrical."[9] Harper's colleague, Mary Ann Shadd Cary, was also commended for her feminine deportment when making public appearances. The delivery of one of her speeches was "modest, and in strict keeping with the popular notions of the 'sphere of women'" one reporter enthused.[10]

The style and rhetoric of enraged male abolitionists was far from "modest and in strict keeping with the popular notions of the 'sphere of women.'" Indeed, it is significant that when Frances Ellen Watkins Harper was perceived as transgressing gendered prescriptions—perhaps because of her "eloquent indignation"—she was accused of being a man.[11] Abrasive, militant, and confrontational, enraged male abolitionists castigated their nation and countrymen for committing both sacred and secular sins. Frederick Douglass's impassioned speech, "What to the Slave is the Fourth of July," delivered in Rochester, New York, on the 5th of July 1852, is a prime example of how male abolitionists made the expression of rage into an art form. "I do not hesitate to declare, with all my soul, that the character and conduct of this nation never looked blacker to me than on the 4th of July!" Douglass thundered.

> Whether we turn to the declarations of the past, or to the professions of the present, the conduct of the nation seems equally hideous and revolting. America is false to the past, false to the present, and solemnly binds herself to be false to the future. Standing with God and the crushed and bleeding slave on this occasion, I will, in the name of humanity which is outraged, in the name of liberty which is fettered, in the name of the constitution and the Bible, which are disregarded and trampled upon,

dare to call in question and to denounce, with all the emphasis I can command, everything that serves to perpetuate slavery—the great sin and shame of America![12]

Repeatedly "dar[ing] to call in question and to denounce" "the great sin and shame of America," male abolitionists "abandoned the restraints of polite discourse and went in for shock-effect statements."[13] They had a particular "fondness for epithet," Benjamin Quarles notes. "[T]hey might label a slaveholder as a man-thief, a child-seller, and a woman-whipper."[14] Enraged contempt was their rhetorical trademark. It is also Harriet Wilson's. With the same fondness for epithet and the same urgent expression of contemptuous rage, she excoriates the hypocrisy of American democracy by dramatizing the ways in which its values, institutions, and practices abandon, brutalize, and ultimately cripple its black female children. Indeed, in Wilson's vision, hypocrisy is the most blatant symptom of the plague that is destroying America. The impetus to expose its corrosive power and punish its practitioners is the force that propels her storytelling.

Assuming the mask of an enraged male abolitionist in order to express the vindictive rage that her culture believes is reserved exclusively for God and his male spokesmen is only one of Harriet Wilson's rhetorical feats. Yet another is that she uses the tactics of abolitionism to indict abolitionism itself. The book's title page is a prime example. With its shocking use of the racist epithet "Nig," the bitter sarcasm of its message that slavery exists in the North, and its inclusion of a poetic epigraph about the oppressive nature of human suffering rendered in the language and imagery of Christian sacrifice, it incorporates the distinguishing features of abolitionist rhetoric. Yet, instead of lambasting the dehumanizing practice of slavery in the South, the jolting language and allusions to human suffering are placed in the service of a different target—exposing the hypocrisy of northern racism, including that of white abolitionists. By situating an enslaved "free black" in a "White House, North," Wilson bitingly mocks the notion that "North" signifies freedom.

Wilson's rage at hypocritical white abolitionists is also evident in the preface, for as some critics have suggested, Wilson's disclaimers ironically mask her actual intentions.[15] Joanne Melish argues, for example, that Wilson's

> demure insistence that she did not intend to "palliate slavery at the South by disclosures of its appurtenances North" served in fact to equate the two conditions, and in immediately casting Mrs. Bellmont's behavior as uncharacteristic of New England—"My mistress was wholly imbued with *southern* principles"—she in fact located such principles squarely

in New England and further eroded the distinction between the "free" and slave states on which New England nationalist assumptions were fondly based.[16]

Moreover, Wilson's appeal to her "colored brethren" for "patronage" not only suggests her identification with the black community; it also confirms her rage at the "good anti-slavery friends at home" for whom she has nothing but contempt. This becomes most evident when, in yet another highly ironic gesture, Wilson assumes the voice and tone of an enraged male abolitionist in order to castigate the enraging behavior of his white colleagues. "[S]ome" of the "strange" "adventures" Frado has after her indentured term expires include encounters with "professed abolitionists, who didn't want slaves at the South, nor niggers in their own houses, North. Faugh! to lodge one; to eat with one; to admit one through the front door; to sit next one; awful!" (129).

The "good anti-slavery friends at home" are racist hypocrites who exclude the author and her autobiographical protagonist from the familial and national homeland. Blinded by self-interest, they embrace imposters—such as Frado's husband—who spout "illiterate harangues" (128) when those "harangues" support their cause, but they disregard authentic sufferers—such as Frado—whose literate testimony and mode of expression do not conform to the standard agenda.[17] Thus, when Wilson appeals solely to her "colored brethren" for patronage in the preface, she engages in an act of vindictive retaliation. Excluding the "professed" abolitionists in the same way they exclude her, she implies that her only hope for "patronage" lies within the black community. In Wilson's world, white abolitionists are enemies not allies.

The Personal Sources of Wilson's Public Rage

Recent scholarship helps us to understand the personal sources of Wilson's public rage. Pursuing Henry Louis Gates Jr.'s initial findings about Harriet Wilson's identity, Barbara White has established that the characters in *Our Nig* are based on actual people.[18] After scouring Milford, New Hampshire, town records, institutional reports, and family histories, White discovered that the Bellmont family—the family with whom Frado comes of age after she is abandoned by her mother—is a pseudonym for a respectable Milford family, the Nehemiah Haywards. Living in the midst of abolitionist activity—as White notes, Milford was "an abolitionist stronghold and stop on the Underground Railroad" (38)—the Haywards had personal connections to abolitionism through both social and familial relations. Indeed, White provides compelling evidence that Rebecca Hayward (the she-devil, Mrs. Bellmont) and one of her children, Jonas Hayward (Lewis Bellmont) may have had "abolitionist sympathies" (37). Nehemiah and Rebecca Hayward were married by a minister who was "such a strong abolitionist that he was elected by antislavery men to the House of Representatives in 1840 and to the New Hampshire State Senate in 1841" (37). And the Hayward family was related through blood ties and marriage to members of the Hutchinson Family Singers, a singing group which used music to promote progressive social reforms such as abolition, woman's rights, and temperance. When the group toured Maryland in the 1840s, Nehemiah and Rebecca's son, Jonas, assumed the role of informal manager, securing accommodations and arranging performance dates.

That members of the family who virtually enslaved the young and vulnerable indentured servant, Harriet Wilson, may have also been "professed abolitionists" is indicative of the most exquisite irony of white abolitionist fervor. Even though many white crusaders advocated the eradication of slavery because it was a moral blight upon the nation, they believed in the immutability of racial difference and engaged in exclusionary practices. In her discussion of racism within the white women's abolitionist movement, Shirley J. Yee explains the logic behind these attitudes and behavior: "That the women of the New York society could believe in unity between themselves and slave women but still exclude black women from their organization reveals that the members clearly distinguished between the slave and the free black, between social equality with blacks and social obligation to the 'poor heart-broken victims' of slavery."[19] These racist beliefs and practices created interracial tension within the abolitionist movement. As Benjamin Quarles notes, black abolitionists abhorred whites' patronizing attitudes, their willingness to engage in segregated activities and associations, their disregard for the rights and status of "free" blacks, and their tendency to privilege abstraction over concrete action.[20] And they complained about it publicly, accusing whites of hating "a man who wears a colored skin" more than they hated slavery, and of "best lov[ing] the colored man at a distance." If white abolitionists wanted to "receive the unwavering confidence of the people of color," one black activist exhorted, they had to "eradicate prejudice from their own hearts."[21]

Harriet Wilson's personal experience profoundly shaped her literary sensibility. Suffering the indignities of dehumanization in a family of "professed" abolitionists during the formative years of her life, Wilson came of age in a disjunctive environment that engendered disjunctive responses. Her consistent use of mockery, irony, and dissemblance stems from her daily experience of mockery, irony, and dissemblance. Transforming her rage into artistic creation enabled her to reconcile the glaring contradictions of her life and culture.

Nothing fuels Wilson's artistry of anger more than her rage at the way in which America deprives its black, female children of its democratic promises. The betrayals her autobiographical protagonist endures as an orphaned child in the "white house, North" are emblematic of the betrayals all young black women endure as orphaned citizens in the national homeland. Abandoned and deceived by mother, husband, "professed" friends, and the republican enterprise, the young black woman is betrayed by family, community, government, and her own body. A casualty of the national "plague" that is infecting the nation, she suffers from a debilitating illness that makes it impossible to achieve independence. The only cure is public testimony in the marketplace animated by angered truth.

Our Nig: Courtroom Drama in Disguise

Couched as an "experiment" executed by a "humble" writer who is "forced" to author her life story as a way of aiding her ailing self and child, *Our Nig* is courtroom drama in disguise. Published two years after the Supreme Court declared in the Dred Scott Decision that blacks had "no rights which white men were bound to respect," Harriet Wilson uses her "crude narrations" not only to "appeal" for economic and psychological "patronage" from her "colored brethren," but also to appeal the ruling of a racist white legal system. Barred from the right of bearing witness in court, Harriet Wilson creates her own courtroom within the pages of her novelized autobiography. Behind the mask of desperate debility, the "invalid" seeking sympathy from the "gentle reader" selects a jury, provides witnesses, evaluates testimony, and metes out justice. As witness, jury, and judge, Wilson denigrates the testimony of her oppressors, reverses their racist logic, and sentences them to public censure. In her courtroom, criminal perpetrators are condemned, not forgiven, and the black woman's quest for vengeance is vindicated.

In *Our Nig*, Wilson argues her case for the moral sanctity of revenge by using two interactions between Frado and Aunt Abby, the white woman who is the equivalent of Mr. Walters in Fanny Fern's *Ruth Hall*. "[A] professor of religion" (45), Aunt Abby is the only member of the Bellmont household to have her "own quarters" (67). As Frado's "sole comforter" (121), she not only "[stands] between [Mrs. Bellmont] and Frado" (67); she is also a conduit of Frado's verbal empowerment. For it is she who unwittingly fosters Frado's "conversion" by taking her out of the house and into "the neighborhood" to "evening meetings" (68); it is she who introduces Frado to the idea that "speak[ing] freely" is a source of power (103).

Ironically, however, it is not Aunt Abby's version of Christianity to which Frado is "converted"; it is the realization that publicly "relat[ing] her experience" is a potent weapon of revenge (103). Immediately after speaking "at the meeting," Frado uses words to resist Mrs. Bellmont's tyranny. Whereas in the past Mrs. B. has "shut her up" by stuffing her mouth with a towel or a wedge of wood, when Frado discovers the ability to articulate resistance through language, she liberates a primary source of power from Mrs. B's control (77). The next time Mrs. B. attempts to beat her, Frado tests her new found weapon and triumphantly discovers that it "had the power to ward off assaults":

> She was sent for wood, and not returning as soon as Mrs. B. calculated, she followed her, and, snatching from the pile a stick, raised it over her.
>
> "Stop!" shouted Frado, "strike me, and I'll never work a mite more for you;" and throwing down what she had gathered, stood like one who feels the stirring of free and independent thoughts.
>
> By this unexpected demonstration, her mistress, in amazement, dropped her weapon, desisting from her purpose of chastisement. Frado walked towards the house, her mistress following with the wood she herself was sent after. She did not know, before, that she had a power to ward off assaults. Her triumph in seeing her enter the door with *her* burden, repaid her for much of her former suffering. (105, Wilson's emphasis)

Connecting the overt expression of anger and "the stirring of free and independent thoughts," Wilson demonstrates that anger and independence are integrally related. Expressing anger assumes the right to judge those who are causing injury; it also assumes that the self is worth defending. Frado finds revenge a gratifying reward for "former suffering" because it is a form of restitution; it equalizes the relationship between the aggrieved and the perpetrator.

Wilson's depiction of Aunt Abby reveals her rage at a middle-class, Christian ethos that advocates self-sacrificing forgiveness and mercy as opposed to self-satisfying punishment and condemnation of one's enemies. When Mary, the daughter who "more nearly resembled [Mrs. Bellmont] in disposition and manners than the others" leaves the Bellmont household, Frado shares her joy with Aunt Abby (25). Excitedly "jump[ing] up and down," she exclaims, "Well, she's gone, gone, Aunt Abby. I hope she'll never come back again" (80). Frado is so ecstatic at the prospect of "some days of peace," it does not occur to her that Aunt Abby might not understand her intense sense of relief (79). She soon learns, however, that Aunt Abby is far from sympathetic; in fact, she is downright disapproving. Informing Frado that her feelings are "wrong," she admonishes her to remember "what our good minister told us last week, about doing good to those that hate us" (80). By having Frado respond: "Didn't I do good, Aunt Abby, when I washed and ironed and packed her old duds to get rid of her?" (81), Wilson makes it clear she does not accept Aunt Abby's view. Indeed, she disavows it even further by concluding the scene with Frado "singing in joyous notes the relief she felt at the removal of one of her tormentors" (81). Doing so, she once again emphasizes Frado's ability to achieve revenge through language. Using song, a significant medium of subversive communication in African American culture, Frado triumphantly has the final word about the moral sanctity of anger and revenge.

Wilson continues to affirm black women's right to vengeful feelings when she describes Frado's reaction to Mary's death. While Aunt Abby and Mr. Bellmont experience Mary's death as a "fresh sorrow" (106); to Frado it "seemed a thanksgiving" (107). She is so delighted by the news that "[e]very hour or two she would pop into Aunt Abby's room" expressing vengeful thoughts "not at all acceptable to the pious, sympathetic dame; but she could not evade them" (107). Although Frado's feelings are not "acceptable" to Aunt Abby, they are to Harriet Wilson. She uses these exchanges between Frado and Aunt Abby to undermine the latter's Jesus-style approach to oppression. Because "doing good to those that hate us" means subjecting oneself to tyranny, Wilson posits angry-god militance as the most effective way to achieve justice in a "two-story white house, North."

Aunt Abby is a symbolic representation of one of the "professed abolitionists" who Wilson finds so abhorrent. As a white woman whose allegiance to a racialized power structure remains unshaken, she is a useful pathway to Frado's empowerment, nothing more. Because she continues to live in a "white house," she is not interested in fostering Frado's independence, only her docile acceptance of racialized relationships. Like James, another one of Frado's ineffectual "protectors" who believes that Frado can achieve "self-reliance" if "the pertness she sometimes exhibited" was "restrained properly," Aunt Abby wants to "restrain" Frado's most important source of survival: her ability to use anger actualized in language as a weapon of revenge (69).

Behind the mask of "Our Nig," Wilson uses Aunt Abby in the same way she uses other white characters in the book: as a way to punish those who have tortured, humiliated, and deceived her. Considered from this perspective, the novel "repays" Wilson the author "for much of her former suffering" (105). Transforming herself into a subject and "her tormentors into objects" is the ultimate form of revenge.[22] Employing this strategy, Wilson not only proves that writing a fictionalized autobiography is a healthy way to manage rage and still remain sane; she also shows why Frado's behavior is an appropriate response for a respectable black woman who lives in "a sneering world" (7) full of "hateful deceivers and crushing arrogance" (6).

In *Our Nig*, Wilson validates a black woman's male-styled, vengeful-God anger. Given that Frado has been subjected to Mary's monstrous behavior since the beginning of her servitude in the Bellmont house, it is perfectly understandable why she "could not evade" vengeful feelings when she learns of Mary's death. Similarly, when Frado "contemplate[s] administering poison to her mistress, to rid herself and the house of so detestable a plague," her idea is not criminal; rather, under the circumstances, it seems to be a reasonable plan of escape (108). Over and over again throughout the text, Wilson establishes a gender-neutral ethical system that rejects a Jesus-style, turn-the-other-cheek model of forgiveness, and replaces it with an angry-God model of punishment and revenge. Black women have every right to feel and express hatred and a desire for vengeance, she asserts, and they, like black men, should use these feelings as weapons against those who build, own, and support the "two-story white houses" in which black people are enslaved.

The end of the novel reinforces this point. At the same time that the "humble" narrator is "[r]eposing on God," asking "sympathy" from her "gentle reader," she also reports that Mrs. B. "passed away" "after an agony in death unspeakable" (130). Here the transformation of the respectable Mrs. H. E. Wilson into the vindictive "Our Nig" is complete. Using the conventions of late-eighteenth-century seduction novels, Wilson punishes her most heinous culprit by making sure she gets her just desserts.[23] Equally significant, she assures readers she is unwilling to forgive: "Frado has passed from [her tormentors'] memories, as Joseph from the butler's, but she will never cease to track them till beyond mortal vision" (131).

"To assume the burden of being a relentless keeper of the truth is to place a higher value on righteous anger and remembrance than on forgiveness," Susan Jacoby notes. "Such people arouse antagonism not only because the world is unprepared to hear what they have to say but also because the personality traits that lend themselves to sharp recollection of past injustice are not considered the most appealing qualities in ordinary social intercourse. . . . [T]here is no question that the act of bearing witness is rooted not only in devotion to justice but also in the psychological need for vindication. But the witness, unlike the destructive avenger, places the drive for vindication in the service of justice rather than in opposition to it."[24] For Harriet Wilson, a "relentless keeper of the truth," vengeance is integral to achieving democratic justice.

In Wilson's courtroom, racist and sexist ideologies and institutions are also tried and condemned. A capitalist democracy that keeps women beholden to exploitative men is a particular target. Indeed, when it comes to economics and marriage, Wilson's view is no different than Lydia Maria Child's and Fanny Fern's. Like them, she abhors women's inability to achieve independence; and like them, she uses a generational motif to criticize a patriarchal culture that regards women as sexual property to be bought, used, and then discarded.

Frado's mother, Mag, is a prime example of this phenomenon. In the first two chapters of *Our Nig*, Wilson records Mag's fate as a victim of a patriarchal, capitalist system in which heterosexual love is the only source of economic support for women. A friendless orphan who is deceived by a man because the relationship "whispered of an elevation before unaspired to; of ease and plenty her simple heart had never dreamed of as hers," Wilson uses Mag's story to dramatize what happens to women when their sexuality is treated as a commodity in an economic system designed by and for men (5–6). Mag's desire for love, security, and protection is so great, Wilson explains, that she is willing to "surrender" her virginity, that "priceless gem, which [the seducer] proudly garnered as a trophy, with those of other victims, and [then] left her to her fate" (6).

As a "fallen" woman who has been impregnated and abandoned, Mag is cast out of the Eden of republican womanhood. She is homeless and alone because "the great bond of union to her former companions was severed" (6). Although she attempts to support herself, economic conditions make it increasingly difficult to secure work. Becoming poorer and poorer, Mag descends "another step down the ladder of infamy" (13) and finally agrees to marry a "kind-hearted African" based solely on economic necessity (9). When this man sickens and dies, Mag is so downtrodden "[s]he had no longings for a purer heart, a better life" (16). Knowing that she cannot care for herself and children without male support, she "entered the darkness of perpetual infamy" by deciding to live with another black man without undergoing "the rite of civilization or Christianity" (16). Poverty eventually forces them to "give the children away" so they can "try to get work in some other place" (16).

Depicting Mag as an embittered woman who is so victimized by poverty that she loses all sense of decency, morality, and maternal feelings, Wilson's central point is that when women are regarded as sexual "toys," they can not be respectable or independent (126). That Frado also experiences seduction, betrayal, and abandonment when she "opened her heart to the presence of love—that arbitrary and inexorable tyrant" is an important message about the ongoing nature of this specifically gendered problem (127). Like her mother and many other women, Frado's only hope for "comfortable support" (127) is through marriage, and like her mother and many other women, Frado is left abandoned with a child "when, of all [times], she most needed the care and soothing attentions of a devoted husband" (134).[25]

Through Mag's and Frado's experience of heterosexual love, Wilson demonstrates how women are betrayed by the promise of heterosexual love in the same way they are betrayed by the nation: they are deceived into believing they will be protected, when in actuality they are vulnerable and powerless. The central difference between Frado and her mother, however, is that even as a child Frado "escaped through the open door" (19). Unwilling to succumb to the tyranny of poverty and abuse, the strong-willed, independently minded Frado always looks for a way out. As a mature woman who is committed to the "steadfast purpose of elevating herself," writing a fictionalized autobiography indicates that she is determined not to repeat her mother's tragic fate (130). Even though her "experiment" failed to provide the immediate "aid" she so desperately needed, the fact that it inscribes a permanent record of the wronged woman's story is an indication that Wilson does disrupt the pernicious cycle, if only on a symbolic level (130).[26]

Another source of Harriet Wilson's ire is the way in which women are denied autonomy in what is supposed to be an egalitarian country. Indeed, *Our Nig* is an expression of rage against stultifying emotional and economic female dependency in the same way *Ruth Hall* is. Neither "sympathetic" white men like Mr. Bellmont, Jack, and James, nor black men like Samuel, the husband who "was kind . . . when at home, but made no provision for his absence," provide protection (127). The "pleasant, . . . placid [and] . . . serious" (46–47) James who pays lip service to Frado's "finer feelings" is a primary target of indictment (74). Even though he is the Christlike figure on whom Frado most relies to "remove her from such severe treatment as she was subject to" (52), and it is he who "longed . . . to take [Frado] under his protection" (72), James ultimately betrays her like all other men because he dies "feeble" and "lame," killed by the same "disease" that is afflicting the nation (67).[27] James's betrayal conveys an important message about male protection: in a patriarchal culture women have no one to rely on but themselves.

Frado's indefatigable effort to resist dependency reveals Wilson's rage at a culture that makes it impossible for women to be self-sufficient. Determined to "[provide] for her own wants" in spite of debilitating illness and lack of resources, Frado values independence as much as Ruth Hall (116). When illness frequently prevents her from earning her own living, and she is forced to rely on others for care and support, "she resolved to feel patient, and remain till she could help herself" (120–21). In the same way Ruth Hall vows that she will steer "her little bark" to "the nearing port of Independence," Frado's "hope that she might yet help herself, impelled her on" (123).

In Wilson's courtroom, white women are as guilty as white men of robbing black women of independence. Wilson's depiction of Mrs. Bellmont as an embodiment of slavery reveals her profound anger at white women who are central participants in a system that deprives black women of humanity, independence, and womanhood. Because she is a "plague," Mrs. Bellmont spreads disease and death wherever she goes; she infects every one around her, including James and Frado. Treating Frado as a workhorse and whipping boy, depriving her of food, clothing, rest, and respect, Mrs. Bellmont ruins Frado's health. When her period of indenture is finally over, Frado can not live independently because "weary sickness wasted her" (122). Symbolic of slavery, Mrs. Bellmont literally makes Frado incapable of caring for herself, let alone her own child.

For Harriet Wilson, illness is a metaphor for the way in which the nation deprives its black female children of self-sufficiency in health, motherhood, and community. Physical disability incurs anger, frustration, and feelings of worthlessness. "In pain, we experience ourselves as helpless, powerless," Giles Milhaven posits. "We experience the other as exercising power over us. Pain is someone stripping us of power and life. Pain is invasion, oppression, by that vague other."[28] In *Our Nig*, the "vague other" is an economic and ideological system that robs black women of humanity. Illness engenders homelessness and dispossession. Because Frado is "[a]ll broken down" (120), she must depend on others to care for her. In this incapacitated state, she is even more vulnerable to betrayal. Accused of being "an imposter" (123) by a caretaker who uses money provided by "charitable public disburses" to "[fill] her coffers" (122), Frado is denied credibility as well as shelter. In yet another ironic reversal, Wilson demonstrates that the real fakery is a pubic aid system that is corrupted by greed and hypocrisy: "Mrs. Hoggs was a lover of gold and silver, and she asked the favor of filling her coffers by caring for the sick" (122).

Wilson's depiction of Mrs. Bellmont's assault on Frado's physical and emotional integrity expresses her profound rage at a system that degenders black women in order to steal the fruits of their labor. By the time she is "seven years old," Frado's labor is "quite indispensable" (30); by the age of fourteen, she is "do[ing] all the washing, ironing, baking, and the common *et cetera* of household duties" (63). Performing the work of "man, boy, housekeeper, domestic, etc." (116), Frado is "the only moving power" both inside and outside the Bellmont household (62). Here Wilson exposes the racialized politics of gender relations that Fanny Fern takes for granted: not only are there no distinctions between "male" and "female" tasks when black women are the laborers; it is black women's work that upholds the white household.[29] Showing how Mrs. Bellmont continually attempts to strip Frado of womanhood by shaving her "glossy ringlets" (68) and depriving her of clothes, Wilson makes it clear that white women consider black women sexual threats to their limited sovereignty. The politics of moral emotionalism that Fanny Fern and other white women freely manipulate is a politics unavailable to black women.

Also unavailable is access to a justice system that guarantees the legal right to equality and freedom. Nowhere is Wilson's rage at the ways in which black women are denied a fair hearing in America's judicial system more apparent than in her depiction of Frado's struggle to establish credibility in the Bellmont household. She uses one scene in particular to dramatize how the oppressors' power to control testimony and determine judgment leads to the perversion and suppression of truth. When the "wilful, determined" Frado (28) and her young tormentor, "the pert, haughty Mary" (27), engage in a power struggle over wits and status, it is Frado, the victor, who is wrongly accused of misdeed. Threatened by Frado's popularity with their peers at school, Mary decides "to use physical force 'to subdue her [rival],' to 'keep her down'" (33). On their way home one day, Mary commands Frado to cross a stream by walking across a "single plank." Yet, although Mary "dragged [Frado] to the edge, and told her authoritatively to go over," because "Nig hesitated, resisted," it is Mary who "lost her footing and plunged into the stream" (33). Embedded in this schoolgirl tussle is a message about racial struggle: cognitive ability coupled with physical resistance disarms powerful opponents.

In this instance, Wilson depicts Frado, the young child who can not depend on achieving justice through institutionalized channels, as a cunning trickster who uses her wiles to withstand assault. By endowing her with such capabilities, Wilson creates a heroine who transcends gendered expectations. Unlike many of her white female contemporaries, she does not divide her female protagonist into two characters, one a paragon of female-gendered virtues and behavior, the other a symbolic representation of the latter's forbidden desire to defy those prescriptions. On the contrary, Wilson unsettles this division by incorporating the qualities of both kinds of female characters in Frado, her feisty, victimized heroine.

Frado both conforms to, and shatters, gendered stereotypes. At the same time that she is a "defenceless girl" (64) who bears her "misery" "with the hope of a martyr" (82–83), she is also a cunning avenger who has the audacity to retaliate against her mistress when the latter attempts to punish her for defying her enslaved status. When Mrs. Bellmont sees "Nig" sitting in her chair at the dinner table, she insists that Frado eat from her dirty plate. Frado responds by having her dog lick it first: "To eat after James, his wife or Jack, would have been pleasant; but to be commanded to do what was disagreeable by her mistress, *because* it was disagreeable, was trying. Quickly looking about, she took the plate, called Fido to wash it, which he did to the best of his ability; then, wiping her knife and fork on the cloth, she proceeded to eat her dinner" (Wilson's emphasis, 71). Wilson's depiction of Frado as a "disconsolate" (41, 96), "frail" (50) child who is also capable of utilizing her "pent up fires" (38) to claim ascendancy in unequal power relations not only sets her apart from her fictional peers; it also allows Wilson to engage in a dialogue with her readers about the propriety of female transgression, especially the quest for vengeance.

Wilson's rewriting of a significant initiation scene in Susan Warner's *The Wide, Wide World* is a telling example of this phenomenon.[30] In Warner's text, the motherless young heroine, Ellen, is victimized by Nancy, the "mischief-making" (213) "bad girl" (126) who embodies all the qualities Ellen attempts to suppress. Impudent, defiant, and vengeful, Nancy is the ultimate representation of the "lawlessness" that Ellen secretly craves (208). Most important, Nancy, unlike Ellen, expresses anger without regret and refuses to practice submissive docility. "Hold your tongue," said Miss Fortune, "and listen to me." "I'll listen, ma'am," said Nancy, "but it's of no use to hold my tongue. I do try, sometimes, but I never could keep it long" (231). Early in the novel, after experiencing a "storm of anger [that] drove over her with such violence that conscience had hardly time to whisper" (117), Ellen encounters "wicked" Nancy (127, 213) by "a little brook" which held "great charms for her" (117).

> At a particular spot, where the brook made one of its sudden turns, Ellen sat down upon the grass, and watched the dark water,—whirling, brawling over the stones, hurrying past her, with ever the same soft pleasant sound, and she was never tired of it. She did not hear footsteps drawing near, and

it was not till some one was close beside her, and a voice spoke almost in her ears, that she raised her startled eyes and saw the little girl who had come the evening before for a pitcher of milk. (117)

Warner associates the "charm" of imaginative indulgence with Nancy, who "ain't a good girl" (115). Ellen can not resist the sensual pleasure of watching the "whirling, brawling" "dark water" in the same way she can she not resist Nancy's invitation to "take [her] all about and show [her] where people live" (118). Knowing that her aunt would not consent, Ellen willfully disobeys her, choosing to satisfy her own pleasure rather than concede to self-denial. "The temptation was too great to be withstood" (118).

Temptation, however, leads to frightful initiation into a world of competing ethical claims, a world in which "pride and passion" associated with the republican imperative of inalienable rights and privileges competes with "reason and conscience" associated with the Christian imperative to be kind to your persecutors (554). Warner signals Ellen's immersion in a highly symbolic brook-crossing scene in which the naive heroine's baptismal plunge signifies the beginning of her awareness that she is at "war with herself" (553).

It is this scene that Harriet Wilson rewrites in *Our Nig*, but for very different purposes. Although she replicates the basic characteristics of Warner's vignette, she changes one crucial element: she reverses tormentor and victim. In *The Wide, Wide World*, when the naive heroine, Ellen, embarks on "her perilous journey over the bridge," it is she and not the black-eyed, bad girl Nancy, who is the victim of trickery. After Nancy taunts Ellen to cross the same way she has, Ellen "[s]lowly and fearfully, and with as much care as possible, . . . set step by step upon the slippery log. Already half of the danger was passed, when, reaching forward to grasp Nancy's outstretched hand, she missed it,—*perhaps* that was Nancy's fault,—poor Ellen lost her balance and went in head foremost" (Warner's emphasis, 125). In Warner's imaginative vision, the girl who is "reward[ed] for her faithful steadiness to duty" (383), the girl who is the "dear," "patient" (384) "*good* child" (Warner's emphasis, 418), is the one who is tricked; it is she who becomes the butt of the bad girl's joke. Equating gullibility, goodness, and victimization, Warner implicitly suggests that succeeding on "perilous journeys" requires bad girl capabilities: defiance of fear, trust in one's own mental and physical agility, and a willingness to engage in power struggles, no matter what the consequences.

Harriet Wilson challenges Susan Warner's equation. In *Our Nig*, Frado, the persecuted good girl, is also the trickster who beats her opponent at her own game. Mary the tormentor, not Frado the sufferer, endures defeat. Here, as in the other significant rebellion scenes in the text, Wilson draws from

African American folk culture to advance the legitimacy of Frado's vengeful behavior. Throughout *Our Nig*, Wilson incorporates trickster tale motifs to express "otherwise inexpressible angers, . . . gnawing hatreds, . . . pent-up frustrations," and "unrestrained fantasies" of revenge in an idiom African Americans understand. Like the southern slaves to whom she feels akin, Wilson derives both personal and political satisfaction from plotting stories that demonstrate how a "weak, relatively powerless" young girl employs the "tactics of trickery and indirection" to triumph over her more power-ful tormentors. Imagining her autobiographical protagonist "outwit[ting] and humilat[ing] the strong" through cunning and stratagem affords Wilson "psychic relief and a sense of mastery" over horrific living conditions. Equally significant, such imaginings convey important lessons about survival and autonomy while reinforcing the notion that she and her African Ameri-can readers belong to a community united by racial struggle.[31]

In the spirit of African American trickster tales, Frado's victory over the "self-willed, domineering" (33) Mary is a literary revenge fantasy, which, as Louise DeSalvo notes, is "a special form of assault, somewhere between verbal abuse and physical violence."[32] Engaging in this "special form of assault" gives Wilson the power to achieve retributive justice. Assuming the role of judge and jury, she determines that Mary's vindictive behavior war-rants equally vindictive punishment: Mary suffers the humiliation of defeat that she intended for Frado. Although "[i]t occurred to Mary that it would be a punishment to Nig to compel her to cross over" the "single plank" that served as a bridge across the stream, it is Frado who ultimately does the punishing. "Mary placed herself behind the child, and, in the struggle to force her over, lost her footing and plunged into the stream" (33). Unlike many of her white peers, Wilson does not mask her desire to secure retribu-tion through literary defamation.

Harriet Wilson's overtly vengeful renderings are anomalous in antebellum women's literature. In *The Wide, Wide World*, for example, Susan Warner never allows Ellen the possibility of revenge, and her "lawless" angry double, Nancy, is eradicated from the text once she is morally transformed. Like Topsy in Harriet Beecher Stowe's *Uncle Tom's Cabin*, Nancy is converted to good girlhood through Christian benevolence. And it is this conversion that allows Ellen to find a more congenial household and community in which she is freed from domestic drudgery: Nancy takes Ellen's place as dutiful laborer in Aunt Fortune's household (486). In *Our Nig*, however, there is no such fantasy of transformation, no alleviation of involuntary servitude: the "bad girl" is not the "good girl's" angry double, nor is she ever redeemed. On the contrary, the "bad girl" is the embodiment of national corrosion who legitimizes the heroine's rightful quest for vengeance, especially because the latter is excluded from achieving justice within institutionally sanctioned white channels.

Harriet Wilson's refusal to dislodge anger and vengeful impulses from her protagonist's sensibility stands in stark contrast to the popular conventions of her era. Again, Susan Warner's *The Wide, Wide World* is an instructive example. Throughout the novel, it is Nancy who connects Ellen to a righteously angry, transgressive self. It is she who has the courage to question the ethics of unjust authority; she who restores justice by giving Ellen what rightfully belongs to her. A significant case in point is that it is "bold, black-eye[d]" Nancy (115) who makes sure Ellen receives her beloved mother's letters which the malicious Aunt Fortune has deliberately kept from her. Commenting on the retrieval, Nancy justifies her defiance. "Well, thought I," Nancy informs Ellen, "Mrs. Van has no right to that any how, and she ain't a going to take the care of it any more; so I just took it up and put it in the bosom of my frock while I looked to see if there was any more for you" (488). Ellen gratefully replies, "I do thank you very much, Nancy . . . I do thank you— though it wasn't right;—but oh, how could she! How could she!" (488).

In this scene, Warner's employment of the language of rights underscores the problematical relationship of this discourse for women. On the one hand, women are bound by the ethics of gendered behavior which outlaw defiant resistance. "[I]t wasn't right" for Nancy to disobey authority. On the other hand, however, women seek an equal right to the republican discourse of inalienable democratic privileges. "[B]ut oh, how could she! How could she!" In Warner's imaginative vision, a bifurcated heroine resolves the dilemma. The rebellious Nancy who embodies "the spirit of '76" secures the restitution that the compliant Ellen desires but is too fearful to actualize.

For Frado, however, restitution is an elusive pursuit. Robbed of the bodily strength needed to secure economic resources, she is "alone in the world" (117), lacking psychic as well as material shelter. The enticing possibility of alternative community never comes to fruition. As a result, Frado does not experience the kind of retributive justice that Ellen ultimately enjoys. Once again, this significant difference between Warner's and Wilson's imaginative visions is foreshadowed in Wilson's revision of the brook-falling incident. In *The Wide, Wide World*, Nancy brings the drenched Ellen to a neighboring house of mercy where she is cleansed and cared for by solicitous protectors. In *Our Nig*, on the other hand, "Mary went to the nearest house, dripping, to procure a change of garments" (34) and Frado returns to the white house of oppression where she is incarcerated (34). While Ellen finds succor in a clean, orderly, loving house, Frado endures abuse in the national house of corruption.

Wilson uses the aftermath of the brook-falling incident to demonstrate the ways in which black women are excluded from the judicial process. Back inside the white house, Frado, not Mary, is put on trial, and Frado's testimony, not Mary's, is invalidated. Subject to an unjust judicial system, Frado is denied rights, representation, and credibility. Here Wilson suggests that trickster tactics that work in the liminal space of nature are ineffective when pitted against institutionalized racist power structures. In the diseased confines of the domestic interior, different trickster strategies are required. It is these strategies—most notably "verbal facility and role playing"—that Harriet Wilson, behind the mask of the author "Our Nig," ultimately employs.[33]

Wilson lambastes black women's exclusion from the American courtroom by depicting the post brook-falling confrontation between Frado, Mary, and Mr. and Mrs. Bellmont as if it were a mock tribunal. As soon as Mary comes "loitering home" and charges that "Nig pushed [her] into the stream!," the accused is "called in from the kitchen" (34). The prosecuting attorney, Mrs. Bellmont, interrogates; the defense attorney, Mr. Bellmont, "quietly" ignores the proceedings. Although Frado takes the stand in her own defense, "passionately" denying the charges and "relat[ing] the occurrence truthfully," she is pronounced guilty without benefit of a jury and punished "inhumanly" (34). "No sooner was [Mr. B] out of sight than Mrs. B and Mary commenced beating [Frado] inhumanly; then propping her mouth open with a piece of wood, shut her up in a dark room, without any supper" (34–35).

By dramatizing Frado's legal disenfranchisement, Wilson reinforces the "damning fact" that Frederick Douglass wants "perpetually told": "The minister of American justice is bound by the law to hear but *one* side; and *that* side, is the side of the oppressor."[34] In the white house, the discrepancy between Mary's and Frado's stories is resolved by violent suppression, not rational argumentation. Because Frado lacks citizenship rights, she has no legal protection or credibility. Mr. Belmont's defense, "How do we know but she has told the truth? I shall not punish her," is meaningless in a biased courtroom in which a guilty verdict has been predetermined (34). His decision to leave "the house, as he usually did when a tempest threatened to envelop him" belies his unwillingness to enforce his convictions (34). As a result, the defendant suffers the indignity of two betrayals: one by a legal system which denies her due process, and the other by those within it who supposedly represent her interests. The latter, Wilson makes clear, is especially traumatic. Mr. Bellmont's betrayal "unintentionally prolonged [Frado's] pain" (35). Later on, however, the case is briefly reopened when sympathetic Jack provides evidence that supports Frado's testimony. He informs his mother that Frado's version of events was corroborated by "the school-children [who] happened to see it all." "Which is most likely to be true," Jack asks, "what a dozen agree they saw, or the contrary?" (35).

Wilson's rendering of this scene conveys three central messages about truth, justice, and censorship. The first is that those in power preserve their power by determining the meaning of "truth" and then making certain that all other interpretations are invalidated. The second is that violence and deprivation are key weapons of suppression. By making explicit the question of how her culture ascertains the nature of truth, Wilson intervenes in a debate traditionally conducted by white men in power. She also demonstrates what happens when black women participate in the discourse. When they speak the truth about their experiences, they are "inhumanly" beaten into silence. In the same way Frado's truth "worked fearfully on Jack," causing him to realize "the perfidy of his sister" and his mother's insensible hatred, black women's truths "work fearfully" on the nation's consciousness (36). In the same way Frado's truth pits white family members against each other causing havoc and disruption, so, too, does black women's truth sever national unity. Black women's truths threaten the hegemony of white supremacy.

Wilson's third message is that disempowered people can advance the truths that their oppressors ruthlessly attempt to censor by utilizing the corroborating testimony of witnesses. The battle over whose truth prevails in the Bellmont household—that of the enslaved or the enslaver—is emblematic of the larger national drama in which abolitionists and pro-slavery factions battle over whose version of reality constitutes truth. The credibility of witnesses, as well as how their testimony is interpreted, are key dueling points. Theodore Weld begins his influential abolitionist text, *American Slavery As It Is* (1839), for example, by stating that "the testimony of a multitude of impartial witnesses" will "disprove [the] assertions" of the "slaveholders and their apologists [who] are volunteer witnesses in their own cause." Because Weld amasses and analyzes the testimony of a legion of witnesses—slaveholders, ambassadors, judges, clergymen, merchants, mechanics, lawyers, physicians, professors, planters, overseers, and drivers—it is he who judges their credibility, and it is he who ultimately has the power to interpret the evidence.[35]

In *Our Nig*, Harriet Wilson employs the same strategy. When she has Jack ask, "Which is most likely to be true, what a dozen agree they saw, or the contrary?" (35), she affirms the abolitionist idea that truth is ascertained by the corroborating testimony of witnesses. Frado's version of events is confirmed by the "school-children [who] happened to see it all" (35); thus readers do not have to accept her word alone. Witnesses provide verification. This example encodes in miniature one of Wilson's most important points:

in order for disempowered people to advocate their version of truth, they must gain credibility by having witnesses corroborate their perception of reality. Adding her testimony to the "accumulations of proof," the "affirmations and affidavits," the "written testimonies and statements of a cloud of witnesses who speak [about] what they know and testify [about] what they have seen," Wilson uses her novelized autobiography to affirm the existence of slavery's "appurtenances North" (preface).[36] The irony is that Harriet Wilson the author creates the witnesses and ultimately judges their integrity.

Appropriating the voice and sensibility of an enraged male abolitionist behind the mask of "Our Nig," Wilson substantiates the claim that the "youthful republic" is being poisoned by the "horrible reptile" of hypocrisy.[37] Her testimony, her truth—in conjunction with that of many others— has the power to overturn the falsehoods promulgated by a racist legal system. By creating a courtroom in the form of a novelized autobiography, Wilson establishes an alternative legal forum through which she can control the meanings of truth and justice. Her reality, as well as her moral judgment of that reality, prevail over that of racist hypocrites.

Claiming authority from neither a male narrator, a patriarchal God, nor patriotic rhetoric, Harriet Wilson provides an enraged critique of the failed promises of American democracy. Behind multiple shifting masks, Wilson creates an autobiographical protagonist who values independence and freedom as much as her militant "colored brethren." By gendering sanctified goals such as the pursuit of literacy and the overt resistance to white tyranny female, Wilson challenges the boundaries between "brethren" and "sisters" in the black community. Her "attempt . . . to be erudite" enables her to utilize anger in the war against gender and racial oppression.

In Wilson's imaginative universe, there is no fantasy of reconciliation. Marriage does not signify reinstatement of community and privilege; belief in God does not authorize public leadership; and poverty and abuse do not lead to an equal partnership in capitalism. The pursuit of vengeance is Wilson's highest priority. "Remembrance is unquestionably a form of revenge," Susan Jacoby notes.[38] As a calculated act of revenge against the people and institutions that deprive black women of inalienable rights and freedom, Our Nig is a perfect illustration of this claim. Like all tricksters, Harriet Wilson refuses "to forget or forgive."[39] Through memory, language, and imagination she creates a courtroom in which she "assert[s] her rights" and sentences her oppressors to perpetual infamy (108). "Never ceas[ing] to track [her tormentors] till beyond mortal vision," she is both witness and judge, and her text, like that of Fanny Fern's, provides a permanent record of damning evidence that is an enraged claim for justice (131).

Our Nig is witness to one woman's struggle against historical erasure and the disease of racism. The two-story white house in which the young Frado is kept in captivity refers to more than domestic enclosure. Embedded in the text are two stories that Harriet Wilson tells about American culture: one story is about an aggrieved woman who has been excluded from America's democratic promises. The other is about the duplicity of storytelling itself. Like all good trickster tales, *Our Nig* is a biting social critique that fosters community, relishes the pursuit of vengeance, and celebrates the restoration of justice.

William Leach notes that the metaphor of a healthy body was a staple of mid-nineteenth-century reform consciousness. "The health of the body and the uses made of it decided whether nations or societies would rise or fall."[40] Envisioning slavery as a plague that infects all American houses, Harriet Wilson portrays a terminally ill national body rent apart by racism and greed. Instead of imagining an alternative America, she deconstructs the existing one. In her nation, illness is a coded way to articulate frustration and rage about the difficulty of effecting social change. Wilson the author resists the illness by managing rage through writing, but the culture at large succumbs to the disease. Yet, while men use cannons and guns on the battlefield, women continue to fight for their nation with words.[41]

Fanny Fern and Harriet Wilson: United and Divided

Published within four years of each other, Fanny Fern's *Ruth Hall* (1855) and Harriet Wilson's *Our Nig; or, Sketches From the Life of a Free Black* (1859) continue the literary nation-building tradition that Lydia Maria Child and Maria W. Stewart establish earlier in the century. Both texts are imaginative records of anger, claims to authorship, and critiques of dependency that use domestic literary conventions and settings to redefine American freedom from a woman-centered perspective. Both authors turn their anger at exclusion into artistry, creating texts that convey inspiring models of self-transformation and public protest. Depicting heroic mothers who struggle to achieve material and psychic freedom for themselves and their children, both novels explode the notion that a nation based on a patriarchal system of economic and social relations can be democratic.

Fanny Fern's and Harriet Wilson's adaptation of elements from woman's fiction and slave narratives indicates the ways in which both genres affected women's literary imaginings in mid-nineteenth-century America. Both *Ruth Hall* and *Our Nig* combine a "trials and tribulations" plot commonly used by domestic fictionalists, with one of the distinguishing features of African American women's slave narratives: a clarion "call for justice, not mere sympathy or pity."[42] Although in white woman's fiction, the heroine's bondage is not literal enslavement, there is an integral relationship between her situation and that of an escaped slave's. Indeed, Nina Baym's observation that white woman's fiction is "full of poverty, coarseness, brutality, exploitation, treachery, pettiness, illness, exhaustion, degradation, and suffering" bears a striking resemblance to the crippled world of the antebellum slave narrative.[43]

Fanny Fern's *Ruth Hall* and Harriet Wilson's *Our Nig* help us to understand the dynamic, interactive exchange between two freedom-struggling genres that use words to build an alternative America. Fanny Fern uses the quintessential African American quest for freedom to interpret gender oppression; Harriet Wilson uses the quintessential white woman's quest for self-actualization to interpret racial oppression. Equally important, these two mid-nineteenth-century women writers create angry protagonists when such an endeavor is still a radical imaginative act.

Arming themselves with anger, words, and imagination, Fanny Fern and Harriet Wilson engage their oppressors in warfare. Rejecting a female-gendered, Jesus-styled, turn-the-other-check noble self-restraint, they use the act of writing as an act of revenge because it is in the written text that a battle for veracity, credibility, and truth is waged; and it is in the written text that their version triumphs. As victims of malice, fraud, and injustice, they know that the act of writing is the equivalent of a public trial for the disenfranchised.

Chronicling an autobiographical protagonist's educational development from a silenced victim confined to narrow, domestic interiors to a speaking subject energized by the presence of a sympathetic audience, both *Ruth Hall* and *Our Nig* use the act of telling as an act of revenge against those who have robbed them of agency, dignity, and a home of their own. As a white woman writing from a disenfranchised, middle-class position, Fern's retribution is achieved by creating a protagonist who has the capacity to buy stock literally in the culture of patriarchal privilege. As an African American woman writing from a position of enforced servitude, Wilson's retribution is achieved by creating a heroine who cultivates the power to control her own destiny, primarily through the mastery of public speech.

Yet, even though both texts chart a female protagonist's journey from silence to speech—from victimization to agency through the power of the written word—their ultimate destinations do not exist in the same imaginative universe. While Fern envisions her heroine disembarking at a secure way-station in a racialized, hierarchical economic system, Wilson envisions hers indicting that very same system because she knows that it is built on the backs of enslaved black women like herself.

Nevertheless, there is one remarkable similarity between Fern's and Wilson's imaginative visions: each responds to historical forces that constrict her autobiographical female protagonist—who is an imaginative rendering of self—through a creative maneuvering that both speaks and silences rage simultaneously. The legacy both authors leave future generations is a permanent record of the oppressions that engendered that rage, and the artistry of anger it inspired.

Conclusion

Making Sure the Anger Holds

Anger stirs and wakes in her; it opens its mouth, and like a hot-mouthed puppy, laps up the dredges of her shame.

Anger is better. There is a sense of being in anger. A reality and presence. An awareness of worth. It is a lovely surging. Her thoughts fall back to Mr. Yacobowski's eyes, his phlegmy voice. The anger will not hold; the puppy is too easily surfeited. Its thirst too quickly quenched, it sleeps. The shame wells up again, its muddy rivulets seeping into her eyes. What to do before the tears come. She remembers the Mary Janes.

—Toni Morrison, *The Bluest Eye* (1970)

The underlying premise of this book is that contemporary feminists must make sure women's anger holds in our scholarship as well as in our politics. When women's anger holds, we work together to locate the multiple sources of our oppressions, analyze how they function, and attempt to eradicate them. When women's anger holds, we avoid Pecola's fate in *The Bluest Eye*: we do not retreat into madness and inarticulation, bereft of voice and community; on the contrary, we use the "awareness of [our] worth" that anger makes possible to fortify our convictions and publicly protest the myriad injustices that still shape our lives as women in the twenty-first century: male dominance, racial discrimination, lack of power over our bodies and economic resources, intellectual devaluation, and domestic violence. "The world would split open," Muriel Rukeyser contends, if women told the truth about their lives.[1] This book suggests that anger is at the heart of women's truths. We split the world open when we explore the ramifications of this finding. Women's anger disturbs the patriarchy.

In *The Female Imagination*, one of the first studies of white women's literature published during the advent of feminism, Patricia Mayer Spacks notes, "Modern feminists as well as nineteenth-century ones have raged about the limitations of female choices; its literary consequences can probably never be fully assessed."[2] More than a quarter of a century later, it is time to modify Spacks's judgment. As I have endeavored to show throughout this study, it *is* possible to assess the literary consequences of women's rage when women's anger becomes a mode of analysis and the basis of an aesthetic. Applying the anger paradigm to discrete historical periods illuminates the artistry of anger women have invented to express the discontent that their culture has historically attempted to suppress. The strategies antebellum women devised, whether conscious or not, reveal a great deal about their imaginative responses to injustice. Speaking through a male voice, assuming a male identity, employing irony, and creating characters such as children, men, and working-class women to ventriloquize their anger, these women writers found a way to leave a historical record of their oppressions as well as of their fantasies of liberation. It is this record that must become part of our historical memory. If it is obscured or erased, we will once again sink into the suffocating quicksand of inarticulation, having to relearn how "to speak / starting with I / starting with *We* / starting as the infant does / with her own true hunger / and pleasure / and rage."[3]

The process of women learning to speak with their "own true" anger has a history, and that history coincides with women's struggle to claim democratic liberty and freedom. A small part of that history is charted in *The Artistry of Anger*. In the antebellum period, a confluence of forces made it possible for women to express their anger behind a variety of masks: the culture's valuing of moral virtue as a bedrock principle of democratic governance; the freedom struggles of women and African Americans, which created a discourse of moral outrage; the Judeo-Christian belief in righteousness; the increase in literacy; and the development of a publishing industry that enabled the circulation of literary texts.

"Consciousness-raising begins with the claiming of public space and political language for what were private feelings and personal sorrows," Peter Lyman argues.[4] Antebellum women claimed a public space in the literary marketplace, and they communicated their private feelings, personal sorrows, and masked volcanic anger in their literature. As Helen Papashvily astutely observed fifty years ago, the domestic novel was one of the primary sites of this communication:

> Nineteenth-century women, if they were to achieve freedom in what seemed to them a hostile world, needed direction, inspiration, appreciation, reassurance, a sense of self-importance and of group unity, a plan of action.
>
> The Seneca Falls Convention supplied this to a few women but uncounted hundreds and thousands more found *their* Declaration of Rights, *their* Statement of Intentions within the pages of the domestic novel. (Papashvily's emphasis)[5]

The domestic novel was not the only medium through which women communicated with each other, however; they also related their psychic and material experiences in slave narratives, spiritual autobiographies, historical novels, speeches, short stories, and poetry. For antebellum women, reading and writing were the equivalent of twentieth-century consciousness-raising groups. Until literal organizations in the post–Civil War years took the place of textual conversations, women communicated their anger to themselves, each other, and their culture through their literature.

"The anger that liberates," Teresa Bernardez writes, "is the conscious response to an awareness of injustices suffered, of losses and grievances sustained and is the result of breaking away and defying the injunction to keep silent about it. The anger that liberates involves self-love and awareness of the responsibility of making choices. . . . It leads to connections with the past, the recovery of painful memories, grieving the losses, assessing the complicity of the person in her own submission and reconstructing the future."[6] The history of women's anger in their literature elucidates the injustices women have suffered, their complicity in their own submission as well as that of others, the losses and grievances that are part of our collective existence. When we write this history, we recover painful memories as well as inspiring inscriptions of struggle. We also ensure that the story of how women have transformed their anger into artistry becomes a permanent part of American history.

Chapter One

1. Lorde, "Uses of Anger," 127; Morgan, "Introduction: The Women's Revolution," xv; Lorde, "Eye to Eye," 145; Lorde, "Uses of Anger," 133.

2. Silver, "Authority of Anger," 367.

3. Kovecses, *Metaphors of Anger*, 11–13, 23. The same information is also presented in Lakoff, *Women, Fire, and Dangerous Things*, 380–409.

4. On doubled characters and retreats into madness, see Gilbert and Gubar, *Madwoman in the Attic*; on diminishing the male, see Papashvily, *All the Happy Endings*, 91, 211; on tears, see Baym, *Woman's Fiction*, 144; and Tompkins, afterword to *The Wide, Wide World*, 599.

5. One of the earliest studies by feminist literary critic and historian Ellen Moers was an essay on Harriet Beecher Stowe, the Brontës, and Getrude Stein entitled "The Angry Young Women." See Bennett, *My Life as a Loaded Gun*; Dobson, *Dickinson and the Strategies of Reticence*; Marcus, *Art and Anger*; Ostriker, *Stealing the Language*; and Washington, " 'Taming All That Anger Down'," 387–405, for representative examples of feminist critical studies that make the issue of women writers' anger central.

6. Gilbert and Gubar, *Madwoman in the Attic*, especially chapter 2, "Infection in the Sentence: The Woman Writer and the Anxiety of Authorship," 45–92.

7. Heilbrun, *Writing a Woman's Life*, 13, 15.

8. Spacks, *The Female Imagination*, 12.

9. Ellman, *Thinking about Women*, 32–33, 29.

10. Millet, *Sexual Politics*, 11.

11. Fetterley, *Resisting Reader*, xii; Rich, "When We Dead Awaken," 35; Fetterley, *Resisting Reader*, xxii.

12. Beal, "Double Jeopardy," 340–53; Hull and Smith, "Introduction: The Politics of Black Women's Studies," xvii.

13. Bell, Parker, and Guy-Sheftall, *Sturdy Black Bridges*, xiv.

14. Walker, "One Child of One's Own," 372; Bambara, *The Black Woman*, 10–11.

15. Walker, "One Child of One's Own," 374.

16. McDowell, "New Directions for Black Feminist Criticism," 187.

17. Barbara Smith, "Toward a Black Feminist Criticism"; McDowell, "New Directions for Black Feminist Criticism"; Washington, " 'The Darkened Eye Restored.' "

18. Washington, " 'The Darkened Eye Restored,' " xix, xvii–xviii.

19. Averill, *Anger and Aggression*, 248, 317–22; Diamond, *Anger, Madness and the Daimonic*, 15; Lerner, *Dance of Anger*, 1; Lyman, "Politics of Anger," 61; Jean Baker Miller, "Construction of Anger in Women and Men," 188–89; Jean Baker Miller, "Revisioning Women's Anger," 1–2.

20. Gaylin, *Rage Within*, 16, 142.

21. Lerner, *Dance of Anger*, 3.

22. Deming, "On Anger," 213.

23. Lorde, "Uses of Anger," 131.

24. Diamond, *Anger, Madness and the Daimonic*, 8, 7, 13.

25. Milhaven, *Good Anger*, 63, 65.

26. Lerner, *Dance of Anger*, 3. Also see Jean Baker Miller, "Construction of Anger in Women and Men," 188–89; Wilt, "Treatment of Anger," 262. In *Anger: The Misunderstood Emotion*, Carol Tavris characterizes anger as "a process, a transaction, a way of communicating" (19).

27. Lorde, "Uses of Anger," 127.

28. Smucker, Martin, and Wilt, "Values and Anger," 129.

29. Lyman, "Politics of Anger," 62; Spelman, "Anger and Insubordination," 266; Milhaven, *Good Anger*, 176–77.

30. Aristotle, *The Art of Rhetoric*, 6, 2:2, p. 142; St. Thomas Aquinas, *Summa Theologiae* Vol. 21 (1a2ae), 46.1, p. 89; St. Thomas Aquinas, *Summa Theologiae* Vol. 44 (2a2ae), 158.1:3, p. 55.

31. Lerner, *Dance of Anger*, 3, 1. Also see Greenspan, *New Approach to Women and Therapy*, and Jean Baker Miller, *Toward a New Psychology of Women*.

32. Milhaven, *Good Anger*, 138; Spelman, "Anger and Insubordination," 270.

33. Tavris, *Anger: The Misunderstood Emotion*, 49–50.

34. Kaplow, "Getting Angry," 37; Scheman, "Anger and the Politics of Naming," 180–81; Bernardez, "Women and Anger," 4; Spelman, "Anger and Insubordination," 267.

35. On repression, suppression, and displacement, see Lerner, *Dance of Anger*; Madow, *Anger*; Marcus, *Art and Anger*; Spelman, "Anger and Insubordination"; and Thomas, "Anger and Its Manifestations."

36. On the importance of creating a public language of anger, see Lyman, "Politics of Anger," and Scheman, "Anger and the Politics of Naming."

37. Stanton, Anthony, and Gage, *History of Woman Suffrage*, vol. 1, 840.

Chapter Two

1. Karcher, "Recovering Nineteenth-Century American Literature," 782; Dobson, "The American Renaissance Reenvisioned," 169. In *19th-Century American Women's Novels: Interpretive Strategies*, Susan Harris intervenes in the signification debate by proposing an

alternative classification system for nineteenth-century women's texts. Distinguishing between "didactic" and "exploratory" fiction, she believes the latter texts contain "a high degree of ambiguity" that encourages "multiple readings," while the former texts tend to "[limit] the interpretations they permit" (40). For helpful considerations of the aesthetic question, see Harris, "'But Is It Any Good?'" and *Nineteenth-Century American Women's Novels*; Lauter, "Is Frances Ellen Watkins Harper Good Enough to Teach?" and "Teaching Nineteenth-Century Women Writers"; and Tompkins, *Sensational Designs*.

2. Baym, *Woman's Fiction*, 22, 11, 15; Kelley, *Private Woman, Public Stage*; Tompkins, *Sensational Designs*, 126; Donovan, *New England Local Color Literature*, 50.

3. For a comprehensive review of how the separate spheres paradigm has been used in women's history scholarship, see Kerber, "Separate Spheres."

4. Baym, *Woman's Fiction*, 19, 21.

5. Kelley, *Private Woman, Public Stage*, 335, 221; Baym, *Woman's Fiction*, 311; Kelley, *Private Woman, Public Stage*, 246.

6. In *Woman's Fiction*, Nina Baym notes that "[d]omesticity is set forth as a value scheme for ordering all of life, in competition with the ethos of money and exploitation that is perceived to prevail in American society. The domestic ideal meant not that woman was to be sequestered from the world in her place at home but that everybody was to be placed in the home, and hence home and the world would become one" (27).

7. On republican motherhood, see Norton, *Liberty's Daughters*, and Kerber, *Women of the Republic*; Hale cited in Hanaford, *Daughters of America*, 24. Hale's emphasis.

8. Published in 1857, the ideas in Mary Still's "Appeal to the females of the African Methodist Episcopal Church," are representative of these attitudes. In her words, "The moral or degraded condition of society depends solely upon the influence of woman, if she be virtuous, pious and industrious, her feet abiding in her own house, ruleing [*sic*] her family as well. Such a woman is like a tree planted by the river side, whose leaves are evergreen; she extends in her neighborhood a healthy influence, and all men calleth her blessed." Cited in Yee, *Black Women Abolitionists*, 46.

9. Wilson, *Our Nig*, 101.

10. Hart, *Female Prose Writers of America*, v.

11. Elbert, *Hunger for Home*, 32; Bronson Alcott cited in ibid., 27.

12. Abba Alcott cited in Barton, *Transcendental Wife*, 138. On the gendered nature of self sacrifice, see Elbert, *Hunger for Home*, 38–39, and Warren, *American Narcissus*.

13. Cheney, *Louisa May Alcott*, 23; Stern, introduction to *Journals of Louisa May Alcott*, 5–6.

14. Alcott, *Journals*, 61–62.

15. Ibid., 165. For a description of the events leading up to Alcott's writing of *Little Women*, see Stern, *Louisa May Alcott*, 161–93; and Showalter, introduction to *Little Women*, xv–xix. Page references from the Penguin reprint edition of *Little Women* are cited parenthetically in the text.

16. Crèvecoeur, *Letters from an American Farmer*, 70. Crèvecoeur's 1782 text is a classic articulation of postrevolutionary national mythmaking.

17. I am especially indebted to Frederick DeNaples, Carol Mason, and Sam Stoloff for helping me formulate this analysis. On the importance of reason in the exercise of virtue, see Takaki, *Iron Cages*, 3–65.

18. Alcott, "Behind a Mask." Page references from the Rutgers University Press reprint edition are cited parenthetically in the text.

19. Collins, "Reminiscences," in Stanton, Anthony, and Gage, *History of Woman Suffrage*, vol. 1, 88. Quoted in Dubois, *Feminism and Suffrage*, 48.

20. Sedgwick, "Cacoethes Scribendi."

21. Sterling, *We Are Your Sisters*, 77, 75; Harriet Jacobs to Amy Post, 25 June [1853], in Sterling, *We Are Your Sisters*, 77; Harriet Jacobs to Amy Post, 21 June [1857], in Jacobs, *Incidents*, 242.

22. Jacobs, *Incidents*, 1.

23. Jacobs to Post, [1852?], in ibid., 232; Jacobs to Post, [1854], in Jacobs, ibid., 237–38.

24. Jacobs to Post, [1854], in ibid., 238; Jacobs to Post, 8 October [1860], in ibid., 246–47.

25. Jacobs to Post, 12 February [1851–52], in Sterling, *We Are Your Sisters*, 74.

26. Paul Lauter briefly discusses how "the problem of a place to live is central to many nineteenth-century women's texts" in "Teaching Nineteenth-Century Women Writers," 290–93.

27. Jacobs, *Incidents*. Page references from the Harvard University Press reprint edition are cited parenthetically in the text.

28. Andrews, *To Tell a Free Story*, 262.

29. Hine, "Rape and the Inner Lives of Black Women," 292, 294.

30. Niemtzow, "The Problematic of Self in Autobiography," 106.

31. Andrews, *To Tell a Free Story*, 278–80. Deborah M. Garfield also comments on this chapter in "Earwitness," 117–19.

32. Masking is a pivotal feature of African American literature. For a sustained study of its development and uses in nineteenth- and twentieth-century African American literature, see Petesch, *A Spy in the Enemy's Country*.

33. Halttunen, *Confidence Men and Painted Women*, 57–58.

34. Ostriker, *Stealing the Language*, 41.

35. See Bennett, *My Life as a Loaded Gun*; Dobson, *Dickinson and the Strategies of Reticence*; Gilbert and Gubar, *Madwoman in the Attic*; and Rich, "Vesuvius at Home" for classic feminist interpretations of Dickinson's masking techniques.

36. Papashvily, *All the Happy Endings*, 195; Douglas, *Feminization of American Culture*; Kelley, *Private Woman, Public Stage*.

37. Harris, *Nineteenth-Century American Women's Novels*, 21; Painter, *Sojourner Truth*, especially 185–99; Peterson, *"Doers of the Word,"* 49.

38. Juster, *Disorderly Women*, 161; Baym, *American Women Writers*, 7–8.

39. Milhaven, *Good Anger*, 138; Spelman, "Anger and Insubordination," 270.

40. Lerner, *Dance of Anger*, 1, 3.

Chapter Three

1. Lydia Maria Child to Mary Preston, 11 June 1826, in *Selected Letters*, 7–8. Discussing the content of this letter, Carolyn Karcher notes that Child "does not divulge" the cause of "her outburst" (*First Woman in the Republic*, 51). In her study of white feminist abolitionists, *The Slavery of Sex*, Blanche Glassman Hersh comments that Lydia Maria Child "used a moderate voice" in public, "but her private correspondence revealed a fierce feminist rage" (197). In the short story, "Cacoethes Scribendi" (1830), Catharine Maria Sedgwick describes a protagonist who "*felt a call* to become an author, and before she retired to bed

she obeyed the call, as if it had been, in truth, a divinity stirring within her" (53). Sedgwick's emphasis.

2. On middle-class identity and formation, see Halttunen, *Confidence Men and Painted Women*, especially 25, 29. In Eliza Leslie's short story, "Mrs. Washington Potts," published in *Godey's Lady's Book* in 1832, one of the American characters asserts that "in our country the only acknowledged distinction should be that which is denoted by superiority of mind and manners" (103). Reprinted in Fetterley, *Provisions*, 75–104.

3. Hart, *Female Prose Writers of America*, 76.

4. Angelina Grimké, *An Appeal to the Women of the Nominally Free States*, cited in Yellin, *Women and Sisters*, 35, and in *Turning the World Upside Down*, 27. Grimké prepared the *Appeal* with assistance from Lucretia Mott, Lydia Maria Child, Abby Kelley, and Grace Douglass.

5. "Oppositional discourse" is Jean Yellin's characterization. *Women and Sisters*, xvii.

6. "The spirit of slavery is here and has been roused to wrath," Angelina Grimké pronounced when a mob prepared to burn the hall in which she spoke. *History of Pennsylvania Hall, Which Was Destroyed by a Mob, on the 17th of May, 1838* (Philadelphia, 1838; reprint, New York: Negro Universities Press, 1969), 123–26, cited in Yellin, *Women and Sisters*, 48–49. Sarah M. Grimké, cited in Yellin, *Women and Sisters*, 44.

7. Sarah Louisa Forten published "An Appeal to Women" under the pseudonym Ada in the *Liberator* 4, no. 5 (1 February 1834): 20. One of the poem's stanzas was used as an epigraph for Angelina Grimké's *An Appeal to the Women of the Nominally Free States*, which was circulated at the Antislavery Convention of American Women held in New York in 1837. The poem is reprinted in Gray, *She Wields a Pen*, 60–61. Todd Gernes discusses Forten and the context in which the poem was written in "Poetic Justice." Also see Yellin, *Women and Sisters*, 58–59.

8. Cited in Sterling, *We Are Your Sisters*, 25. See testimony of women who engaged in physical confrontations with masters and mistresses in ibid., 27, 56, 59, 61. More often than not, the women were brutally punished for their audacity. In *Labor of Love, Labor of Sorrow*, Jacqueline Jones notes that "a systemic survey of the [Works Progress Administration Federal Writer's Project] slave narrative collection reveals that women were more likely than men to engage in 'verbal confrontations and striking the master but not running away,' probably because of their family responsibilities" (21). Enslaved men and women also resisted, of course, through covert, nonviolent actions, including caring for their own families, singing in code, transmitting stories and knowledge through oral culture, and withholding their labor by engaging in deception and subterfuge.

9. Elizabeth Perry to Correspondent, 11 March 1844, in Cashin, *Our Common Affairs*, 140.

10. Cashin, *Our Common Affairs*, 14; Chestnut, *A Diary from Dixie*, 21–22, cited in Yee, *Black Women Abolitionists*, 43.

11. For ex-slave women's testimony of white women's acts of cruelty, see Sterling, *We Are Your Sisters*, 9, 10. Garfield, "Earwitness," 114–15. Like Deborah Garfield, Cynthia Davis, in her essay "Speaking the Body's Pain," suggests that Harriet Wilson's descriptions of Mrs. Belmont's brutality against Frado in *Our Nig* "bear chilling similarities to classic depictions of rape" (397). For a discussion of the literary representation of the white mistress in Jacobs's *Incidents* and Elizabeth Keckley's *Behind the Scenes: Thirty Years as a Slave and Four Years in the White House*, see Gwin, "Green-eyed Monsters of the Slavocracy."

12. Kemble, 17–22 March 1839, 182. The letters comprise *The Journal of a Residence on A Georgian Plantation*, which was not published until 1863 (see Kemble, *The American Journals*).

13. Maria Louisa C. Marshall to Eliza Chotard Gould, 19 December 1826; Diary of Lucy Muse Walton Fletcher, 15 December 1856. Fletcher's emphasis. In Cashin, *Our Common Affairs*, 132, 151.

14. Diary of Lucy Muse Walton Fletcher, 2 February 1857; 15 December 1856, in Cashin, *Our Common Affairs*, 153, 152, respectively. Fletcher's emphasis.

15. Child, *The Mother's Book*, 2. Subsequent references are cited parenthetically in the text.

16. Kerber, *Women of the Republic*, 11.

17. See Rose, "Conduct Books for Women, 1830–1860," for a discussion of the ways in which issues of patriotism and virtue influenced the delineation of women's ideal behavior in antebellum "conduct-of-life books."

18. *The Colored American*, 17 November 1838, 2. I am indebted to Joanne Melish for supplying me with this source.

19. Beecher, *Treatise on Domestic Economy for the Use of Young Ladies at Home and at School*, 13. Excerpts are reprinted in Boydston, Kelley, and Margolis, *Limits of Sisterhood*, 130–37. Quotation is on 133. According to Beecher's biographer, Kathryn Kish Sklar, *The Treatise* "was reprinted nearly every year from 1841 to 1856" (151). See her *Catharine Beecher: A Study in American Domesticity*, as well the excellent introductions to primary sources in *Limits of Sisterhood* for an assessment of Beecher's intellectual and literary contributions to nineteenth-century American culture.

20. Beecher, *Treatise*, in Boydston, Kelley, and Margolis, *Limits of Sisterhood*, 134. Child, *The Mother's Book*. "Gentleness, patience, and love, are almost everything in education; especially to those helpless little creatures, who have entered into a world where everything is new and strange to them" (2).

21. Seneca, "On Anger," 209.

22. Writing to her brother, Lydia Maria Child maintained: "The aristocratic principle, unable to act openly, disguises itself, and sends its poison from under a mask." Lydia Maria Child to Convers Francis, 19 September 1833; Lydia Maria Child to Charlotte Phelps, 2 January 1834, in *Selected Letters*, 41, 28.

23. Stearns and Stearns, *Anger*, 36–37. Also see Peter N. Stearns, *American Cool*, 16–94.

24. Nehemiah 5:1, 6, 7, 11, 12. In his analysis of the meanings and representations of anger in the Old Testament, Bruce Edward Baloian discusses at length the ways in which Biblical texts emphasize the importance of reason when human beings encounter anger-producing situations. See his *Anger in the Old Testament*, especially 28–29, 45–46, 149–51.

25. Baloian, *Anger in the Old Testament*, 149–50; Artistotle, *The Art of Rhetoric*, section 6, 2.2., p. 142; Aristotle, *The Nicomachean Ethics*, II.7, p. 41–42; St. Thomas Aquinas, *Summa Theologiae*, Vol. 44 (2a2ae. 155–70), article 2 reply, 57.

26. Stearns and Stearns, *Anger*, 47; see also Stearns, *American Cool*, 29.

27. Amanda M. Hughes to Mary Hughes, 12 January 1858, cited in Cashin, *Our Common Affairs*, 77.

28. Charlotte Forten Grimké, 6 July 1862, in *Journals*, 370; cited in Anna B. Warner, *Susan Warner* [Elizabeth Wetherll], 109. Subsequent page references are cited parenthetically in the text.

29. In the afterword to the Feminist Press reprint of *The Wide, Wide World*, Jane Tompkins discusses the relationship between Susan Warner's life and that of Ellen Montgomery's, the novel's central protagonist. In her view, "the conditions of Susan Warner's life . . . were, in the directest possible way, the inspiration for her work" (586). In a sympathetic reading of the novel, Tompkins notes that "In the final chapter, Warner gives her heroine everything that she herself wanted and couldn't get: city living, wealth and position, relief from household cares, people who adore her, and marriage to an all-powerful protector" (601). For an extended analysis of the gendered significance of the novel's self-sacrificing ethic, see Tompkins, *Sensational Designs*, 147–85.

30. Lydia Sigourney, *Letters to Mothers* (1838), cited in Faragher, Buhle, Czitrom, and Armitage, *Out of Many*, 455.

31. Sedgwick, *The Power of Her Sympathy*, 51.

32. For the creation of class identity, see Halttunen, *Confidence Men and Painted Women*; for a discussion of class issues, see Stearns, *American Cool*, 41–42, 64–65.

33. See Harris, *Nineteenth-Century American Women's Novels*, and Stewart, "The Wild Side of *The Wide, Wide World*," for illuminating discussions of the ways in which female working-class characters function as subversive forces in Fanny Fern's *Ruth Hall* and Susan Warner's *Wide, Wide World*, respectively.

34. Boylan, "Benevolence and Antislavery Activity," 130–31. See Horton, "Freedom's Yoke," and Yee, *Black Women Abolitionists*, on the racial significance of gender conventions in the "free" black community.

35. *Freedom's Journal*, 20 April 1827, p. 24, cited in Yee, *Black Women Abolitionists*, 45. In *We Are Your Sisters*, Dorothy Sterling notes that "the early black newspapers published innumerable articles on what was called woman's sphere, some reprinted from the white press." By the 1840s, however, with the emergence of the woman's rights movement and the vocal assertions of "progressive black spokespersons," they "virtually disappeared" (220).

36. Charlotte Forten Grimké, 5 June 1854, 10 August 1854, in *Journals*, 67, 95.

37. *Liberator*, 28 July 1832, cited in Winch, " 'You Have Talents,' " 107.

38. Sarah Forten to Angelina Grimké, 15 April 1837, in Sterling, *We Are Your Sisters*, 125. In this letter, Forten is responding to Grimké's request that she tell her about the "effects" racial prejudice has had on her. Often working together on antislavery committees, the two women formed a close bond, which they sustained through the course of their lifetimes. Some of their correspondence is included in Sterling, *We Are Your Sisters*, 124–26, 130–32. For information on the Forten women, see entries in *Black Women in America: An Historical Encyclopedia*, edited by Darlene Clark Hine, Elsa Barkley Brown, and Rosalyn Terborg-Penn (Bloomington: Indiana University Press, 1993).

39. Sarah Forten to Angelina Grimké, 15 April 1837, in Sterling, *We Are Your Sisters*, 124.

40. Charolotte Forten Grimké, 4 September 1857, 5 February 1857, in *Journals*, 255, 189–90, respectively. Grimké's emphasis.

41. Sarah L. Forten, in Sterling, *We Are Your Sisters*, 127; Charlotte Forten Grimké, 18 June 1857, in *Journals*, 230. Grimké's emphasis.

42. Charlotte Forten Grimké, 5 August 1854, in *Journals*, 94.

43. 5 September 1854, in ibid., 98.

44. 4 July 1857, in ibid., 235. For other entries in which Grimké records paralysis of speech, see 66, 87, 230.

45. Charlotte Forten Grimké, 17 August 1862, 8 August 1854, 4 October 1857, 11 October 1857, in ibid., 376, 95, 260, 261.

46. Charlotte Forten Grimké, 15 July 1854, in ibid., 86–87.

47. Charlotte Forten Grimké, 30 June 1854, in ibid., 80. Fanny Fern, "Gail Hamilton," in Parton, *Eminent Women of the Age*, 208.

48. Lydia Maria Child's diary entry is included in Lerner, *The Female Experience*, 124–26. I am indebted to Thadious Davis for directing me to this source.

49. Charlotte Forten Grimké, 7 August 1857, 15 June 1858, in *Journals*, 245, 316. For Grimké's assessment of her work as inferior, see entries on 310–11, 318, 326, 351, 399, 407, and 422.

50. On Truth, see Painter, "Difference, Slavery, and Memory," and *Sojourner Truth*; on Black women and verbal resistance, see Mullen, "Runaway Tongue." Jean Yellin comments on Jacobs's shift in tone in the introduction to *Incidents*, xxi.

51. Braxton, *Black Women Writing Autobiography*, 21.

52. Lucy Stone's remarks were made at the National Woman's Rights Convention, held in Cincinnati, Ohio, in 1855. Included in Schneir, *Feminism*, 106–9.

53. Stewart, *Productions*, 16, 54–55.

54. Aristotle maintains that men get angry when their desires are thwarted and the opposite of what they expect occurs. *Rhetoric* 2.2. Also see Denham and Bultemeier, "Anger: Targets and Triggers," 73; Madow, *Anger*, 99; Valentis and Devane, *Female Rage*, 5; Weiss, *The Anger Trap*, 12, 90.

55. "As daughters of a despised race, it becomes a duty . . . to cultivate the talents entrusted to our keeping, that by so doing, we may break down the strong barrier of prejudice." From the constitution of a Female Literary Society. Cited in Sterling, *We Are Your Sisters*, 110. Frances Ellen Watkins Harper, "Oh, How I Miss New England," in the *Liberator*, 23 April 1858, reprinted in Foster, *A Brighter Coming Day*, 46–47. Harriet Beecher Stowe recalls her response to hearing the Declaration of Independence read aloud when she was a child. "I had never heard it before, and even now had but a vague idea of what was meant by some parts of it. Still I gathered enough from the recital of the abuses and injuries that had driven my nation to this course to feel myself swelling with indignation, and ready with all my little mind and strength to applaud the concluding passage . . . I was as ready as any of them to pledge my life, fortune, and sacred honor for such a cause. The heroic element was strong in me, having come down by ordinary generation from a long line of Puritan ancestry, and just now it made me long to do something, I knew not what: to fight for my country, or to make some declaration on my own account." Cited in Annie Fields, *Life and Letters of Harriet Beecher Stowe*, 28–29.

56. Horton, "Freedom's Yoke," 71. In *Black Women Abolitionists*, Yee makes a similar point: "[E]ven those [black men] who supported black women's participation in non-traditional activities also endorsed strict standards of female deportment, especially in interaction with the men of their race" (8). Yee writes that "For black women, public speaking gradually became socially acceptable, as long as they stopped short of direct criticism of black men or challenges to male authority" (127). According to Horton, Sojourner Truth was one of the "few black women [who] were outspoken in their condemnation of the burdens placed on them by sex and race . . . By the end of the nineteenth century, other black women like Mary Church Terrell and Anna Cooper

took up [Truth's discourse], but during the ante-bellum years few spoke publicly in opposition to the subordinate position they were urged to assume in black society." "Freedom's Yoke," 72.

57. Stanton, Anthony, and Gage, *History of Woman Suffrage*, vol. 1, 523 and 852, respectively. The latter quote is from an article in the *Star*, which reported on the Syracuse National Convention, held on September 8th, 9th, and 10th, 1852.

58. Jean Baker Miller, *Toward a New Psychology of Women*, 5–9.

59. For an in-depth analysis of public responses to the antebellum woman's rights movement, see Hoffert, *When Hens Crow*, 91–115.

60. Stanton, Anthony, and Gage, *History of Woman Suffrage*, vol. 1, 523. For information on Elizabeth Oakes Smith's role in the woman's rights movement, see the entry on her in *Notable American Women*, vol. 3; Russo and Kramarae, introduction to *The Radical Women's Press of the 1850s*; and Conrad, *Perish the Thought*. Oakes Smith also wrote fiction and poetry. For an analysis of her poetry, see Walker, *The Nightingale's Burden*.

61. Stanton, Anthony, and Gage, *History of Woman Suffrage*, vol. 1, 14.

Chapter Four

1. Lydia Maria Child to Rufus Wilmot Griswold, October 1846 [?], in Child, *Selected Letters*, 232.

2. Lydia Maria Child, *Hobomok, A Tale of Early Times*. Page references from the Rutgers University reprint edition of the novel, *Hobomok and Other Writings on Indians*, are cited parenthetically in the text.

3. Carolyn Karcher also reads Mary's rebellion in this way, noting that she "returns to the Puritan community on her own terms, unscathed by her violation of its taboos against miscegenation and divorce. Far from paying any price for her transgressions, she finds herself rewarded by the unprecedented opportunity to remarry." Introduction to *Hobomok and Other Writings on Indians*, xxxii.

4. Carolyn Karcher sees "the experience of being denied the education lavished on her brother" as pivotal to Child's emerging "feminist consciousness." Introduction to *Hobomok and Other Writings on Indians*, x. For information on white women's education in this period, see Conrad, *Perish the Thought*; Kelley, *Private Woman, Public Stage*; Kerber, *Women of the Republic*; and Norton, *Liberty's Daughters*.

5. Deborah Pickman Clifford's and Carolyn Karcher's scrupulously researched biographies provide information that enables this interpretation of Child's feelings. In addition, several fine literary studies include rich biographical detail. See, for example, Patricia Holland's essays; Carolyn Karcher's introduction to *Hobomok and Other Writings on Indians*; and William S. Osborne, *Lydia Maria Child*. The edition of Child's selected letters edited by Milton Meltzer and Patricia G. Holland also contains a valuable biographical narrative.

6. Child, *Selected Letters*, 1. The letter was written to Lucy Osgood, a childhood friend. See also Clifford, *Crusader for Freedom*, 5–19; Karcher, *First Woman in the Republic*, 3–6.

7. Quoted in Clifford, *Crusader for Freedom*, 5.

8. For a compelling analysis of the ways in which "the other" is portrayed in selected nineteenth-century texts, see Herzog, *Women, Ethnics, and Exotics*.

9. On Child's early reading, education, and influences, see Clifford, *Crusader for*

Freedom, and Karcher, *First Woman in the Republic*. On the Puritan uses of Biblical typology as a mode of history writing, see Slotkin, *Regeneration through Violence*.

10. Child's emphasis. *Selected Letters*, 2.

11. See especially the letter of 15 April 1863 in which Child memorializes her brother's role in her life by stating, "I owe my own literary tendencies entirely to his early influence.... Such developement [*sic*] as my mind has attained, I attribute to the impulse thus early given by his example and sympathy." Child, *Selected Letters*, 426.

12. Meltzer and Holland write that Child "decided to be baptized in her brother's church and gave herself a new name" sometime in late 1821 or early 1822 when she began living with him. Child, *Selected Letters*, 3. Clifford, however, believes that the new name was acquired when Child was baptized as an orthodox Congregationalist, when she visited her old home. According to Clifford, Child eventually adopted neither her father's nor her brother's religion, but chose one of her own. She notes that although Child attended her brother's services and participated in his church's community affairs, it was the Swedenborgian Church that she joined. *Crusader for Freedom*, 35–38.

13. Letter to Theodore Tilton, 27 May 1866. Child, *Selected Letters*, 460.

14. I am indebted to Daniel Ross for this insight.

15. Letter to Rufus Griswold, October 1846 [?]; letter to Mary Preston [her sister], 11 June 1826. "If people knew half the extent of my vehement and impetuous temperament, they would give me credit for governing myself as well as I do. 'What's *done*, we partly may compute, but know not what's *resisted*' " (Child's emphasis). *Selected Letters*, 232, 7–8, respectively.

16. In later years, Child attributed a review of James Wallis Eastburn and Robert Sands's narrative poem, "Yamoyden, A Tale of the Wars of King Philip: in Six Cantos" as her immediate inspiration. "[O]ne Sunday noon, I took up the N. American Review, and read Mr. Palfrey's review of Yamoyden, in which he eloquently describes the adaptation of early N. England history to the purposes of fiction.... There were at that time scarcely any American books. Cooper's and Mrs. Sedgwick's had not appeared. I finished Hobomok in six weeks. Hasty, imperfect, and crude as it was, it excited a great deal of interest, under the then existing circumstances. Upon the strength of it, the Boston fashionables took me up, and made a 'little wee bit' of a lion of me." Letter to Rufus Griswold October [?] 1846 [?], *Selected Letters*, 232.

Carolyn Karcher discusses the parallels of title, plot, characterizations of Indians, and Shakespearian influences between "Yamoyden" and *Hobomok*. She concludes, however, that Child's foregrounding of patriarchal oppression makes the two texts "substantially" different. Introduction to *Hobomok and Other Writings on Indians*, xviii–xix.

17. Letter to George Ticknor, 29 March 1825, *Selected Letters*, 3–4. Also see Holland, "Lydia Maria Child As a Nineteenth-Century Professional Author"; Clifford, *Crusader for Freedom*, 34–45; Karcher, *First Woman*, 38–40; and Kelley, *Private Woman, Public Stage*, especially 180–214. According to Kelley, for a young woman in the early decades of the nineteenth century to conceive of herself as a "creator of culture" was a "revolutionary act" because it "represented the boldest and most presumptuous act of all on a female's part." Trained to think of themselves in subordinate, domestic roles, to conceive of themselves "as legitimate creators of culture would have required a leap of vision that could only have drawn upon a confidence and a faith in their own ability and power to create and shape their own lives." Kelley, *Private Woman, Public Stage*, 181, 183.

18. Karcher, *First Woman*, 1.

19. Ibid., 37.

20. I am indebted to Frederick DeNaples for helping me formulate these ideas.

21. According to Cathy Davidson, although anonymous and pseudonymous author-ship in the early republic was a common occurrence for both men and women, there were "psychological pressures operating specifically upon the woman author" that men did not have to confront, such as the belief that authorship threatened women's domes-tic roles (32). See *Revolution and the Word*, 31–37. Also see Kelley, *Private Woman, Public Stage*, especially 111–37, for a discussion of anonymity from a gendered perspective.

22. Carolyn Karcher also discusses Child's subversive narrative strategies, as well as her historical sources. See introduction to *Hobomok and Other Writings on Indians*.

23. Baym, *Novels, Readers, and Reviewers*, 106 and 42, respectively. For an extended discussion of these issues, see especially 82–107.

24. "Lines Suggested on Reading 'An Appeal to Christian Women of the South,'" 17–19. In "Poetic Justice: Sarah Forten, Eliza Earle, and the Paradox of Intellectual Prop-erty," Todd Gernes argues that this poem was authored by a white Quaker woman, Eliza Earle, and not by African American abolitionist Sarah L. Forten as previous scholars have assumed.

25. See Exodus 15:27 and 16:3.

26. It is significant that contemporary male reviewers praised Child's portrayal of the women in this scene because they regarded Mrs. Conant and Lady Arabella as ideal self-sacrificing wives. Karcher, introduction to *Hobomok and Other Writings on Indians*, xxxiv–xxxv.

27. Allusions to circles recur throughout the text. See, for example, pages 36, 78, 114, 117, 122, 125.

28. Karcher, introduction to *Hobomok and Other Writings on Indians*, xxv.

29. In "The American Eve," Leland S. Person Jr. notes that this "scene has many characteristics of a dream, an escape from oppressive social order into an imaginative wilderness where repressed desires can be liberated" (681–82).

30. Karcher argues that Brown and Hobomok "function as doubles rather than rivals" (xxx) because both "represent a fusion of nature and culture" (xxix) that Mary Conant finds particularly appealing. Introduction to *Hobomok and Other Writings on Indians*. While I, too, see Brown and Hobomok as doubles, unlike Karcher, I don't see them as "merg-ing" into one another. Rather, I see Child using their doubled characterizations as a way of engaging in an intertextual dialogue about gender, privilege, and sacrifice.

31. I am indebted to Thadious Davis for pointing out the birth imagery in this scene. For a rich and nuanced discussion of the importance of imagining "new plots" for women's lives, see Heilbrun, *Writing a Woman's Life*.

32. Child's use of language makes it clear that she genders nature female. "Silently Mary gazed on the going down of that bright planet, and tree and shrub bowed low their spangled plumes in homage to her retiring majesty, till her oblique rays were only to be seen in faint and scattered radiance, on the cold, smooth surface of the earth" (88). To situate Child's gendered vision of nature within larger American literary traditions, see Annette Kolodny's two studies, *The Lay of the Land* and *The Land Before Her*.

33. In *The Ignoble Savage*, Louise K. Barnett notes that Hobomok is a stereotypical "good Indian" because his primary concern is to help whites. As an Indian who sees "Indianness through white eyes," he sacrifices his own future for the sake of whites (90–95). While

Barnett's study enables placing Child's depiction of Native Americans within a broader literary context, it does not address the question of how "literary racism" is depicted differently by male and female authors. For another interpretation of Hobomok as "Indian in name only," see William Osborne's chapter on *Hobomok* in *Lydia Maria Child*, 39–54. Osborne suggests that in order "to forestall her readers' protests over miscegenation, [Child] uncolors" Hobomok so he can be considered "an acceptable suitor" (50).

34. In Leland Person Jr.'s study of the way in which "male and female attitudes toward miscegenation" differ in various "frontier fiction," he argues that "the successful marriages between white women and Indian men (in works by Catharine Maria Sedgwick and Lydia Maria Child) suggest terms for an alternative, female frontier fantasy—a pact between Indians and women, an Eden from which Adam rather than Eve has been excluded." "The American Eve," 670. Also see Karcher's introduction to *Hobomok and Other Writings on Indians* on this point.

35. It is clear that Child understood the notion of reverence as a relationship in which one party had more power than the other. In *Hobomok*, when she describes the ordination of a teacher and a pastor, she notes that "with many a low courtesy and reverential bow, were the gentlemen in black saluted as they passed along" (63). Much later in her life, in an apologetic letter to the composer Philip Heinrich, she uses the term reverence to express feelings of deference, admiration, and awe. Although she is taking pains to explain why she did not see him when he called—"I found myself under the necessity of adopting the invariable rule of never seeing strangers, & you came under this rule"—it is worth noting that twenty-one years after the publication of *Hobomok* she still sees artists as male. "All artists are to me as brothers, and to musicians, in particular, I would be most kind and respectful; for my reverence for their divine art amounts almost to worship." "Your composition is of course far above my comprehension; but I will not 'transfer it to some practical votary of art,' because I would like to keep it, as a memorial of your talent, and of your kind and flattering attention to one whose love and reverence for the Art so immeasurably transcends her knowledge." *Selected Letters*, 219–21.

36. The term is Ann duCille's. For a trenchant analysis of the way in which people of color are inadvertently "otherized" in contemporary historical narrative see her essay, "'Othered' Matters."

37. Harris, *Nineteenth-Century American Women's Novels*, especially pages 19–21.

38. I am indebted to Jane Gerhard for my analysis in this section because it was her insight that Mary's marriage to Hobomok allows her to "dream of a non-hierarchical relationship" with a man who provides "a new model of masculinity," one that is "in harmony with women and not setting itself above them," that prompted my interpretation of Hobomok as an alternative lover.

39. Lerner, *Dance of Anger*; Madow, *Anger*, especially chapter 1, "How to Recognize Anger"; Gaard, "Anger Expressed/Repressed"; Marcus, *Art and Anger*.

40. See Salvino, "The Word in Black and White"; and Takaki, *Iron Cages*.

Chapter Five

1. Stewart's meditations were originally published in 1832 in a twenty-eight-page pamphlet that contained fourteen poems and seven prayers. They were then included in *Productions of Mrs. Maria W. Stewart, Presented to the First African Baptist Church & Society, of the*

City of Boston (Boston: Friends of Freedom and Virtue, 1835). In addition to the meditations and prayers, *Productions* also includes what was originally a pamphlet, "Religion and the Pure Principles of Morality, The Sure Foundation on Which We Must Build," and the texts of four lectures: "Lecture, Delivered at the Franklin Hall, Boston, Sept. 21, 1832," "An Address, Delivered Before the Afric-American Female Intelligence Society, of Boston," "An Address Delivered at the African Masonic Hall, Boston, Feb. 27, 1833," "Mrs. Stewart's Farewell Address To Her Friends in the City of Boston, Delivered September 21, 1833." The text concludes with a poem, "The Negro's Complaint." *Productions* is now reprinted in *Spiritual Narratives*, which is part of The Schomburg Library of Nineteenth-Century Black Women Writers Series. Page references are from the reprint edition, which is a duplication of the original. For the publication history of Stewart's texts, see Marilyn Richardson's invaluable introductions to another edition of Stewart's essays and speeches, *Maria W. Stewart: America's First Black Woman Political Writer*.

2. Richardson, *Maria W. Stewart*, 9–10, 5, 7, respectively.

3. Moses, *Black Messiahs*. Moses defines the "Black Jeremiad" as "the constant warnings issued by blacks to whites, concerning the judgment that was to come for the sin of slavery" (30–31).

4. Juster, *Disorderly Women*, 7, 209.

5. Swerdlow, "Abolition's Conservative Sisters," 32, 44.

6. Marilyn Richardson notes that although Stewart "did not pursue a public speaking career" in New York, "according to the advertisements for the 1879 edition of her work, she did lecture" while there. She points out, however, that since no new lectures were included in her republished text, it is likely that Stewart used previous material. See introductions in Richardson, *Maria W. Stewart*, 27.

7. Reprinted in ibid., 98–109.

8. "Biographical Sketch" by Louise Hatton, republished in Richardson, *Maria W. Stewart*, 93. After receiving a government pension based on her late husband's service in the War of 1812, Stewart republished *Productions* in 1879, re-titling it *Meditations From The Pen of Mrs. Maria W. Stewart*. The only difference between the two editions is that the later one contains the brief biographical sketch as well as letters from friends and colleagues who testify to her character and accomplishments. Louise Hatton contributes one of the testimonials. See Richardson, *Maria W. Stewart*, Part II: Later Life, 79–109, for invaluable contextual information.

9. Hatton in Richardson, *Maria W. Stewart*, 92; Richardson, *Maria W. Stewart*, 7; Hatton in ibid., 92. Marilyn Richardson notes that Stewart's experience was not atypical in this period. White people frequently used the opportunity of "free" black men's deaths to gain control of their property (7). In *"Doers of the Word,"* Carla Peterson notes that before her marriage Stewart was a member of the "steadily growing subaltern class of unschooled and unskilled black laborers who inhabited the northeastern states at the turn of the century" (56).

10. Stewart, "Sufferings during the War," in Richardson, *Maria W. Stewart*, 98.

11. Hatton in Richardson, *Maria W. Stewart*, 91; Stewart, "Sufferings," 100, in ibid. In *"Doers of the Word,"* Carla Peterson discusses Stewart's "repeated dislocations" while in Washington, noting that Stewart's "affiliation with the Episcopal Church, the 'white folks' church," alienated her from the black community (207). In addition, Stewart was refused support from the white community because of her race. "[D]enied financial aid

by the Episcopal Church because of her blackness and by the black churches because of her commitment to Episcopalianism," Peterson writes, "Stewart could find no local place within which to situate her Sunday school and was eventually forced to hold prayer meetings in her own 'dwelling-house' " (208).

12. The Garrison and Crummell letters are reprinted in Richardson, *Maria W. Stewart*, 89–90 and 93–94, respectively.

13. For information about black women's literary societies, see Sterling, *We Are Your Sisters*, 109–13; Gerda Lerner, *Black Women in White America*, 435–40; and Yee, *Black Women Abolitionists*, 60–85. Stewart's participation in the Ladies Literary Society is noted by Richardson, *Maria W. Stewart*, 27, and Sterling, *We Are Your Sisters*, 158.

14. See note 8.

15. Stewart, preface to *Meditations From The Pen of Mrs. Maria W. Stewart*, reprinted in Richardson, *Maria W. Stewart*, 87.

16. William Lloyd Garrison in Richardson, *Maria W. Stewart*, 90. See his letter of commendation, which is included in the 1879 edition of Stewart's texts.

17. Ibid., 18–19.

18. In her consideration of Maria Stewart as a black nationalist, Lora Romero also notes Stewart's utilization of different discourses. Stewart "speaks both masculinist and womanist languages of black nationalism," Romero argues (*Home Fronts*, 69).

19. For a succinct summary of the doctrine of influence, see Woloch, *Women and the American Experience*, chapter 5: "Sarah Hale and the Ladies Magazine" (97–112). Also see Douglas, *The Feminization of American Culture*, for a more partisan view. Woloch points out that "[t]he power of female influence was never fully defined: it was so awesome, it defied description" (103).

20. Sarah Hale quoted in Woloch, *Women and the American Experience*, 103.

21. "Religion and The Pure Principles of Morality" was originally published in the *Liberator* and then as a twelve-page pamphlet in 1831. Stewart later included it, along with the meditations, in *Productions*.

22. See William Andrews's introduction to *Sisters of the Spirit* and Jean McMahon Humez's introduction to *Gifts of Power* for a discussion of other black women who found personal and political empowerment through religion. Also see Sue E. Houchins's introduction to *Spiritual Narratives* for a more general discussion.

23. More than twenty years later, Harriet Jacobs employs the same technique when she, too, appeals to "virtuous readers" who have no idea of "what it is to be a slave; to be entirely unprotected by law or custom; to have laws reduce you to the condition of chattel, [and to be] entirely subject to the will of another" (*Incidents*, 55).

24. These quotations are from a letter to the editor of the *Liberator*. The letter is not included in *Productions*, but Richardson reprinted it in *Maria W. Stewart*, 43.

25. Franklin, *Autobiography*, 75.

26. An abridged version of the "Pastoral Letter of the Massachusetts Congregationalist Clergy, 1837" is reprinted in Kraditor, *Up From the Pedestal*, 50–52.

27. In a chapter titled "Finding a Voice to Answer the Moral Call," in their study, *Declarations of Independence: Women and Political Power in Nineteenth Century American Fiction* (38–69), Barbara Bardes and Suzanne Gossett trace the ambivalent portrayal of "lecturesses," convincingly demonstrating the "social tension" that was generated by women's public speaking. According to their sources, "The right of women to influence politics by

speaking from the public platform became a heated issue during the 1830s and remained a source of tension in American culture until the Civil War" (38).

28. Reprinted in Richardson, *Maria W. Stewart*, 90.

29. In his study of David Walker, *To Awake My Afflicted Brethren: David Walker and the Problem of Antebellum Slave Resistance*, Peter Hinks notes that "the mass of blacks" did not subscribe to the values that David Walker and Maria W. Stewart were advocating. "Many were neither church-going nor temperate, and they were not committed to study and displayed little interest in adopting the reformers' prescriptions for self-improvement" (85).

30. Sterling, *We Are Your Sisters*, 157; Gerda Lerner, *Black Women in White America*, 83; Fetterley, *Provisions*, 61; Loewenberg and Bogin, *Black Women in Nineteenth-Century American Life*, 184; Richardson, *Maria W. Stewart*, 24, 25. In *Black Women Abolitionists*, Shirley J. Yee writes that "In 1831 in Boston, an audience of black men jeered and threw rotten tomatoes at Maria Miller Stewart when she delivered an address to black men that criticized them for failing to follow basic Christian principles of thrift, sobriety, and hard work" (115). Although she cites Sterling as her source, there is no mention of men throwing tomatoes in Sterling's narrative, nor in the Stewart excerpt she introduces.

31. Yee, *Black Women Abolitionists*, 4.

32. Richardson, *Maria W. Stewart*, 20, 24.

33. Peterson, *"Doers of the Word,"* 58; Stewart, "Sufferings during the War," in Richardson, *Maria W. Stewart*, 99.

34. Kerber, *Women of the Republic*, 206; Conrad, *Perish the Thought*, 95.

35. In her analysis of the gendered nature of women's conversion experiences in the nineteenth century, Barbara Leslie Epstein points out that "the desire to rebel against God's authority often became the paramount issue" for women (*Politics of Domesticity*, 47). She also notes that "The moment of conversion came when . . . the desire to rebel was replaced by the desire to obey" (58). Susan Juster also analyzes gender differences in conversion narratives. She notes that "By 1800 two distinct models of conversion, one male and one female, existed side by side in evangelical stories of religious transformation" (*Disorderly Women*, 181). Also see William Andrews's introduction to *Sisters of the Spirit* for a discussion of the "Afro-American Spiritual Autobiography Tradition," 10–16.

36. Marilyn Richardson interprets the "uncharacteristic serenity of tone" in the Farewell Address as a sign that Stewart had decided to "annihilate her public persona." She goes on to note that Stewart speaks as if she were "one dying into a new life." See introduction in Richardson, *Maria W. Stewart*, 27.

37. "Biographical Sketch by Louise Hatton," in ibid., 93. "I found out from all the old personal friends of Mrs. Stewart, that she was then, as now, a very devout Christian lady, a leader in all good movements and reforms, and had no equal as a lecturer and authoress in her day."

38. Both of these documents are reprinted in Schneir, *Feminism*, 3–4, 77–82.

Chapter Six

1. Stanton, "Ruth Hall." For information about the role of the *Una* in the antebellum woman's rights movement, see Conrad, *Perish the Thought*, 157–82, and Russo and Kramarae, introduction to *Radical Women's Press*.

2. Geary, "The Domestic Novel as a Commercial Commodity," 383. According to Geary, this is stated in the author's book contract. See her essay for details and analysis of the multifaceted campaign.

3. Ibid., 387, 388–89. Fanny Fern was a pseudonym for Sara Payson Willis. Joyce Warren's interpretation of these events differs slightly from Geary's. In her biography of Fern, *Fanny Fern: An Independent Woman*, Warren writes that the publishers "responded to the critics who had insisted on reading the book as autobiography" with suggestive hints about its autobiographical nature (123). Thus Warren does not attribute full responsibility to the publishers for revealing Fern's identity.

4. Although *The Life and Beauties of Fanny Fern* was originally published anonymously, scholars have identified William U. Moulton, the editor of the *True Flag*, as its author. See Adams, *Fanny Fern, or a Pair of Flaming Shoes*, 10; Geary, "The Domestic Novel as a Commercial Commodity," 390; Warren, *Independent Woman*, 123–24.

5. Both Linda Huf in *A Portrait of the Artist as a Young Woman: The Writer as Heroine in American Literature*, 17–35, and Joyce Warren in the introduction to the American Women Writers reprint edition of *Ruth Hall*, ix–xxxix, and *Fanny Fern: An Independent Woman*, 120–42, provide a critical assessment of *Ruth Hall*'s reception by quoting liberally from contemporary reviews. The quotations I have used are cited in Huf, 17, 20. They were originally published in *The Life and Beauties of Fanny Fern* and *Putnam's Monthly* 5 (1855): 216, respectively.

6. From a review in the *New Orleans Crescent City* (January 1855). Cited in Warren, *Independent Woman*, 125–26.

7. *Una* 3, no. 2 (February 1855): 25. Cited in Russo and Kramarae, *Radical Women's Press*, 29.

8. Many historians have explored the integral relationship between the abolitionist and woman's rights movements. See, for example, DuBois, *Feminism and Suffrage*; Flexner, *Century of Struggle*; and Hersh, *Slavery of Sex*.

9. Stanton, "Ruth Hall."

10. Dall, "Ruth Hall."

11. Another of Fern's contemporaries, Grace Greenwood, also shared this view. In an essay on Fern, Greenwood writes: "As a novelist, she is somewhat open to the charge of exaggeration, and she is not sufficiently impersonal to be always artistic. Her own fortunes, loves, and hates live again in her creations,—her heroines are her doubles." "Fanny Fern—Mrs. Parton," in Parton, *Eminent Women of the Age*, 82.

12. In their historical study of anger, Carol Zisowitz Stearns and Peter N. Stearns theorize that "the growth of capitalism" may have been a significant factor in the development of an ideology of anger control. They note that many scholars "have seen an association between investment capitalism, with its need to defer gratification, and the development of a modern personality that emphasizes impulse control and introspection." *Anger: The Struggle for Emotional Control in America's History*, 34. Also see Halttunen, *Confidence Men and Painted Women*.

13. Stearns and Stearns, *Anger*, 42.

14. Ibid., 48. In her study of "sentimental culture," Halttunen also notes that "Above all, the sentimental woman was instructed to exercise moral self-control. Passions, especially envy and anger, were believed to be injurious to the skin" (*Confidence Men*, 88).

15. Foster, *Witnessing Slavery*, 16. Excerpts from William Craft and Ellen Craft's narra-

tive, *Running a Thousand Miles for Freedom; or, The Escape of William and Ellen Craft from Slavery* (1860) are reprinted in Loewenberg and Bogin, *Black Women in Nineteenth-Century American Life*, 104–23.

16. Starling, *The Slave Narrative*, 129.

17. Baym, *Woman's Fiction*, 252.

18. Russo and Kramarae, *Radical Women's Press*, 9.

19. Byerman, "We Wear the Mask"; Foster, *Witnessing Slavery*; Olney, "'I Was Born.'"

20. Welter, "Feminization of American Religion," 138. Also see Douglas, *Feminization of American Culture*; Perry Miller, "From Edwards to Emerson"; and John L. Thomas, "Romantic Reform in America."

21. Welter, "Feminization of American Religion," 138.

22. Warren, *Independent Woman*, 86–89, 107–16.

23. Cited in Warren, *Independent Woman*, 93.

24. In *Witnessing Slavery*, Frances Smith Foster discusses the "four chronological phases" of the nineteenth-century slave narrative: loss of innocence, the decision to seek freedom, the escape, and freedom obtained. She points out that this sequence of events "is informed by the Judeo-Christian mythological structure," which "follows a progression from innocence to the knowledge of evil, repentance and conversion, the resistance of sin, and salvation" (84).

25. Fanny Fern, *Ruth Hall*. Page references from the Rutgers University reprint edition are cited parenthetically in the text.

26. Franklin, *Autobiography*, 22, 76–77.

27. For an overview of the history of women's waged labor, see Kessler-Harris, *Out to Work: A History of Wage-Earning Women in the United States*. For an imaginative construction of the range of employments open to antebellum white middle-class women, see Louisa May Alcott's autobiographical novel, *Work: A Story of Experience*.

28. Fern's imaginative reconstruction of this exchange between herself and her editor/writer brother, Nathaniel Parker Willis, has parallels to Louisa May Alcott's exchange with the publisher James T. Fields. Early in Alcott's career, Fields wrote: "Stick to your teaching Miss Alcott. You can't write." Alcott responded to Fields in much the same way Fern responded to Willis: "I went back to my writing, which pays much better, though Mr. F[ields] did say, 'Stick to your teaching; you can't write.' Being wilful, I said, 'I won't teach; and I can write, and I'll prove it.'" The Fields letter is quoted in Madeline Stern's introduction to *Behind a Mask: The Unknown Thrillers of Louisa May Alcott*, xiii, and Alcott's response is in her May 1862 journal entry, reprinted in *The Journals of Louisa May Alcott*, 109. For details of Fern's relationship with her brother, see Warren, *Independent Woman*, and Kelley, *Private Woman, Public Stage*, 196–98.

29. Baym, *Woman's Fiction*, 251 and 252, respectively.

30. Warren, introduction to *Ruth Hall and Other Writings*, xxv. Analyzing the passage cited above, Warren notes that the repetition of the three sentences beginning with "I" demonstrate Ruth Hall's newfound determination to chart her own course to independence.

31. *Ladies Magazine* 2 (January 1829): 393–95. Cited in Cott, *The Bonds of Womanhood*, 96.

32. From Grimké, *Letters on the Equality of the Sexes and the Condition of Woman* (1838), reprinted in Schneir, *Feminism*, 38.

33. For a Bakhtinian reading of the function of voice in *Ruth Hall*, see Susan Harris,

"Inscribing and Defining: The Many Voices of Fanny Fern's *Ruth Hall*," in *Nineteenth-Century American Women's Novels*, 111–27.

34. Although scholars have noted Ruth's monumental change after she decides to become a writer, none that I am aware of have related it to her ability to express anger. In "'The Scribbling Women' and Fanny Fern: Why Women Wrote," Ann Douglas [Wood], for example, writes that *Ruth Hall* contains two Ruth's—the naive, "sentimental" dependent daughter and wife whose experiences are chronicled in the first half of the novel, and the "shrewd, bitter, business-oriented and aggressive woman" who becomes a successful writer in the second half (21). The scene in which Ruth declares, "I can do it, I feel it, I will do it," Douglas observes, marks the turning point. What Douglas glosses over, however, is that Ruth's self-conscious recognition and expression of anger are significant parts of her conversion experience.

35. Adrienne Rich's insights about Emily Dickinson are relevant to Fern's characterization of Ruth as a seemingly "placid" woman who in actuality is "a smouldering volcano." In "Vesuvius at Home: The Power of Emily Dickinson," Rich analyzes the "images, codes, metaphors, strategies, [and] points of stress" (158) in Dickinson's work, noting that "The woman who feels herself to be Vesuvius at home has need of a mask, at least, of innocuousness and of containment" (169).

36. In *A Portrait of the Artist as a Young Woman*, Linda Huf also discusses Ruth's changing conception of freedom by pointing out Fern's use of bird imagery in several prominent scenes. She notes that Ruth's "escape to freedom is indicated in terms of flying and birds. . . . [A]s a wife Ruth is a caged or domestic bird; as a widow, a crippled or wounded bird; and finally as a writer, a high-flying soaring bird" (25–26).

37. The phrase "self-definition and verbal power" is Susan Harris's. See *Nineteenth-Century American Women's Novels*, 112.

38. "Placing his hand on mine, smiling at me / in such a way that I was reassured, / he led me in, into those mysteries." Dante Alighieri, *Inferno*, Canto III, reprinted in *World Masterpieces: Through the Renaissance*, edited by Maynard Mack (New York: W. W. Norton and Co., 1973), 859–60.

39. Mary Kelley convincingly argues that Fern was not the only white nineteenth-century woman writer who disguised her literary ambitions by imagining that she was serving the needs of her family when she really wanted to satisfy her own desires. Kelley notes that many "literary domestics" insisted that they were writing strictly because of dire financial circumstances. *Private Woman, Public Stage*, 164–79. Also see Claudia Tate, "Allegories of Black Female Desire," for another perspective on this issue.

40. That Fern deliberately chose to capitalize the word independence indicates how much she wanted to stress its importance as a goal for women.

41. When discussing Fern's depiction of Mrs. Skiddy, Susan Harris notes that "As with many other women's novels of the mid-nineteenth century, the unacknowledged model for the successful heroine's behavior is the lower-class woman, whose status frees her from the gender definitions and restrictions of the middle and upper-middle classes" (*Nineteenth-Century American Women's Novels*, 122).

42. For an analysis of the racist effects of "the expansive, imperial project of sentimentalism," see Wexler, "Tender Violence." To place Fern's depiction of African-Americans in a larger context, see Cohn, "The Negro Character."

43. For other examples of this phenomenon see Castiglia, "In Praise of Extra-Vagrant Women."

44. Rowlandson, *A Narrative of Captivity and Restauration*, 78.

45. Mr. Hall says "That tells the whole story" ten times. See pages 46, 47, 56, 62, 63, 66, 70, 118, 139.

46. On Fern's popularity see Warren, *Independent Woman*, and Kelley, *Private Woman*, especially chapter 1, "The Fanny Fern," 3—27. We get a sense of how popular *Ruth Hall* was by Grace Greenwood's comment to Fern that "the first novel [her daughter] ever read was your 'Ruth Hall'. She was about eight years old." Quoted in Warren, *Independent Woman*, n. 4, 357.

47. From Fred Louis Patte's condescending dismissal of "the rage of the scorned author" (*The Feminine Fifties*, 120), to Ann Douglas's [Wood's] contention that Fern "cries from the rooftops what other women writers hardly wished to whisper in the basement" ("The 'Scribbling Women'," 13), to Judith Fetterley's observation that it is "anger [that] provides the connective tissue that links" Fern's seemingly disparate styles (*Provisions*, 246), to Lauren Berlant's insight that "Fern frequently registers her rage at how isolation and monotony of women's lives threaten them mentally" ("The Female Woman," 450), there is agreement among scholars that Fern's anger is readily discernible, and that, in fact, it marks the singularity of her style as well her achievement. Also see Harris, *Nineteenth-Century American Women's Novels*, 111, 114.

48. Greenwood, "Fanny Fern—Mrs. Parton," 83, 75, 76—77, respectively.

49. Ibid., 78, 83—84.

Chapter Seven

1. Harriet E. Wilson, *Our Nig*. Page references to the Vintage Books edition are cited parenthetically in the text.

2. Jacoby, *Wild Justice*, 355. "The anger that proceeds from unredressed suffering can be more terrifying than the original facts of suffering; moreover, the outraged, as distinct from the ostensibly detached, witness not only expects us to listen but also to *do something* about the wrongs that have been enumerated" (Jacoby's emphasis).

3. In his investigation of extant copies of *Our Nig*, Eric Gardner has determined that most of the first owners of the book were white middle-class readers who were under the age of twenty. Gardner theorizes that the book may have been a childhood gift and read as an instruction manual fostering moral Christian development ("'This Attempt of Their Sister,'" 238—39). See Elrod, "Harriet Wilson and the White Reader," for an analysis of the ways in which "particular moments and sections in the text reveal . . . Wilson's shifting position, or her changing voice, as she addresses the white reader over the course of the narrative" (298).

4. In the preface to the *Appeal* (1836), Child writes: "Reader I beseech you not to throw down this volume as soon as you have glanced at the title. Read it, if your prejudices will allow, for the very truth's sake:—If I have the most trifling claims upon your good will, for an hour's amusement to yourself, or benefit to your children, read it for my sake:— Read it, if it be merely to find fresh occasion to sneer at the vulgarity of the cause:— Read it, from sheer curiosity to see what a woman (who had much better attend to her

household concerns) will say upon such a subject:—Read it, on any terms, and my purpose will be gained."

5. The authorship and meaning of the letters in the appendix have been the subject of debate in Wilson scholarship. Some scholars, such as Henry Louis Gates Jr. and Barbara White, assume that the letters are written by Wilson's acquaintances and, as such, provide important biographical information. Other scholars, such as William Andrews and Elizabeth Breau, suggest that the letters "may be fictive documents composed by Wilson herself" (Andrews, "Novelization of Voice," n. 7, 34). In this case, as Breau argues, the letters can be regarded as a subversive feat on Wilson's part: not only does she parody slave narrative conventions by authoring her own verifying documents; she also places the testimonials by unknown authenticators at the end of her book, not at the beginning (Breau, "Identifying Satire," 458).

6. Gates, introduction to *Our Nig*, li; Tate, "Allegories of Black Female Desire," 113–14.

7. Melish, *Disowning Slavery*, 283.

8. Cited in *Provincial Freeman*, 7 March 1857, *Black Abolitionist Papers*, reel 10, fr. 0571, quoted in Yee, *Black Women Abolitionists*, 119.

9. *Portland Daily Press*, in *The Underground Rail Road* by William Still (Philadelphia: Porter and Coates, 1872), 760, cited in Boyd, *Discarded Legacy*, 42; Grace Greenwood, *Philadelphia Independent*, in Still, *Underground Rail Road*, 779–80, cited in Boyd, *Discarded Legacy*, 43.

10. Cited in *Provincial Freeman*, 7 March 1857, *Black Abolitionist Papers*, reel 10, fr. 0097, quoted in Yee, *Black Women Abolitionists*, 119.

11. The phrase "eloquent indignation" is William C. Nell's. In a letter published in the *Liberator* in 1858, Nell describes Harper's public speaking at an event that focused on a black man's betrayal of two fugitive slaves as "one of her very best outbursts of eloquent indignation" (quoted in Frances Smith Foster, *A Brighter Coming Day*, 17). In the *Underground Rail Road*, William Still includes a letter from Harper in which she writes: "I don't know but that you would laugh if you were to hear some of the remarks which my lectures call forth: 'She is a man,' again 'She is not colored, she is painted'" (772). Commenting on these responses, Hazel Carby notes that although "Frances Harper fought for and won the right to be regarded as a successful public lecturer," she was still hampered by gender and race discrimination (*Reconstructing Womanhood*, 66).

12. Douglass, "What to the Slave Is the Fourth of July?" 1739.

13. Quarles, *Black Abolitionists*, 15.

14. Ibid.

15. Breu, "Identifying Satire," 456–57; Melish, *Disowning Slavery*, 283.

16. Melish, *Disowning Slavery*, 283.

17. As Barbara White notes, "Samuel [Frado's husband] had no trouble getting an audience from abolitionists, for they were 'hungry' for his lies; they preferred his story to hers, even when hers was both highly literate and based on true experience" ("*Our Nig* and the She-Devil," 40).

18. Ibid. Subsequent page references for this article are cited parenthetically in the text.

19. Yee, *Black Women Abolitionists*, 92.

20. Quarles, *Black Abolitionists*, 47–53.

21. Nathaniel Paul in a speech delivered at the Albany Anti-Slavery Society, 1838. *The*

Friend of Man (Utica), 14 March, 1838, cited in Quarles, *Black Abolitionists*, 47; Samuel Ringgold Ward in a letter to the *Anti-Slavery Standard*, 2 July 1840, cited in Quarles, *Black Abolitionists*, 47; *Northern Star and Freeman's Advocate*, 3 March 1842, cited in Quarles, *Black Abolitionists*, 48. Also see Horton and Horton, *In Hope of Liberty*, 220–21.

22. Gates, introduction to *Our Nig*, li.

23. See, for example, the conclusions of *Charlotte Temple* by Susanna Rowson (1791) and *The Coquette* by Mrs. Hannah Webster Foster (1797). Both novels end with the seducer's guilt, remorse, and punishment.

24. Jacoby, *Wild Justice*, 358.

25. One of the most articulate silences in *Our Nig* is Wilson's rage at Samuel, the black man who betrays Frado and colludes with hypocritical whites.

26. In the introduction to *Our Nig*, Henry Louis Gates reports that "a systematic search of all extant copies of black and reform newspapers and magazines in circulation contemporaneously with the publication of *Our Nig* yielded not one notice or review, nor did searches through the Boston, Massachusetts, dailies and the Amherst, New Hampshire, *Farmer's Cabinet*" (xxix–xxx). Thus he concludes that sales of the book did not help Wilson "maintain" her son's life. George Mason Wilson "succumbed to 'Fever' " "five months and twenty-four days after the publication of *Our Nig*" (xii). Also see Gates's "Parallel Discursive Universes: Fictions of the Self in Harriet E. Wilson's *Our Nig*," in *Figures in Black*.

27. Wilson repeatedly refers to Frado's hope that James will "rescue" her. See pages 63, 65, 70, 72, and 95.

28. Milhaven, *Good Anger*, 170–71.

29. See Jones, *Labor of Love, Labor of Sorrow*, for an extensive analysis of these issues.

30. Susan Warner, *The Wide, Wide World*. Page references for the Feminist Press reprint edition are cited parenthetically in the text.

31. Levine, *Black Culture*, 118, 103, 131, 112, 115, respectively.

32. DeSalvo, *Conceived With Malice*, 16.

33. Levine, *Black Culture*, 128.

34. Douglass, "What to the Slave Is the Fourth of July?" 1743. Douglass's emphasis.

35. Theodore Weld, *American Slavery As It Is* (New York: 1839), 9–10, reprinted in Grant, *Black Protest*, 72–75.

36. Ibid., 74.

37. Douglass, "What to the Slave Is the Fourth of July?" 1748.

38. Jacoby, *Wild Justice*, 1.

39. Levine, *Black Culture*, 117.

40. Leach, *True Love*, 21.

41. For illuminating analyses of the political import of women's writing during the Civil War, see Sizer, *Political Work of Northern Women Writers*, and Young, *Disarming the Nation*.

42. Baym, *Woman's Fiction*; Andrews, introduction to *Six Women's Slave Narratives*, xxxv.

43. Baym, *Woman's Fiction*, 24.

Conclusion

1. "What would happen if one woman told the truth about / her life? / The world would split open." These lines are from Muriel Rukeyser's poem, "Kathe Kollwitz."

Louise Bernikow uses them as an epigraph to her collection of women's poetry, which she titles *The World Split Open*.

2. Spacks, *Female Imagination*, 285.

3. Piercy, "Unlearning to Not Speak."

4. Lyman, "The Politics of Anger," 69.

5. Papashvily, *All the Happy Endings*, xvii.

6. Bernardez, "Women and Anger," 5.

BIBLIOGRAPHY

Ada. "Lines Suggested on Reading 'An Appeal to Christian Women of the South' by A. E. Grimke." In *Black Sister: Poetry by Black American Women, 1746–1980*, edited by Erlene Stetson, 17–19. Bloomington: Indiana University Press, 1981. Originally published in *Liberator* 6 (October 29, 1836).

Adams, Florence Bannard. *Fanny Fern, or a Pair of Flaming Shoes*. West Trenton, N.J.: Hermitage Press, 1966.

Alcott, Louisa May. "Behind a Mask, or, A Woman's Power." 1866. Reprinted in *Alternative Alcott*, edited by Elaine Showalter, 97–202. New Brunswick, N.J.: Rutgers University Press, 1988.

———. "Hospital Sketches." 1863. Reprinted in *Alternative Alcott*, edited by Elaine Showalter, 3–73. New Brunswick, N.J.: Rutgers University Press, 1988.

———. *The Journals of Louisa May Alcott*. Edited by Joel Myerson and Daniel Shealy. Boston: Little, Brown and Co., 1989.

———. *Little Women*. 1868. Reprint, with introduction by Elaine Showalter, New York: Penguin Books, 1989.

———. *Work: A Story of Experience*. 1873. Reprint, New York: Schocken Books, 1977.

Ammons, Elizabeth. *Conflicting Stories: American Women Writers at the Turn into the Twentieth Century*. New York: Oxford University Press, 1991.

Anderson, Benedict. *Imagined Communities: Reflections on the Origin and Spread of Nationalism*. New York: Verso, 1983.

Anderson, Bonnie S. *Joyous Greetings: The First International Women's Movement: 1830–1860*. New York: Oxford University Press, 2000.

Anderson, Douglas. *A House Undivided: Domesticity and Community in American Literature*. Cambridge: Cambridge University Press, 1990.

Andrews, William. Introduction to *Sisters of the Spirit: Three Black Women's Autobiographies of the Nineteenth Century*. Bloomington: Indiana University Press, 1986.

———. Introduction to *Six Women's Slave Narratives*. New York: Oxford University Press, 1988.

———. "The Novelization of Voice in Early African American Narrative." *PMLA* 105, no. 1 (January 1990): 23–34.

———. *To Tell a Free Story: The First Century of Afro-American Autobiography, 1760–1865*. Urbana: University of Illinois Press, 1986.

Aquinas, St. Thomas. *Summa Theologiae*. Vol. 21, *Fear and Anger*. Translation, introduction, notes, and glossary by John Patrick Reid, O.P. New York: McGraw-Hill, 1965.

———. *Summa Theologiae*. Vol. 44, *Well-Tempered Passion*. Translation, introduction, notes, and glossary by Thomas Gilby, O.P. New York: McGraw-Hill, 1971.

Aristotle. *The Art of Rhetoric*. Translated, with an introduction and notes by H. C. Lawson-Tancred. New York: Penguin Books, 1991.

———. *The Nicomachean Ethics*. Translated, with an introduction by David Ross, revised by J. L. Ackrill and J. O. Urmson. New York: Oxford University Press, 1998.

Armstrong, Nancy. *Desire and Domestic Fiction: A Political History of the Novel*. New York: Oxford University Press, 1987.

Auerbach, Nina. *Communities of Women: An Idea in Fiction*. Cambridge, Mass.: Harvard University Press, 1978.

Averill, James R. *Anger and Aggression: An Essay on Emotion*. New York: Springer-Verlag, 1982.

Baker, Paula. "The Domesticization of Politics: Women and American Political Society, 1870–1920." *American Historical Review* 89, no. 3 (June 1984): 620–47.

Baloian, Bruce Edward. *Anger in the Old Testament*. New York: Peter Lang, 1992.

Bambara, Toni Cade, ed. *The Black Woman: An Anthology*. New York: Mentor, 1970.

Banta, Martha. *Imaging American Women: Idea and Ideals in Cultural History*. New York: Columbia University Press, 1987.

Bardes, Barbara, and Suzanne Gossett. *Declarations of Independence: Women and Political Power in Nineteenth Century American Fiction*. New Brunswick, N.J.: Rutgers University Press, 1990.

Barnett, Louise K. *The Ignoble Savage: American Literary Racism, 1790–1890*. Westport, Conn.: Greenwood, 1975.

Barton, Cynthia. *Transcendental Wife: The Life of Abigail May Alcott*. New York: University Press of America, 1996.

Bauer, Dale M. *Feminist Dialogics: A Theory of Failed Community*. New York: State University of New York, 1988.

Bauermeister, Erica R. "*The Lamplighter*, *The Wide, Wide World* and *Hope Leslie*: Reconsidering the Recipes for Nineteenth-Century American Women's Novels." *Legacy* 8, no. 1 (Spring 1991): 17–28.

Baym, Nina. *American Women Writers and the Work of History, 1790–1860*. New Brunswick, N.J.: Rutgers University Press, 1995.

———. *Novels, Readers, and Reviewers: Responses to Fiction in Antebellum America*. Ithaca, N.Y.: Cornell University Press, 1984.

———. *Woman's Fiction: A Guide to Novels by and about Women in America, 1820–1870*. Ithaca, N.Y.: Cornell University Press, 1978.

Beal, Frances M. "Double Jeopardy: To Be Black and Female." In *Sisterhood Is Powerful: An Anthology of Writings from the Women's Liberation Movement*, edited by Robin Morgan, 340–53. New York: Random House, 1970.

Beecher, Catharine, and Harriet Beecher Stowe. *The American Woman's Home*. 1869. Reprint, with an introduction by Joseph Van Why, Hartford, Conn.: Harriet Beecher Stowe Center, 1975.

Belenky, Mary Field, Blythe McVicker Clinchy, Nancy Rule Goldberger, and Jill Mattuck Tarule. *Women's Ways of Knowing: The Development of Self, Voice, and Mind*. New York: Basic Books, 1986.

Bell, Roseann P., Bettye J. Parker, and Beverly Guy-Sheftall, eds. *Sturdy Black Bridges: Visions of Black Women in Literature*. Garden City, N.Y.: Anchor Books, 1979.

Bennett, Paula. *My Life as a Loaded Gun: Female Creativity and Feminist Poetics*. Boston: Beacon Press, 1986.

Benstock, Shari, ed. *The Private Self: Theory and Practice of Women's Autobiographical Writings*. Chapel Hill: University of North Carolina Press, 1988.

Berg, Barbara. *The Remembered Gate: Origins of American Feminism—The Woman and the City, 1800–1860*. New York: Oxford University Press, 1978.

Berlant, Lauren. "The Female Woman: Fanny Fern and the Form of Sentiment." *American Literary History* 3, no. 3 (Fall 1991): 429–54.

———. "The Female Complaint." *Social Text* 19/20 (1988): 237–59.

Bernardez, Teresa. "Women and Anger: Cultural Prohibitions and the Feminine Ideal." Jean Baker Miller Training Institute Working Paper no. 31. Wellesley, Mass.: Stone Center for Developmental Services and Studies, 1988.

Bernikow, Louise, ed. *The World Split Open: Four Centuries of Women Poets in England and America, 1552–1950*. New York: Vintage Books, 1974.

Blair, Karen. *The Clubwoman as Feminist: True Woman Redefined, 1868–1914*. New York: Holmes and Meier, 1980.

Bloch, Ruth H. "The Gendered Meanings of Virtue in Revolutionary America." *Signs* 13, no. 1 (1987): 37–58.

Bordin, Ruth. *Women and Temperance: The Quest for Power and Liberty, 1873–1900*. Philadelphia: Temple University Press, 1980.

Boyd, Melba Joyce. *Discarded Legacy: Politics and Poetics in the Life of Frances E. W. Harper, 1825–1911*. Detroit: Wayne State University Press, 1994.

Boydston, Jean, Mary Kelley, and Anne Margolis, eds. *The Limits of Sisterhood: The Beecher Sisters on Women's Rights and Woman's Sphere*. Chapel Hill: University of North Carolina Press, 1988.

Boylan, Anne M. "Benevolence and Antislavery Activity among African American Women in New York and Boston, 1820–1840." In *The Abolitionist Sisterhood*, edited by Jean Fagan Yellin and John C. Van Horne, 119–37. Ithaca, N.Y.: Cornell University Press, 1994.

Branch, Douglas E. *The Sentimental Years: 1836–1860*. New York: Hill and Wang, 1934.

Braxton, Joanne M. *Black Women Writing Autobiography: A Tradition within a Tradition*. Philadelphia: Temple University Press, 1989.

Braxton, Joanne M., and Andree Nicola McLaughlin, eds. *Wild Women in the Whirlwind: Afra-American Culture and the Contemporary Literary Renaissance*. New Brunswick, N.J.: Rutgers University Press, 1990.

Breau, Elizabeth. "Identifying Satire: *Our Nig.*" *Callaloo* 16, no. 2 (Spring 1993): 455–65.

Brodhead, Richard H. *Cultures of Letters: Scenes of Reading and Writing in Nineteenth-Century America*. Chicago: University of Chicago Press, 1993.

Brodzki, Bella, and Celeste Schenck, eds. *Life/Lines: Theorizing Women's Autobiography*. Ithaca, N.Y.: Cornell University Press, 1988.

Broude, Ann. *Radical Spirits: Spiritualism and Women's Rights in 19th-Century America*. Boston: Beacon Press, 1989.

Brown, Gillian. *Domestic Individualism: Imagining Self in Nineteenth-Century America*. Berkeley: University of California Press, 1991.

———. "Getting in the Kitchen with Dinah: Domestic Politics in *Uncle Tom's Cabin.*" *American Quarterly* 36 (Fall 1984): 503–23.

Brown, Herbert Ross. *The Sentimental Novel in America, 1789–1860*. Durham, N.C.: Duke University Press, 1940.

Buhle, Mari Jo. *Women and American Socialism, 1870–1920*. Urbana: University of Illinois Press, 1981.

Buhle, Mari Jo, and Paul Buhle, eds. *The Concise History of Woman Suffrage*. Urbana: Univeristy of Illinois Press, 1978.

Burack, Cynthia. *The Problem of the Passions: Feminism, Psychoanalysis, and Social Theory*. New York: New York University Press, 1994.

Byerman, Keith. "We Wear the Mask: Deceit as Theme and Style in Slave Narratives." In *The Art of Slave Narrative*, edited by John Sekora and Darwin T. Turner, 70–82. Macomb: Western Illinois University, 1982.

Campbell, Anne. *Men, Women, and Aggression*. New York: Basic Books, 1993.

Carby, Hazel V. *Reconstructing Womanhood: The Emergence of the Afro-American Woman Novelist*. New York: Oxford University Press, 1987.

Cashin, Joan E. *Our Common Affairs: Texts from the Old South*. Baltimore, Md.: Johns Hopkins University Press, 1996.

Castiglia, Christopher. "In Praise of Extra-Vagrant Women: *Hope Leslie* and the Captivity Romance." *Legacy* 6 (Fall 1989): 3–16.

Chambers-Schiller, Lee Virginia. *Liberty: A Better Husband: Single Women in America, The Generations of 1780–1840*. New Haven, Conn.: Yale University Press, 1984.

Cheney, Ednah D. *Louisa May Alcott*. 1890. Reprint, New York: Chelsea House, 1980.

Chevigny, Belle Gale. *The Woman and the Myth: Margaret Fuller's Life and Writings*. Old Westbury, N.Y.: Feminist Press, 1976.

Child, L. Maria. *An Appeal in Favor of That Class of Americans Called Africans*. 1836. Reprint, New York: Arno Press, 1968.

———. *Hobomok, A Tale of Early Times*. 1824. Reprinted in *Hobomok and Other Writings on Indians*, edited and introduction by Carolyn L. Karcher. New Brunswick, N.J.: Rutgers University Press, 1986.

———. *The Mother's Book*. 1831. Reprint, Old Saybrook, Conn.: Applewood Books, 1992.

———. *Selected Letters, 1817–1880*. Edited by Milton Meltzer and Patricia G. Holland. Amherst: University of Massachusetts Press, 1982.

Clifford, Deborah Pickman. *Crusader for Freedom: A Life of Lydia Maria Child*. Boston: Beacon Press, 1992.

Clinton, Catherine. *The Plantation Mistress: Women's World in the Old South*. New York: Pantheon, 1982.

Cogan, Frances B. *All-American Girl: The Ideal of Real Womanhood in Mid-Nineteenth Century America*. London: University of Georgia Press, 1989.

Cohn, Jan. "The Negro Character in Northern Magazine Fiction in the 1860s." *New England Quarterly* 43 (1970): 572–92.

Collins, Patricia Hill. *Black Feminist Thought: Knowledge, Consciousness, and the Politics of Empowerment*. London: Harper Collins Academic, 1990.

Conrad, Susan. *Perish the Thought: Intellectual Women in Romantic America, 1830–1860*. New York: Oxford University Press, 1977.

Cott, Nancy F. *The Bonds of Womanhood: "Woman's Sphere" in New England, 1780–1835*. New Haven, Conn.: Yale University Press, 1977.

———. *The Grounding of Modern Feminism*. New Haven, Conn.: Yale University Press, 1987.

Cott, Nancy F., and Elizabeth Pleck, eds. *A Heritage of Her Own*. New York: Simon and Schuster, 1980.

Coultrap-McQuin, Susan. *Doing Literary Business: American Women Writers in the Nineteenth Century*. Chapel Hill: University of North Carolina Press, 1990.

Crèvecoeur, J. Hector St. John de. *Letters from an American Farmer*. 1782. Reprint, New York: Penguin Books, 1986.

Curry, Leonard P. *The Free Black in Urban America 1800–1850: The Shadow of the Dream*. Chicago: University of Chicago Press, 1981.

Curry, Renee R., and Terry L. Allison, eds. *States of Rage: Emotional Eruption, Violence, and Social Change*. New York: New York University Press, 1996.

Dall, Caroline Healey. "Ruth Hall." *Una* (March 1855): 42–43.

Davidson, Cathy, ed. *Reading in America: Literature and Social History*. Baltimore, Md.: Johns Hopkins University Press, 1989.

———. *Revolution and the Word: The Rise of the Novel in America*. New York: Oxford University Press, 1986.

Davis, Angela Y. *Women, Race and Class*. New York: Vintage Books, 1981.

Davis, Charles T., and Henry Louis Gates Jr., eds. *The Slave's Narrative*. New York: Oxford University Press, 1985.

Davis, Cynthia. "Speaking the Body's Pain: Harriet Wilson's *Our Nig*." *African American Review* 27, no. 3 (1993): 391–404.

Dearborn, Mary. *Pocahontas's Daughters: Gender and Ethnicity in American Culture*. New York: Oxford University Press, 1986.

"Declaration of Sentiments." 1848. Reprinted in *Feminism: The Essential Historical Writings*, edited and with an introduction and commentaries by Miriam Schneir, 76–82. New York: Vintage Books, 1972.

Degler, Carl N. *At Odds: Women and the Family in America from the Revolution to the Present*. New York: Oxford University Press, 1980.

Deming, Barbara. "On Anger." In *We Are All Part of One Another: A Barbara Deming Reader*, edited by Jane Meyerding with a foreword by Barbara Smith, 207–17. Philadelphia: New Society Publishers, 1984.

Denham, Gayle, and Kaye Bultemeier. "Anger: Targets and Triggers." In *Women and Anger*, edited by Sandra P. Thomas. New York: Springer Publishing, 1993.

DeSalvo, Louise. *Conceived with Malice*. New York: Dutton, 1994.

Diamond, Stephen A. *Anger, Madness and the Daimonic: The Psychological Genesis of Violence, Evil, and Creativity*. Albany, N.Y.: State University of New York Press, 1996.

Dickinson, Emily. *The Complete Poems of Emily Dickinson*. Edited by Thomas H. Johnson. Boston: Little, Brown and Company, 1960.

Dobson, Joanne. "The American Renaissance Reenvisioned." In *The (Other) American Traditions*, edited by Joyce W. Warren, 164–82. New Brunswick, N.J.: Rutgers University Press, 1993.

———. *Dickinson and the Strategies of Reticence: The Woman Writer in Nineteenth-Century America*. Bloomington: Indiana University Press, 1989.

———. "The Hidden Hand: Subversion of Cultural Authority in Three Mid-Nineteenth-Century American Women's Novels." *American Quarterly* 39 (Summer 1986): 230–42.

Donovan, Josephine. *Feminist Theory: The Intellectual Traditions of American Feminism*. New York: Frederick Ungar, 1985.

———. *New England Local Color Literature: A Woman's Tradition*. New York: Frederick Ungar, 1983.

Douglas, Ann [Wood]. *The Feminization of American Culture*. New York: Knopf, 1977.

———. "The Literature of Impoverishment: The Women Local Colorists in America 1865–1914." *Women's Studies* 1 (1972): 3–45.

———. "Mrs. Sigourney and the Sensibility of the Inner Space." *New England Quarterly* 45 (1972): 163–81.

———. "The 'Scribbling Women' and Fanny Fern: Why Women Wrote." *American Quarterly* 23 (September 1971): 3–14.

Douglass, Frederick. "What to the Slave Is the Fourth of July?" 1852. Reprinted in *The Heath Anthology of American Literature*, 2nd ed., vol. 1, 1732–51. Lexington, Mass.: D. C. Heath and Co., 1994.

Dublin, Thomas. *Women at Work: The Transformation of Work and Community in Lowell, Massachusetts, 1826–1860*. New York: Columbia University Press, 1979.

Dubois, Ellen. *Feminism and Suffrage: The Emergence of an Independent Women's Movement in America, 1848–1869*. Ithaca, N.Y.: Cornell University Press, 1978.

Dubois, Ellen, and Vicki L. Ruiz, eds. *Unequal Sisters: A Multicultural Reader in U.S. Women's History*. New York: Routledge, 1990.

DuCille, Ann. "'Othered' Matters: Reconceptualizing Dominance and Difference in the History of Sexuality in America." *Journal of the History of Sexuality* 1, no. 1 (July 1990): 102–27.

Eagleton, Terry. *Literary Theory: An Introduction*. Minneapolis: University of Minnesota Press, 1983.

Echols, Alice. "The Demise of Female Intimacy in the Twentieth Century." University of Michigan Occasional Papers in Women's Studies, no. 6. Ann Arbor: Women's Studies Program, University of Michigan, 1978.

Ehrenreich, Barbara, and Deidre English. *For Her Own Good: 150 Years of Experts' Advice to Women*. Garden City, N.Y.: Anchor Press, 1978.

Elbert, Sarah. *A Hunger for Home: Louisa May Alcott's Place in American Culture*. New Brunswick, N.J.: Rutgers University Press, 1987.

Ellmann, Mary. *Thinking about Women*. New York: Harcourt Brace Jovanovich, 1968.

Elrod, Eileen Razzari. "Harriet Wilson and the White Reader: Authority and Audience in *Our Nig*." *Prospects* 24 (1999): 297–310.

Emerson, Ralph Waldo. *Selections from Ralph Waldo Emerson*. Edited by Stephen E. Whicher. Boston: Houghton Mifflin, 1957.

Epstein, Barbara. *The Politics of Domesticity: Women, Evangelism and Temperance in Nineteenth Century America*. Middletown, Conn.: Wesleyan University Press, 1981.

Faragher, John Mack, Mary Jo Buhle, Daniel Czitrom, and Susan H. Armitage. *Out of Many: A History of the American People*. Englewood Cliffs, N.J.: Prentice Hall, 1994.

Fawcett, John. *On Anger*. Philadelphia: William Duane, 1809.

Fern, Fanny. "Independence." *New York Ledger* (30 July 1859). Reprinted in *Fanny Fern: An Independent Woman*, edited by Joyce W. Warren, 314–15. New Brunswick, N.J.: Rutgers University Press, 1992.

———. *Ruth Hall*. 1855. Reprint, with an introduction by Joyce Warren, New Brunswick, N.J.: Rutgers University Press, 1986.

Ferrero, Pat, Elaine Hedges, and Julie Silber. *Hearts and Hands: The Influence of Women and Quilts on American Society*. San Francisco: Quilt Digest Press, 1987.

Fetterley, Judith. "Impersonating 'Little Women': The Radicalism of Alcott's *Behind a Mask*." *Women's Studies* 10 (1983): 1–14.

———, ed. *Provisions: A Reader from 19th-Century American Women*. Bloomington: Indiana University Press, 1985.

———. *The Resisting Reader: A Feminist Approach to American Fiction*. Bloomington: Indiana University Press, 1978.

Fields, Annie, ed. *Life and Letters of Harriet Beecher Stowe*. Boston: Houghton, Mifflin and Co., 1898.

Fields, Barbara J. "Ideology and Race in American History." In *Region, Race, and Reconstruction: Essays in Honor of C. Vann Woodward*, edited by C. Vann Woodward, J. Morgan Kousser, and James M. McPherson, 143–77. New York: Oxford University Press, 1982.

Filene, Peter. *Him / Her / Self: Sex Roles in Modern America*. Baltimore, Md.: Johns Hopkins University Press, 1986.

Fisher, Philip. *Hard Facts*. New York: Oxford University Press, 1985.

Flexner, Eleanor. *Century of Struggle: The Woman's Rights Movement in the United States*. New York: Atheneum, 1974.

Flynn, Elizabeth A., and Patrocinio P. Schweickart, eds. *Gender and Reading: Essays on Readers, Texts, and Contexts*. Baltimore, Md.: Johns Hopkins University Press, 1986.

Foreman, P. Gabrielle. "The Spoken and the Silenced in *Incidents in the Life of a Slave Girl* and *Our Nig*." *Callaloo* 13, no. 2 (Spring 1990): 313–20.

Foster, Frances Smith, ed. *A Brighter Coming Day: A Frances Ellen Watkins Harper Reader*. New York: Feminist Press, 1990.

———. *Witnessing Slavery: The Development of Ante-bellum Slave Narratives*. Wesport, Conn.: Greenwood Press, 1979.

———. *Written by Herself: Literary Production by African American Women, 1746–1892*. Bloomington: Indiana University Press, 1993.

Foster, Hannah Webster. *The Coquette*. 1797. Reprint, New York: Oxford University Press, 1986.

Fox-Genovese, Elizabeth. *Within the Plantation Household: Black and White Women of the Old South*. Chapel Hill: University of North Carolina Press, 1988.

Franklin, Benjamin. *Autobiography*. 1791. Reprint, Boston: Houghton Mifflin, 1958.

Freedman, Estelle. "Separatism as Strategy: Female Institution Building and American Feminism, 1870–1930." *Feminist Studies* 5 (Fall 1979): 512–29.

Freibert, Lucy M., and Barbara A. White, eds. *Hidden Hands: An Anthology of American Women Writers, 1790–1870*. New Brunswick, N.J.: Rutgers University Press, 1985.

Gaard, Greta Claire. "Anger Expressed/Repressed: Novels by White, Middle-Class, American Women Writers, 1850–Present." Ph.D. diss., University of Minnesota, 1989.

———. " 'Self-Denial Was All the Fashion': Repressing Anger in *Little Women*." *Papers on Language and Literature: A Journal for Scholars and Critics of Language and Literature* 27, no. 1 (Winter 1991): 3–19.

Gardner, Eric. " 'This Attempt of Their Sister': Harriet Wilson's *Our Nig* from Printer to Readers." *New England Quarterly* 66, no. 2 (June 1993): 226–46.

Garfield, Deborah M. "Earwitness: Female Abolitionism, Sexuality, and *Incidents in the Life of a Slave Girl*." In *Harriet Jacobs and Incidents in the Life of a Slave Girl*, edited by Deborah M. Garfield and Rafia Zafar, 100–130. Cambridge: Cambridge University Press, 1996.

Gates, Henry Louis, Jr. *Figures in Black: Words, Signs, and the "Racial" Self*. New York: Oxford University Press, 1987.

———. Introduction to *Our Nig*, by Hariett Wilson. New York: Vintage Books, 1983.

———. *The Signifying Monkey: A Theory of Afro-American Literary Criticism*. New York, Oxford University Press, 1988.

Gates, Henry Louis, Jr., and David Ames Curtis. "Establishing the Identity of the Author of *Our Nig*." In *Wild Women in the Whirlwind: Afra-American Culture and the Contemporary Literary Renaissance*, edited by Joanne M. Braxton and Andree Nicola McLaughlin, 48–69. New Brunswick, N.J.: Rutgers University Press, 1990.

Gates, Henry Louis, Jr., and Charles T. Davis, eds. "Introduction: The Language of Slavery." In *The Slave's Narrative*, xi–xxxiv. New York: Oxford University Press, 1985.

Gaylin, Willard. *The Rage Within: Anger in Modern Life*. New York: Penguin Books, 1984.

Geary, Susan. "The Domestic Novel as a Commercial Commodity: Making a Best Seller in the 1850s." *Papers of the Bibliographical Society of America* 70, no. 3 (1976): 365–93.

Gernes, Todd S. "Genealogical Anxiety, Literary Production and Difference of Color: Mary Virginia Woods, Charlotte Forten Grimké and Angelina Weld Grimké." Paper presented at the annual meeting of the American Studies Association, New Orleans, Louisiana, 2 November 1990.

———. "Poetic Justice: Sarah Forten, Eliza Earle, and the Paradox of Intellectual Property." *New England Quarterly* 71, no. 2 (June 1998): 229–66.

Giddings, Paula. *When and Where I Enter: The Impact of Black Women on Race and Sex in America*. New York: Morrow, 1984.

Gilbert, Sandra M., and Susan Gubar. *The Madwoman in the Attic: The Woman Writer and the Nineteenth Century Literary Imagination*. New Haven, Conn.: Yale University Press, 1974.

———. *Sexchanges*. Vol. 2 of *No Man's Land: The Place of the Woman Writer in the Twentieth Century*. New Haven, Conn.: Yale University Press, 1989.

———. *The War of the Words*. Vol. 1 of *No Man's Land: The Place of the Woman Writer in the Twentieth Century*. New Haven, Conn.: Yale University Press, 1988.

Gilligan, Carol. *In a Different Voice: Psychological Theory and Women's Development*. Cambridge, Mass.: Harvard University Press, 1982.

Ginzberg, Lori. *Women and the Work of Benevolence: Morality, Politics and Class in the 19th-Century US*. New Haven, Conn.: Yale University Press, 1990.

Gordon, Linda. *Woman's Body, Woman's Right: A Social History of Birth Control in America*. New York: Penguin Books, 1976.

Grant, Joanne. *Black Protest: History, Documents, and Analyses*. New York: Fawcett Premier, 1968.

Gray, Janet, ed. *She Wields a Pen: American Women Poets of the Nineteenth Century*. Iowa City: University of Iowa Press, 1997.

Greenspan, Miriam. *A New Approach to Women and Therapy*. New York: McGraw Hill, 1983.

Greenwood, Grace. "Fanny Fern—Mrs. Parton." In *Eminent Women of the Age; Being Narratives of the Lives and Deeds of the Most Prominent Women of the Present Generation*, edited by James Parton, 66–84. Hartford, Conn.: S. M. Betts and Co., 1868.

Grimké, Charlotte Forten. *The Journals of Charlotte Forten Grimké*. Edited by Brenda Stevenson. New York: Oxford University Press, 1988.

Gwin, Minrose G. "Green-eyed Monsters of the Slavocracy: Jealous Mistresses in Two Slave Narratives." In *Conjuring: Black Women, Fiction, and Literary Tradition*, edited by Marjorie Pryse and Hortense J. Spillers, 39–52. Bloomington: Indiana University Press, 1985.

Halttunen, Karen. *Confidence Men and Painted Women: A Study of Middle-Class Culture in America, 1830–1870*. New Haven, Conn.: Yale University Press, 1982.

Hanaford, Phebe. *Daughters of America, or, Women of the Century*. Augusta, Maine: True and Co., 1882.

Hardesty, Nancy. *Women Called to Witness: Evangelical Feminism in the Nineteenth Century*. Nashville: Abingdon Press, 1984.

Harper, Frances Ellen Watkins. "Liberty for Slaves." 1857. Reprinted in *The Rhetoric of Struggle: Public Address by African American Women*, edited by Robbie Jean Walker, 37–40. New York: Garland Press, 1992.

Harris, Susan K. " 'But Is It Any Good?': Evaluating Nineteenth-Century American Women's Fiction." *American Literature* 63, no. 1 (March 1991): 43–61. Reprinted in *The (Other) American Traditions*, edited by Joyce W. Warren, 263–79, New Brunswick, N.J.: Rutgers University Press, 1993.

———. *Nineteenth-Century American Women's Novels: Interpretive Strategies*. Cambridge: Cambridge University Press, 1990.

Hart, John S.. *The Female Prose Writers of America*. Philadelphia: E. H. Butler and Co., 1857.

Hedges, Elaine, and Ingrid Wendt, eds. *In Her Own Image: Women Working in the Arts*. Old Westbury, N.Y.: Feminist Press, 1980.

Hedrick, Joan D. *Harriet Beecher Stowe: A Life*. New York: Oxford University Press, 1994.

Heilbrun, Carolyn. *Writing a Woman's Life*. New York: Norton, 1988.

Hersh, Blanche Glassman. *The Slavery of Sex: Feminist-Abolitionists in America*. Urbana: University of Illinois Press, 1978.

Herzog, Kristin. *Women, Ethnics, and Exotics: Images of Power in Mid-Nineteenth-Century American Fiction*. Knoxville: University of Tennessee Press, 1983.

Hewitt, Nancy. *Women's Activism and Social Change: Rochester, New York 1822–1872*. Ithaca, N.Y.: Cornell University Press, 1984.

Hine, Darlene Clark. "Rape and the Inner Lives of Black Women in the Middle West: Preliminary Thoughts on the Culture of Dissemblance." 1989. Reprinted in *Unequal Sisters: A Multi-Cultural Reader in U.S. Women's History*, edited by Ellen Carol Dubois and Vicki L. Ruiz, 292–97. New York: Routledge, 1990.

Hinks, Peter P. *To Awake My Afflicted Brethren: David Walker and the Problem of Antebellum Slave Resistance*. University Park: Pennsylvania State University Press, 1997.

Hoffert, Sylvia D. *When Hens Crow: The Woman's Rights Movement in Antebellum America*. Bloomington: Indiana University Press, 1995.

Holland, Patricia. "Lydia Maria Child." *Legacy* 5, no. 2 (Fall 1988): 45–53.

——. "Lydia Maria Child As a Nineteenth-Century Professional Author." *Studies in the American Renaissance* (1981): 157–67.

Horton, James Oliver. "Freedom's Yoke: Gender Conventions among Antebellum Free Blacks." *Feminist Studies* 12, no. 1 (Spring 1986): 53–76.

Horton, James Oliver, and Lois E. Horton. *In Hope of Liberty: Culture, Community and Protest Among Northern Free Blacks, 1700–1860*. New York: Oxford University Press, 1997.

Houchins, Sue E. Introduction to *Spiritual Narratives*. New York: Oxford University Press, 1988.

Huf, Linda. *A Portrait of the Artist as a Young Woman: The Writer as Heroine in American Literature*. New York: Frederick Ungar Publishing, 1983.

Hull, Gloria T., and Barbara Smith. "Introduction: The Politics of Black Women's Studies." In *All the Women Are White, All the Blacks Are Men, But Some of Us Are Brave: Black Women's Studies*, edited by Gloria T. Hull, Patricia Bell Scott, and Barbara Smith, xvii–xxxii. Old Westbury, N.Y.: Feminist Press, 1982.

Humez, Jean McMahon. Introduction to *Gifts of Power: The Writings of Rebecca Jackson, Black Visionary, Shaker Eldress*. Amherst: University of Massachusetts Press, 1981.

Iverson, Lucille, and Kathryn Ruby, eds. *We Become New: Poems by Contemporary American Women*. New York: Bantam Books, 1975.

Jack, Dana Crowley. *Behind the Mask: Destruction and Creativity in Women's Aggression*. Cambridge, Mass.: Harvard University Press, 1999.

Jacobs, Harriet A. *Incidents in the Life of a Slave Girl*. 1861. Reprint, with introduction and editing by Jean Fagan Yellin, Cambridge, Mass.: Harvard University Press, 1987.

Jacoby, Susan. *Wild Justice: The Evolution of Revenge*. New York: Harper and Row, 1983.

Jelinek, Estelle C. *The Tradition of Women's Autobiography: From Antiquity to the Present*. Boston: Twayne Press, 1986.

——. *Women's Autobiography: Essays in Criticism*. Bloomington: Indiana University Press, 1980.

Jones, Jacqueline. *Labor of Love, Labor of Sorrow: Black Women, Work and the Family from Slavery to the Present*. New York: Vintage Books, 1985.

Jordan, Winthrop D. *White Over Black: American Attitudes toward the Negro, 1550–1812*. Baltimore, Md.: Penguin Books, 1958.

Juster, Susan. *Disorderly Women: Sexual Politics and Evangelicalism in Revolutionary New England*. Ithaca, N.Y.: Cornell University Press, 1994.

Kaplan, Fred. *Sacred Tears: Sentimentality in Victorian Literature*. Princeton, N.J.: Princeton University Press, 1987.

Kaplow, Susi. "Getting Angry." 1971. Reprinted in *Radical Feminism*, edited by Anne Koedt, Ellen Levine, and Anita Rapone, 36–47. New York: Quadrangle, 1973.

Karcher, Carolyn. *The First Woman in the Republic: A Cultural Biography of Lydia Maria Child*. Durham, N.C.: Duke University Press, 1994.

———. Introduction to *Hobomok and Other Writings on Indians*. New Brunswick, N.J.: Rutgers University Press, 1986.

———. "Rape, Murder, and Revenge in 'Slavery's Pleasant Homes.'" *Women's Studies International Forum* 9 (Fall 1986): 323–32.

———. "Recovering Nineteenth-Century American Literature: The Challenge of Women Writers." *American Literature* 66, no. 4 (December 1994): 781–93.

Kelley, Mary. *Private Woman, Public Stage: Literary Domesticity in Nineteenth-Century America*. New York: Oxford University Press, 1984.

Kemble, Fanny. *The American Journals*. Edited by Elizabeth Mavor. London: Weidenfeld and Nicolson, 1990.

Kennedy, Gwynne. *Just Anger: Representing Women's Anger in Early Modern England*. Carbondale: Southern Illinois University Press, 2000.

Kerber, Linda. "Can a Woman Be an Individual? The Limits of Puritan Tradition in the Early Republic." *Texas Studies in Literature and Language* 1 (1983): 165–78.

———. "Daughters of Columbia: Educating Women for the Republic." In *Our American Sisters*, edited by Jean E. Friedman and William G. Shade, 76–92. Boston: Allyn and Bacon, 1976.

———. "Separate Spheres: Female Worlds, Woman's Place: The Rhetoric of Women's History." *Journal of American History* 75 (June 1988): 9–39.

———. *Women of the Republic: Intellect and Ideology in Revolutionary America*. Chapel Hill: University of North Carolina Press, 1980.

Kessler, Carol Farley. Introduction to *The Story of Avis*, by Elizabeth Stuart Phelps. 1877. Reprint, New Brunswick, N.J.: Rutgers University Press, 1985.

Kessler-Harris, Alice. *Out to Work: A History of Wage-Earning Women in the United States*. New York: Oxford University Press, 1982.

Kilcup, Karen L., ed. *Nineteenth-Century American Women Writers: A Critical Reader*. Malden, Mass.: Blackwell Publishers, 1998.

Kolodny, Annette. *The Land Before Her: Fantasy and Experience of the American Frontiers, 1630–1860*. Chapel Hill: University of North Carolina Press, 1984.

———. *The Lay of the Land: Metaphor as Experience and History in American Life and Letters*. Chapel Hill: University of North Carolina Press, 1975.

Kovecses, Zoltan. *Metaphors of Anger, Pride, and Love: A Lexical Approach to the Structure of Concepts*. Amsterdam: John Benjamins Publishing, 1986.

Kraditor, Aileen S. *Ideas of the Woman Suffrage Movement, 1890–1920*. New York: Columbia University Press, 1965.

———, ed. *Up From the Pedestal: Selected Writings in the History of American Feminism*. Chicago: Quadrangle Books, 1968.

Lakoff, George. *Women, Fire, and Dangerous Things: What Categories Reveal about the Mind*. Chicago: University of Chicago Press, 1987.

Lashgari, Deirdre. *Violence, Silence, and Anger: Women's Writing as Transgression*. Charlottesville: University Press of Virginia, 1995.

Lauter, Paul. *Canons and Contexts*. New York: Oxford University Press, 1991.

———. "Is Frances Ellen Watkins Harper Good Enough to Teach?" *Legacy* 5, no. 1 (Spring 1988): 27–32.

———. "Race and Gender in the Shaping of the American Literary Canon: A Case Study from the Twenties." *Feminist Studies* 9 (1983): 435–63.

———. "Teaching Nineteenth-Century Women Writers." In *The (Other) American Traditions*, edited by Joyce W. Warren, 280–301. New Brunswick, N.J.: Rutgers University Press, 1993.

Leach, William. *True Love and Perfect Union: The Feminist Reform of Sex and Society*. New York: Basic Books, 1980.

Leavitt, Judith Walzer. *Brought to Bed: Childbearing in America, 1750–1950*. New York: Oxford University Press, 1986.

Lebsock, Suzanne. *Free Women of Petersburg: Culture in a Southern Town, 1784–1860*. New York: Norton, 1984.

Lerner, Gerda, ed. *Black Women in White America: A Documentary History*. New York: Vintage Books, 1972.

———. *The Female Experience: An American Documentary*. Indianapolis: Bobbs-Merill Educational Publishing, 1977.

———. *The Majority Finds Its Past: Placing Women in History*. New York: Oxford University Press, 1979.

Lerner, Harriet Goldhor. *The Dance of Anger: A Woman's Guide to Changing the Patterns of Intimate Relationships*. New York: Harper and Row, 1985.

Leverenz, David. *Manhood and the American Renaissance*. Ithaca, N.Y.: Cornell University Press, 1989.

Levine, Lawrence W. *Black Culture and Black Consciousness: Afro-American Folk Thought from Slavery to Freedom*. New York: Oxford University Press, 1977.

Lewis, Jan. "The Republican Wife: Virtue and Seduction in the Early Republic." *William and Mary Quarterly* 44 (October 1987): 689–720.

Life and Beauties of Fanny Fern. New York: H. Long and Brother, 1855.

Loewenberg, Bert James, and Ruth Bogin, eds. *Black Women in Nineteenth-Century American Life: Their Words, Their Thoughts, Their Feelings*. University Park: Pennsylvania State University Press, 1976.

Lorde, Audre. "Eye to Eye: Black Women, Hatred, and Anger." 1983. Reprinted in *Sister Outsider: Essays and Speeches*, 145–75. Freedom, Calif.: Crossing Press, 1984.

———. "The Uses of Anger: Women Responding to Racism." 1981. Reprinted in *Sister Outsider: Essays and Speeches*, 124–33. Freedom, Calif.: Crossing Press, 1984.

Lyman, Peter. "The Politics of Anger: On Silence, Ressentiment, and Political Speech." *Socialist Review* 11, no. 3 (May–June 1981): 55–74.

Lystra, Karen. *Searching the Heart: Women, Men, and Romantic Love in 19th-Century America*. New York: Oxford University Press, 1989.

Mabee, Carleton, and Susan Mabee Newhouse. *Sojourner Truth: Slave, Prophet, Legend*. New York: New York University Press, 1993.

McDowell, Deborah. "New Directions for Black Feminist Criticism." 1980. Reprinted in *The New Feminist Criticism: Essays on Women, Literature, and Theory*, edited by Elaine Showalter, 186–99. New York: Pantheon Books, 1985.

McDowell, Deborah, and Arnold Rampersand, eds. *Slavery and the Literary Imagination*. Baltimore, Md.: Johns Hopkins University Press, 1989.

McLoughlin, William G. "Charles Grandison Finney." In *Antebellum Reform*, edited by David Brion Davis, 97–107. New York: Harper and Row, 1967.

——. *Revivals, Awakenings, and Reform: An Essay on Religion and Social Change in America, 1607–1977*. Chicago: University of Chicago Press, 1978.

McNall, Sally Allen. *Who Is in the House? A Psychological Study of Two Centuries of Women's Fiction in America, 1795 to the Present*. New York: Elsevier, 1981.

Madow, Leo. *Anger*. New York: Charles Scribner's Sons, 1972.

Marcus, Jane. *Art and Anger: Reading Like a Woman*. Columbus: Ohio State University Press, 1988.

Matthews, Glenna. *Just a Housewife: The Rise and Fall of Domesticity in America*. New York: Oxford University Press, 1987.

Meese, Elizabeth A. *Crossing the Double-Cross: The Practice of Feminist Criticism*. Chapel Hill: University of North Carolina Press, 1986.

Melish, Joanne Pope. *Disowning Slavery: Gradual Emancipation and "Race" in New England, 1780–1860*. Ithaca, N.Y.: Cornell University Press, 1998.

Milhaven, Giles J. *Good Anger*. Kansas City, Mo.: Sheed and Ward, 1989.

Miller, Jean Baker. "The Construction of Anger in Women and Men." In *Women's Growth in Connection: Writings from the Stone Center*, edited by Judith V. Jordan, Alexandra G. Kaplan, Jean Baker Miller, Irene P. Silver, and Janet L. Surrey. New York: Guilford Press, 1991.

——. *Toward a New Psychology of Women*. Boston: Beacon Press, 1976.

Miller, Jean Baker, and Janet L. Surrey. "Revisioning Women's Anger: The Personal and the Global." Jean Baker Miller Training Institute Working Paper no. 43. Wellesley, Mass.: Stone Center for Developmental Services and Studies, 1990.

Miller, Nancy K. *Getting Personal: Feminist Occasions and Other Autobiographical Acts*. New York: Routledge, 1991.

Miller, Perry. "From Edwards to Emerson." In *Errand into the Wilderness*, 184–203. Cambridge, Mass.: Harvard University Press, 1956.

Millett, Kate. *Sexual Politics*. New York: Avon Books, 1969.

Moers, Ellen. "The Angry Young Women." *Harpers* 227 (December 1973): 88–95.

——. *Literary Women: The Great Writers*. Garden City, N.Y.: Doubleday, 1977.

Morantz-Sanchez, Regina Markell. *Sympathy and Science: Women Physicians in American Medicine*. New York: Oxford University Press, 1985.

Morgan, Robin. "Introduction: The Women's Revolution." In *Sisterhood Is Powerful: An Anthology of Writings from the Women's Liberation Movement*, edited by Robin Morgan, xiii–xli. New York: Random House, 1970.

Morrison, Toni. *The Bluest Eye*. New York: Pocket Books, 1970.

——. "The Site of Memory." In *Inventing the Truth: The Art and Craft of Memoir*, edited and introduction by William Zinser, 103–24. Boston: Houghton Mifflin Co., 1987.

Moses, Wilson Jeremiah. *Black Messiahs and Uncle Toms: Social and Literary Manipulations of a Religious Myth*. University Park: Pennsylvania State University Press, 1982.

Mullen, Harryette. "Runaway Tongue: Resistant Orality in *Uncle Tom's Cabin, Our Nig, Incidents in the Life of A Slave Girl*, and *Beloved*." In *The Culture of Sentiment: Race, Gender, and Sentimentality in 19th-Century America*, edited by Shirley Samuels, 244–64. New York: Oxford University Press, 1992.

Murphy, Ann B. "The Borders of Ethical, Erotic, and Artistic Possibilities in *Little Women*." *Signs* 15 (Spring 1990): 562–85.

Niemtzow, Annette. "The Problematic of Self in Autobiography: The Example of the Slave Narrative." In *The Art of Slave Narrative: Original Essays in Criticism and Theory*, edited by John Sekora and Darwin T. Turner, 96–109. Macomb: Western Illinois University, 1982.

Norton, Mary Beth. *Liberty's Daughters: The Revolutionary Experience of American Women, 1750–1800*. Boston: Little, Brown and Co., 1980.

Olney, James. " 'I Was Born': Slave Narratives, Their Status as Autobiography and as Literature." In *The Slave's Narrative*, edited by Charles T. Davis and Henry Louis Gates Jr., 148–75. New York: Oxford University Press, 1985.

Olsen, Tillie. *Silences*. New York: Delta/Seymour Lawrence, 1965.

Osborne, William. *Lydia Maria Child*. Boston: G. K. Hall and Co., 1980.

Ostriker, Alicia Suskin. *Stealing the Language: The Emergence of Women's Poetry in America*. Boston: Beacon Press, 1986.

Painter, Nell Irvin. "Difference, Slavery, and Memory: Sojourner Truth in Feminist Abolitionism." In *The Abolitionist Sisterhood*, edited by Jean Fagan Yellin and John C. Van Horne, 139–58. Ithaca, N.Y.: Cornell University Press, 1994.

———. *Sojourner Truth: A Life, a Symbol*. New York: W. W. Norton and Co., 1996.

Papashvily, Helen Waite. *All the Happy Endings: A Study of the Domestic Novel in America, the Women Who Wrote It, the Women Who Read It, in the Nineteenth Century*. New York: Harper and Brothers Press, 1956.

Parker, Gail. Introduction to *Oven Birds: American Women on Womanhood, 1820–1920*. New York: Anchor Books, 1972.

Parton, James, ed. *Eminent Women of the Age; Being Narratives of the Lives and Deeds of the Most Prominent Women of the Present Generation*. Hartford, Conn.: S. M. Betts and Co., 1868.

Pattee, Fred Lewis. *The Feminine Fifties*. New York: D. Appleton-Century, 1940.

Person, Leland, Jr. "The American Eve: Miscegenation and a Feminist Frontier Fiction." *American Quarterly* 37 (1985): 668–85.

Peterson, Carla. *"Doers of the Word": African American Women Speakers and Writers in the North (1830–1860)*. New York: Oxford University Press, 1995.

Petesch, Donald A. *A Spy in the Enemy's Country: The Emergence of Modern Black Literature*. Iowa City: University of Iowa Press, 1989.

Pfister, Joel, and Nancy Schnog, eds. *Inventing the Psychological: Toward a Cultural History of Emotional Life in America*. New Haven, Conn.: Yale University Press, 1997.

Piercy, Marge. "Unlearning to Not Speak." In *We Become New: Poems by Contemporary American Women*, edited by Lucille Iverson and Kathryn Ruby. New York: Bantam Books, 1975.

Pratt, Annis. *Archetypal Patterns in Women's Fiction*. Bloomington: Indiana University Press, 1981.

Pyrse, Marjorie, and Hortense J. Spillers, eds. *Conjuring: Black Women, Fiction, and Literary Tradition*. Bloomington: Indiana University Press, 1985.

Quarles, Benjamin. *Black Abolitionists*. New York: Oxford University Press, 1969.

Radway, Janice A. *Reading the Romance: Women, Patriarchy, and Popular Literature*. Chapel Hill: University of North Carolina Press, 1984.

Reynolds, David S. *Beneath the American Renaissance: The Subversive Imagination in the Age of Emerson and Melville*. Cambridge, Mass.: Harvard University Press, 1988.

Rhodes, Jane. *Mary Ann Shadd Cary: The Black Press and Protest in the Nineteenth Century*. Bloomington: Indiana University Press, 1998.

Rich, Adrienne. "Disloyal to Civilization: Feminism, Racism, Gynephobia." 1978. Reprinted in *On Lies, Secrets, and Silence: Selected Prose, 1966–1978*, 275–310. New York: W. W. Norton and Co., 1979.

———. *Of Woman Born: Motherhood as Experience and Institution*. New York: W. W. Norton, 1976.

———. "Vesuvius at Home: The Power of Emily Dickinson." 1975. Reprinted in *On Lies, Secrets, and Silence: Selected Prose, 1966–1978*, 157–83. New York: W. W. Norton and Co., 1979.

———. "When We Dead Awaken: Writing as Re-Vision." 1971. Reprinted in *On Lies, Secrets, and Silence: Selected Prose, 1966–1978*, 33–49. New York: W. W. Norton and Co., 1979.

Richardson, Marilyn, ed. *Maria W. Stewart: America's First Black Woman Political Writer*. Bloomington: Indiana University Press, 1987.

Romero, Lora. *Home Fronts: Domesticity and Its Critics in the Antebellum United States*. Durham, N.C.: Duke University Press, 1997.

Rorty, Amelie Oksenberg, ed. *Explaining Emotions*. Berkeley: University of California Press, 1980.

Rose, Jane E. "Conduct Books for Women, 1830–1860: A Rationale for Women's Conduct and Domestic Role in America." In *Nineteenth-Century American Women and Literacy*, edited by Catherine Hobbs. Charlottesville: University Press of Virginia, 1995.

Rothman, Ellen. *Hands and Hearts: A History of Courtship in America*. New York: Basic Books, 1984.

Rowlandson, Mary. *A Narrative of the Captivity and Restauration of Mrs. Mary Rowlandson*. 1682. Reprint, Tucson, Ariz.: American Eagle Publications, 1988.

Rowson, Susanna. *Charlotte Temple*. 1791. Reprint, New York: Oxford University Press, 1986.

Ruether, Rosemary Radford, and Rosemary Skinner Keller, eds. *Women and Religion in America: The Nineteenth Century, a Documentary History*. San Francisco: Harper and Row, 1981.

Russ, Joanna. *How to Suppress Women's Writing*. Austin: University of Texas Press, 1983.

Russo, Ann, and Cheris Kramarae. Introduction to *The Radical Women's Press of the 1850s*. New York: Routledge, 1991.

Ryan, Mary. *Cradle of the Middle Class: The Family in Oneida County, New York, 1790–1865*. New York: Cambridge University Press, 1984.

———. "The Power of Women's Networks: A Case Study of Female Moral Reform in Antebellum America." *Feminist Studies* 5 (Spring 1979): 66–86.

———. *Womanhood in America: From Colonial Times to the Present.* New York: Franklin Watts, 1983.

———. *Women in Public: Between Banners and Ballots, 1825–1880.* Baltimore, Md.: Johns Hopkins University Press, 1990.

Sahli, Nancy. "Smashing: Women's Relationships before the Fall." *Chrysalis* 8 (Summer 1979): 17–29.

Salvino, Dana Nelson. "The Word in Black and White: Ideologies of Race and Literacy in Antebellum America." In *Reading in America: Literature and Social History*, edited by Cathy N. Davidson, 140–56. Baltimore, Md.: Johns Hopkins University Press, 1989.

Sanchez-Eppler, Karen. "Bodily Bonds: The Intersecting Rhetorics of Feminism and Abolition." *Representations* 24 (Fall 1988): 28–59.

Scheman, Naomi. "Anger and the Politics of Naming." In *Women and Language in Literature and Society*, edited by Sally McConnell-Ginet, Ruth Borker, and Nelly Furman, 174–87. New York: Praeger Special Studies, 1980.

Schlesinger, Elizabeth Bancroft. "Fanny Fern: Our Grandmothers' Mentor." *New York Historical Society Quarterly* 38 (October 1954): 518–19.

Schneir, Miriam, ed. *Feminism: The Essential Historical Writings.* New York: Vintage Books, 1972.

Schnog, Nancy. "Changing Emotions: Moods and the Nineteenth-Century Woman Writer." In *Inventing the Psychological*, edited by Joel Pfister and Nancy Schnog, 84–109. New Haven, Conn.: Yale University Press, 1997.

Sedgwick, Catharine Maria. "Cacoethes Scribendi." 1830. Reprinted in *Provisions: A Reader from 19th-Century American Women*, edited and introduction by Judith Fetterley, 41–59. Bloomington: Indiana University Press, 1985.

———. *Hope Leslie.* 1827. Reprint, edited and introduction by Mary Kelley, New Brunswick, N.J.: Rutgers University Press, 1987.

———. *The Power of Her Sympathy: The Autobiography and Journal of Catharine Maria Sedgwick.* Edited and introduction by Mary Kelley. Boston: Massachusetts Historical Society, 1993.

Seneca. "On Anger." In *Moral Essays*, vol. 1, translated by John W. Basore. Cambridge, Mass.: Harvard University Press, 1963.

Shockley, Ann Allen, ed. *Afro-American Women Writers, 1746–1933.* New York: New American Library, 1988.

Showalter, Elaine. *The Female Malady: Women, Madness, and English Culture, 1830–1980.* New York: Pantheon Books, 1985.

———. Introduction to *Alternative Alcott.* New Brunswick, N.J.: Rutgers University Press, 1988.

———. Introduction to *Little Women.* New York: Penguin Books, 1989.

———, ed. *The New Feminist Criticism: Essays on Women, Literature, and Theory.* New York: Pantheon Books, 1985.

———. *Sister's Choice: Tradition and Change in American Women's Writing.* Oxford: Clarendon Press, 1991.

Silver, Brenda R. "The Authority of Anger: *Three Guineas* as Case Study." *Signs* 16, no. 2 (1991): 340–70.

Six Women's Slave Narratives. Edited and introduction by William L. Andrews. New York: Oxford University Press, 1988.

Sizer, Lyde Cullen. *The Political Work of Northern Women Writers and the Civil War, 1850–1872*. Chapel Hill: University of North Carolina Press, 2000.

Sklar, Katherine Kish. *Catharine Beecher: A Study in American Domesticity*. New York: W. W. Norton and Co., 1973.

Slotkin, Richard. *Regeneration through Violence: The Mythology of the American Frontier, 1600–1860*. Middletown, Conn.: Wesleyan University Press, 1973.

Smith, Barbara. "Toward a Black Feminist Criticism." 1977. Reprinted in *The New Feminist Criticism*, edited by Elaine Showalter, 168–85, New York: Pantheon Books, 1985.

Smith, Sidonie. *A Poetics of Women's Autobiography: Marginality and the Fictions of Self Representation*. Bloomington: Indiana University Press, 1987.

Smith, Valerie. " 'Loopholes of Retreat': Architecture and Ideology in Harriet Jacobs's *Incidents in the Life of A Slave Girl*." In *Reading Black, Reading Feminist*, edited by Henry Louis Gates Jr., 212–26. New York: Meridian, 1990.

Smith-Rosenberg, Carroll. *Disorderly Conduct: Visions of Gender in Victorian America*. New York: Oxford University Press, 1985.

Smucker, Carol, June Martin, and Dorothy Wilt. "Values and Anger." In *Women and Anger*, edited by Sandra P. Thomas. New York: Springer Publishing, 1993.

Spacks, Patricia Meyer. *The Female Imagination*. New York: Anchor Books, 1972.

Spelman, Elizabeth V. "Anger and Insubordination." In *Women, Knowledge and Reality: Explorations in Feminist Philosophy*, edited by Ann Garry and Marilyn Pearsall, 263–73. New York: Unwin Hyman, 1989.

Stansell, Christine. *City of Women: Sex and Class in New York 1789–1860*. Urbana: University of Illinois Press, 1987.

Stanton, Elizabeth Cady. "Ruth Hall." *Una* (February 1855): 29–30.

Stanton, Elizabeth Cady, Susan B. Anthony, Matilda Joslyn Gage. *History of Woman Suffrage*. Rochester, N.Y.: Susan B. Anthony, Charles Mann, 1881–1922.

Starling, Marion Wilson. *The Slave Narrative: Its Place in American History*. 2nd ed. Washington, D.C.: Howard University Press, 1988.

Stearns, Carol Zisowitz, and Peter N. Stearns. *Anger: The Struggle for Emotional Control in America's History*. Chicago: University of Chicago Press, 1986.

Stearns, Peter N. *American Cool: Constructing a Twentieth-Century Emotional Style*. New York: New York University Press, 1994.

Sterling, Dorothy. *Ahead of Her Time: Abby Kelley and the Politics of Antislavery*. New York: W. W. Norton, 1991.

———, ed. *We Are Your Sisters: Black Women in the Nineteenth Century*. New York: W. W. Norton, 1984.

Stern, Madeleine, ed. *Behind a Mask: The Unknown Thrillers of Louisa May Alcott*. New York: William Morrow, 1975.

———. Introduction to *The Journals of Louisa May Alcott*, edited by Joel Myerson and Daniel Shealy. Boston: Little, Brown and Co., 1989.

———. *Louisa May Alcott: A Biography*. 1950. Reprint, New York: Random House, 1996.

———. *Plots and Counterplots: More Unknown Thrillers of Louisa May Alcott*. New York: Popular Library, 1976.

Stetson, Erlene, ed. *Black Sister: Poetry by Black American Women, 1746–1980*. Bloomington: Indiana University Press, 1981.

Stewart, Maria W. *Maria W. Stewart: America's First Black Woman Political Writer*. Edited and introduction by Marilyn Richardson. Bloomington: Indiana University Press, 1987.

——. *Productions of Mrs. Maria W. Stewart, Presented to the First African Baptist Church & Society, of the City of Boston*. 1835. Reprinted in *Spiritual Narratives*, with an introduction by Sue E. Houchins, New York: Oxford University Press, 1988.

Stewart, Veronica. "The Wild Side of *The Wild, Wide World*." *Legacy* 11, no. 1 (1994): 1–16.

Still, William. *The Underground Railroad*. 1872. Reprint, New York: Arno Press, 1968.

Stowe, Harriet Beecher. *Uncle Tom's Cabin*. 1852. Reprint, edited and introduction by Ann Douglas, New York: Penguin Books, 1981.

Swerdlow, Amy. "Abolition's Conservative Sisters: The Ladies New York City Anti-Slavery Societies, 1834–1840." In *The Abolitionist Sisterhood*, edited by Jean Fagan Yellin and John C. Van Horne, 31–44. Ithaca, N.Y.: Cornell University Press, 1994.

Takaki, Ronald. *Iron Cages: Race and Culture in Nineteenth Century America*. Seattle: University of Washington Press, 1979.

Tate, Claudia. "Allegories of Female Black Desire; or, Rereading Nineteenth-Century Sentimental Novels of Black Female Authority." In *Changing Our Own Words: Essays on Criticism, Theory, and Writing by Black Women*, edited by Cheryl A. Wall, 98–126. New Brunswick, N.J.: Rutgers University Press, 1989.

Tavris, Carol. *Anger: The Misunderstood Emotion*. New York: Simon and Schuster, 1982.

Terborg-Penn, Rosalyn, ed. *The Afro-American Woman: Struggles and Images*. London: Kennikat Press, 1978.

Thomas, John L. "Romantic Reform in America, 1815–1865." In *Ante-Bellum Reform*, edited by David Brion Davis, 153–76. New York: Harper and Row, 1967.

Thomas, Sandra P. "Anger and Its Manifestations in Women." In *Women and Anger*, edited by Sandra P. Thomas. New York: Springer Publishing, 1993.

Todd, Janet. *Feminist Literary History*. New York: Routledge, 1988.

Tolstoi, Leo. *What Is Art?* In *The Complete Works of Lyof W. Tolstoi*. New York: Thomas Y. Crowell and Co., 1899.

Tompkins, Jane. Afterword to *The Wide, Wide World*, by Susan Warner. New York: Feminist Press, 1987.

——. "Me and My Shadow." *New Literary History* 19 (Autumn 1987): 169–78.

——. *Sensational Designs: The Cultural Work of American Fiction, 1790–1860*. New York: Oxford University Press, 1985.

Turning the World Upside Down: The Anti-Slavery Convention of American Women. Introduction by Dorothy Sterling. New York: Feminist Press, 1987.

Valentis, Mary, and Anne Devane. *Female Rage: Unlocking Its Secrets, Claiming Its Power*. New York: Carol Southern Books, 1994.

Voloshin, Beverly, R. "The Limits of Domesticity: The Female Bildungsroman in America, 1820–1870." *Women's Studies* 10 (1984): 283–302.

Von Hallberg, Robert, ed. *Canons*. Chicago: University of Chicago Press, 1983.

Walker, Alice. "In Search of Our Mother's Gardens." In *In Search of Our Mother's Gardens: Womanist Prose*, 231–43. San Francisco: Harvest/HBJ, 1983.

——. "One Child of One's Own: A Meaningful Digression Within The Work(s)."

1979. Reprinted in *In Search of Our Mother's Gardens*, 361–83. San Francisco: Harvest/HBJ, 1983.

Walker, Cheryl. *The Nightingale's Burden: Women Poets and American Culture Before 1900*. Bloomington: Indiana University Press, 1982.

Walker, David. *Appeal in Four Articles*. 1829. Reprinted in *One Continual Cry*, edited by Herbert Aptheker. New York: Arno Press, 1965.

Walker, Robbie Jean, ed. *The Rhetoric of Struggle: Public Address by African American Women*. New York: Garland Press, 1992.

Wall, Cheryl A., ed. *Changing Our Own Words: Essays on Criticism, Theory, and Writing by Black Women*. New Brunswick, N.J.: Rutgers University Press, 1989.

Warner, Anna B. *Susan Warner [Elizabeth Wetherell]*. New York: G. P. Putnam's Sons, The Knickerbocker Press, 1909.

Warner, Susan. *The Wide, Wide World*. 1850. Reprint, with an afterword by Jane Tompkins, New York: Feminist Press, 1987.

Warren, Joyce W. *The American Narcissus: Individualism and Women in Nineteenth-Century American Fiction*. New Brunswick, N.J.: Rutgers University Press, 1984.

———. *Fanny Fern: An Independent Woman*. New Brunswick, N.J.: Rutgers University Press, 1992.

———. Introduction to *Ruth Hall and Other Writings*. New Brunswick, N.J.: Rutgers University Press, 1988.

———, ed. *The (Other) American Traditions: Nineteenth-Century Women Writers*. New Brunswick, N.J.: Rutgers University Press, 1993.

Washington, Mary Helen. "'The Darkened Eye Restored': Notes toward a Literary History of Black Women." In *Invented Lives*, xv–xxxi. Garden City, N.Y.: Anchor Press, 1987.

———."'Taming All That Anger Down': Rage and Silence in the Writing of Gwendolyn Brooks." In *Invented Lives: Narratives of Black Women, 1860–1960*, 387–405. Garden City, N.Y.: Anchor Press, 1987.

Weiss, Elizabeth. *The Anger Trap: Intimate Insights on Women's Anger*. New York: Philosophical Library, 1984.

Welter, Barbara. *Dimity Convictions: The American Woman in the Nineteenth Century*. Columbus: Ohio University Press, 1975.

———. "The Feminization of American Religion: 1800–1860." In *Clio's Consciousness Raised: New Perspectives on the History of Women*, edited by Mary Hartman and Lois W. Banner, 137–57. New York: Harper, 1974.

Wexler, Laura. "Tender Violence: Literary Eavesdropping, Domestic Fiction, and Educational Reform." *Yale Journal of Criticism* 5, no. 1 (1991): 151–87.

White, Barbara A. *Growing Up Female: Adolescent Girlhood in American Fiction*. Westport, Conn.: Greenwood Press, 1985.

———. "*Our Nig* and the She-Devil: New Information about Harriet Wilson and the 'Bellmont' Family." *American Literature* 65, no. 1 (March 1993): 19–52.

White, Deborah Gray. *Ar'n't I a Woman?: Female Slaves in the Plantation South*. New York: Norton, 1985.

Wilson, Harriet. *Our Nig, or Sketches From the Life of A Free Black*. 1859. Reprint, with introduction by Henry Louis Gates Jr., New York: Vintage Books, 1983.

Wilt, Dorothy. "Treatment of Anger." In *Women and Anger*, edited by Sandra P. Thomas. New York: Springer Publishing, 1993.

Winch, Julie. " 'You Have Talents—Only Cultivate Them': Philadelphia's Black Female Literary Societies and the Abolitionist Crusade." In *The Abolitionist Sisterhood*, edited by Jean Fagan Yellin and John C. Van Horne, 101–18. Ithaca, N.Y.: Cornell University Press, 1994.

Woloch, Nancy. *Women and the American Experience*. New York: Knopf, 1984.

Yaeger, Patricia. *Honey-Mad Women: Emancipatory Strategies in Women's Writing*. New York: Columbia University Press, 1988.

Yee, Shirley J. *Black Women Abolitionists: A Study in Activism, 1828–1860*. Knoxville: University of Tennessee Press, 1992.

Yellin, Jean Fagan. Introduction to *Incidents in the Life of a Slave Girl*, by Harriet A. Jacobs. Reprint, Cambridge, Mass.: Harvard University Press, 1987.

———. *Women and Sisters: The Anti-Slavery Feminists in American Culture*. New Haven, Conn.: Yale University Press, 1989.

Yellin, Jean Fagan, and John C. Van Horne, eds. *The Abolitionist Sisterhood: Women's Political Culture in Antebellum America*. Ithaca, N.Y.: Cornell University Press, 1994.

Young, Elizabeth. *Disarming the Nation: Women's Writing and the American Civil War*. Chicago: University of Chicago Press, 1999.

Zagarell, Sandra A. "Narrative of Community: The Identification of a Genre." *Signs* 13, no. 3 (Spring 1988): 498–527.

Zinsser, William. *Inventing the Truth: The Art and Craft of Memoir*. Boston: Houghton Mifflin, 1987.

and folk theory of anger, 6–7; anger as
dangerous animal, 7; and national selfhood, 142

Anger paradigm: and women's literature,
5, 7, 10, 194; and corrosive vs. generative anger, 11; and communication of
anger, 12; and antebellum period, 16,
19–40, 194

*Anger: The Struggle for Emotional Control in
America's History* (Stearns and Stearns),
49–50

Antebellum period: and anger paradigm,
16, 19–40, 194; gendered ideologies of,
19, 38, 48, 50–51, 61; and suppression of
anger, 41–67

Appeal in Favor of Americans Called Africans
(Child), 166, 215–16 (n. 4)

Aquinas, Saint Thomas, 13, 50, 51

Aristocratic principle, 49, 202 (n. 22)

Aristotle, 13, 50, 51, 204 (n. 54)

Asian Americans, 19

Bambara, Toni Cade, 9

Baym, Nina, 21–22, 39, 80, 143, 149, 190,
199 (n. 6)

Beecher, Catherine, 48–49

"Behind a Mask, or, A Woman's Power"
(Alcott), 30–33, 37

Bernardez, Teresa, 15, 195

Bible: and anger, 50, 51, 202 (n. 24); and
Child, 75, 78, 83; and Stewart, 104, 117,
119, 120, 127, 128; and gendered ideologies, 123–24; and Wilson, 167, 168

Black men: and black women's literature,
9–10, 64–65; and nation-building
project, 53; and economics, 53, 64, 179;
and gendered ideologies, 64, 204–5
(n. 56); and Stewart, 114–15, 117, 125, 211
(n. 30)

Black Woman, The: An Anthology (Bambara),
9

Black women: and unexpressed anger, 4;
and black feminist scholarship, 8–10;
and republican womanhood, 23–24;
and moral role, 23–24, 199 (n. 8); and
Jacobs, 34, 35, 36; and rape, 36–37, 53;

and abolitionism, 43, 44, 173; and suppression of anger, 44–45; anger
directed at white women, 44–45, 62–
63, 120–21, 180–81, 201 (n. 8); white
women's anger towards, 45–46, 165, 181;
and nation-building project, 48, 53, 63;
and gendered ideologies, 48, 54, 64,
204–5 (n. 56); and gender injustice, 54,
57, 58–60, 61, 105; and racial injustice,
54–58, 60, 63, 64–65; and repression of
anger, 54–58, 62; and expressions of
anger, 56, 57, 125–26; and economics,
62, 120; and evangelicalism, 104–6; and
Fern, 148, 155–56; and democracy, 174;
and vengeance, 176, 177; and justice,
186–87

Black women's literature: and black men,
9–10, 64–65; and moral emotionalism,
24–25; and Jacobs, 33–37; and masking
techniques, 38–39, 57, 58; and slavery,
61

Bluest Eye, The (Morrison), 193–94

Boylan, Anne M., 53–54

Braxton, Joanne, 61

Brontë, Charlotte, 32

Brown, Gillian, 22

Calvinism, 74, 78, 99, 143–44, 156–57

Carby, Hazel, 22

Cashin, Joan E., 45

Characters, fictional: doubled, 7, 89–90,
95–99, 207 (n. 30); and expressions of
anger, 53, 194; and gender bias in
reviewers, 80

Chesnut, Mary Boykin, 45

Child, Lydia Maria: and analysis of
anger, 5; and expressions of anger, 16–
17, 40, 41–42, 47, 49, 66, 72, 95, 132,
139; and nation-building project, 17,
47, 49, 74, 78–79, 83–84, 85, 132, 189;
and anger at exclusion, 17, 72, 74, 77–
78, 80, 81, 92, 132; and moral emotionalism, 24, 99; and Jacobs, 33; and
masking techniques, 39, 72, 77, 79–
100; Cornish compared to, 54; and
gender injustice, 59, 72, 80, 84, 92, 132;

98, 100, 132; and Stewart, 102, 103, 107, 108–9, 118–19, 128, 132; and white women, 128

Elaw, Zilpha, 105

Elbert, Sarah, 26

Ellman, Mary, 8

Exploratory fiction, 16, 21, 198 (n. 1)

Expressions of anger: and women's literature, 5, 6, 25, 194; and feminist scholarship, 6–8, 10, 14–15, 193–94; and justice, 10, 11, 12–13, 14, 29, 139–40, 144, 194, 195; and power relations, 10–11, 13–15, 40, 42, 98, 194; and independent selfhood, 13–14, 39–40; and public anger, 12, 25; and antebellum period, 16, 22–23; and Child, 16–17, 40, 41–42, 47, 49, 66, 72, 95, 132, 139; and Stewart, 16–17, 40, 66, 103–5, 108, 113–16, 121–23, 125–28, 130–32, 139; and Fern, 16–17, 40, 66, 133, 136–43, 138, 149, 150, 155, 157–58, 160, 190, 191, 214 (n. 34), 215 (n. 47); and Wilson, 16–17, 40, 66, 133, 171, 175, 190, 191; and nation-building project, 20, 63–64; and analysis of anger, 21; and gendered ideologies, 23, 25, 42, 125–26, 133, 138, 140, 142, 144, 150, 160; and domestic literature, 23, 142, 143, 195; and Alcott, 26, 27, 64; and Jacobs, 26; and economics, 40, 52, 62, 194; and social class, 42, 52, 57, 95–98, 141, 155, 214 (n. 41); and middle class, 43, 46, 60, 143, 144, 147, 155, 157, 160; and fictional characters, 53, 194; and black women, 56, 57, 125–26; and abolitionism, 60, 139, 140, 143, 170–71; and white women, 104, 140, 143, 144, 147, 160, 162

"Farewell Address" (Stewart), 110, 127–31

Female Imagination, The (Spacks), 194

Female Prose Writers of America, The (Hart), 25

Feminism and feminist scholarship: and connotations of anger, 4; and expressions of anger, 6–8, 10, 14–15, 193–94; and independent selfhood, 8, 14; and

images of black women, 8–10; and racism, 10; and power relations, 11, 14; and nineteenth-century women's literature, 20; and white women's literature, 22; and masking techniques, 38

Fern, Fanny: and analysis of anger, 5; and expressions of anger, 16–17, 40, 66, 133, 136–43, 138, 149, 150, 155, 157–58, 160, 190, 191, 214 (n. 34), 215 (n. 47); and anger at exclusion, 17, 138, 145, 160, 189; and economics, 24, 145, 147–49, 151–52, 155, 157, 178, 179, 189, 190; and moral emotionalism, 24, 181; and masking techniques, 39, 137, 144, 154, 155, 157, 161; as pseudonymous author, 137, 212 (n. 3); and slave narratives, 139, 145–46, 162, 189–90; and interpretation of history, 145, 146; and access to anger, 146, 150; and justice, 162, 188. See also *Ruth Hall* (Fern)

Fetterley, Judith, 8

Folk theory of anger, 6–7

Forten, Sarah Louisa, 44, 55, 56

Foster, Frances Smith, 142, 213 (n. 24)

Franklin, Benjamin, 122, 137, 147

Free blacks: and republican womanhood, 23; and nation-building project, 48, 53; and middle class, 53–54, 57, 58, 60–61; and gendered ideologies, 56, 64; and economics, 62; slaves compared to, 118–19; and Wilson, 164, 171; and abolitionism, 173

Fuller, Margaret, 20, 139

Garfield, Deborah, 45

Garrison, William Lloyd, 108, 124, 130

Gates, Henry Louis, Jr., 172, 217 (n. 26)

Gendered ideologies: of anger, 5–7, 16, 42, 49–53, 65; and women's literature, 8, 23, 65; and black women's literature, 9–10; and righteous anger, 13, 16, 43, 61, 62, 170; and self entitlement, 13–14; and access to anger, 14; and repression of anger, 14, 15, 29; and nation-building project, 16, 19, 26, 28–29, 47–49, 51, 61–63; of antebellum period, 19, 38, 48,

50–51, 61; and economics, 19–20, 35, 52, 65, 152, 178; and labor, 20, 148, 164; and expressions of anger, 23, 25, 42, 125–26, 133, 138, 140, 142, 144, 150, 160; and Alcott, 26, 27, 28–29; and freedom, 26, 32; and masking techniques, 38; and black women, 48, 54, 64, 204–5 (n. 56); and racial boundaries, 48, 64; and politics, 51, 123–24, 210–11 (n. 27); and abolitionism, 60, 61; and slavery, 61, 64, 164; and black men, 64, 204–5 (n. 56); and religion, 65, 143–44; and evangelicalism, 105, 106; and Stewart, 110–11, 123, 125–28, 131–32; and Fern, 138, 145, 149–52; and democracy, 146; and Wilson, 167, 169–70, 181–82

Gender injustice: and feminism, 4; and power relations, 11, 15; and expressions of anger, 11, 15, 43, 44; and women's literature, 22; and black women, 54, 57, 58–60, 61, 105; and Child, 59, 72, 80, 84, 92, 132; and white women, 64; and woman's rights movement, 66; and Stewart, 103, 127, 128, 130, 132; and Stanton, 139, 141; and Fern, 153, 190

Gender relations: and women's literature, 23; and Alcott, 32; and Jacobs, 35; and masking techniques, 39; and expressions of anger, 42, 43; and gendered ideologies, 62; and black women, 64; and Child, 72, 98; and Stewart, 103, 105

Gilbert, Sandra M., 7

Gothic literature, 166

Greek/Roman philosophy, 50

Greenwood, Grace, 160–61, 212 (n. 11)

Grimké, Angelina, 43, 55, 56, 57, 123, 124, 139

Grimké, Charlotte Forten, 52, 54, 56–60

Grimké, Sarah, 43–44, 57, 123, 124, 139, 150

Griswold, Rufus, 71, 76

Gubar, Susan, 7

Hale, Sarah J., 23, 110

Halttunen, Karen, 38

Hamilton, Gail, 59

Harper, Frances Ellen Watkins, 60, 63, 135, 170, 216 (n. 11)

Harris, Susan, 22, 38, 94

Hart, John S., 25

Hatton, Louise, 107, 108, 109

Hayward, Jonas, 173

Hayward, Nehemiah, 172–73

Hayward, Rebecca, 173

Heilbrun, Carolyn, 7

Hine, Darlene Clark, 36–37

Hobomok (Child): and anger paradigm, 5; and moral emotionalism, 24; and masking techniques, 39, 72, 77, 79–100; and male narrator, 39, 79–82, 86; Child's opinion of, 71; and politics, 71–72, 77, 79, 85, 97; and displacement of anger, 72, 75, 90, 91, 92; and expressions of anger, 72, 91, 95–99; and Native Americans, 72–73, 75, 78, 86, 88–95, 97–100, 207–8 (n. 33), 208 (n. 34); and rebellion against white patriarchal captivity, 73, 74, 78, 79, 80–87, 90, 92, 205 (n. 3); and spatial themes, 73, 77, 85–88, 94; and captivity motifs, 73, 78, 80, 84, 85, 95; and women's education, 74, 87, 98, 100; inspiration for, 76, 206 (n. 16); and anger at exclusion, 77–78, 80, 81, 92, 132; and gender injustice, 80, 92; deer hunt in, 88–91; and doubled characters, 89–90, 95–99

Horton, James Oliver, 64

House as metaphor: and Alcott, 29–30; and Jacobs, 34–36; and Child, 73–74

Hull, Gloria T., 8

Hutchinson Family Singers, 173

Incidents in the Life of a Slave Girl (Jacobs), 34–37, 45

"Independence" (Fern), 136

Industrialization, 23, 51, 142

Inferno (Dante), 152

Irish immigrants, 52, 53

Jacobs, Harriet, 20, 25–26, 33–37, 44, 45, 60–61

25; and Alcott, 26, 28–29; and women's literature, 39, 132; and republican motherhood, 47–48; and suppression of anger, 47–50; and women's expectations, 63; and evangelicalism, 106; and woman's rights movement, 132, 139

Native Americans: and democracy, 19; and social class, 53; and Child, 72–73, 75, 78, 81, 86, 88–95, 207–8 (n. 33), 208 (n. 34)

Natural rights philosophy, 141

Nell, William C., 124

Niemtzow, Annette, 37

Northrup, Solomon, 139

Oakes Smith, Elizabeth, 66

Oppression: and women's literature, 4, 15–16, 194; women's response to, 7; and communication of anger, 12; and justice, 13; and repression of anger, 14, 56; and expressions of anger, 40, 139, 141; and gendered ideologies, 51, 54; and nation-building project, 63; and Child, 79, 82, 83, 87, 92, 95; and Stewart, 104, 112, 127; and Fern, 136, 162, 190, 191; and Wilson, 165, 171, 174, 176, 187, 188, 190, 191

Ostriker, Alicia, 38

Our Nig (Wilson): and anger paradigm, 5; and moral emotionalism, 24–25; and masking techniques, 39, 169, 174, 176–77, 188; and Stewart, 163; and slavery, 164; and credibility, 164, 168, 180, 181, 186–88; and righteous anger, 165, 177; and personas, 166; and suppression of anger, 168; and abolitionism, 172–73; and vengeance, 174–75, 177, 184–85; as courtroom drama, 174–89; and economics, 178, 179–80, 185; and heterosexual love, 178–79; and rebellion scenes, 183–84; and domestic literature, 189–90; and nation-building, 189; and racism, 189

Painter, Nell, 38

Papashvily, Helen, 38, 195

Patriarchal power: and Lorde, 4; and Wilson, 24, 178, 179, 189; and Jacobs, 33; and righteous anger, 42; and gendered ideologies, 51, 61; and Child, 73, 74, 78, 79, 80–87, 90, 92, 205 (n. 3); and Stewart, 103, 105, 106, 110, 123, 124, 130, 164; and Fern, 137, 138, 147, 150, 151, 157, 189, 190

Peterson, Carla, 38, 126

Politics: and women's literature, 4, 5, 6, 22, 40; and feminist scholarship, 7–8; and expression of anger, 11, 17, 141; and women's access to anger, 14, 146; and moral emotionalism, 24, 25, 99; and Alcott, 31, 32; and Jacobs, 35; and masking techniques, 39; and suppression of anger, 42, 49; and women's role in nation-building project, 47–48, 64; and gendered ideologies, 51, 123–24, 210–11 (n. 27); and black women, 64; and Child, 71–72, 77, 85, 97; and Stewart, 102, 104, 109–23, 127–28, 164; and Fern, 137, 146, 162, 181; and Wilson, 165, 170, 181, 184

Post, Amy, 33

Power relations: and analysis of anger, 5–6; and black women's literature, 10; and expressions of anger, 10–11, 13–15, 40, 42, 98, 194; and subordination, 11, 65–66; and communication of anger, 12; and vengeance, 13; and suppression of anger, 14–15; and women's literature, 23; and masking techniques, 37; between black and white women, 45; and white women, 46–47, 52, 62; and gendered ideologies, 51; and woman's rights movement, 65; and Child, 91, 92–95, 208 (n. 35); and Stewart, 103; and Wilson, 175, 181, 182, 187, 190. *See also* Patriarchal power

Productions (Stewart), 109

Prose Writers of America (Griswold), 71

Public anger: and women's literature, 5, 15–16; and expressions of anger, 12, 25; and social change, 15; and Child, 78; and Stewart, 106–9, 123–28, 130;

158; and domestic literature, 189–90; and nation-building project, 189

Sarton, May, 7
Scheman, Naomi, 15
Sedgwick, Catherine Maria, 33
Seduction novels, 177
Selfhood: and feminism, 8, 14; and expressions of anger, 11, 13–14, 39–40; and repression of anger, 15; and domestic literature, 22, 149; and women's literature, 23; and Jacobs, 36, 37; and masking techniques, 38, 39; and Child, 72, 76, 85; and Stewart, 112, 128–29, 130, 131; and anger metaphors, 142; and Fern, 150, 153; and Wilson, 175
Self-governance, 50–51, 53–56, 61
Seneca, 49
Seneca Falls Convention, 32, 132–33, 195
Sentimental literature, 16, 20–21, 38
Separate spheres paradigm, 21–22, 63, 64, 85
Sexual Politics (Millet), 8
Shadd Cary, Mary Ann, 170
Slave narratives: and nation-building project, 26, 132; and Fern, 139, 145–46, 162, 189–90; and domestic literature, 141; and expressions of anger, 142–43, 195; and Wilson, 166, 189–90, 216 (n. 5); and white women's literature, 190; chronological phases of, 213 (n. 24)
Slaves and slavery: and anger at exclusion, 7; and righteous anger, 16; and democracy, 19; and women's literature, 23; and Jacobs, 33–37; and insurrections, 34; and morality, 43; and expressions of anger, 44, 140; white women's collusion in system, 44–46, 120, 180; and social class, 53; and black women's literature, 61; and gendered ideologies, 61, 64, 164; and black women's disappointment, 63–64; free blacks compared to, 118–19; and Stewart, 118; and Stanton, 139; white women compared to, 139–40; and Wilson, 164, 167, 171, 180, 184, 189

Smith, Barbara, 8, 9
Social change: and expressions of anger, 11; and public anger, 15; and righteous anger, 51; and Child, 93; and Stewart, 103, 109–23; and Fern, 155; and Wilson, 189
Social class: and power relations, 6, 15, 47, 62; and moral emotionalism, 25; and nation-building project, 28; and democracy, 29–30; and Alcott, 29–32; and Jacobs, 35; and suppression of anger, 42; and expressions of anger, 42, 52, 57, 95–98, 141, 155, 214 (n. 41); and gendered ideologies, 51–52, 53, 62; and woman's rights movement, 66; and evangelicalism, 105; and Stewart, 120
Spacks, Patricia Meyer, 7, 194
Spelman, Elizabeth V., 13, 15
Stanton, Elizabeth Cady, 136–37, 139–42, 159, 161, 162
Starling, Marion, 143
Stearns, Carol Zisowitz, 49–50, 51, 142
Stearns, Peter N., 49–50, 51, 142
Sterling, Dorothy, 125
Stewart, Maria W.: and anger paradigm, 5; and expressions of anger, 16–17, 40, 66, 103–5, 108, 113–16, 121–23, 125–28, 130–32, 139; and moral emotionalism, 24, 110–13; and masking techniques, 39, 102, 103–4, 106, 116, 121, 123, 126–27, 130, 132, 164; and black women's opportunities, 62; and democracy, 101, 102, 111, 116–20, 164; and interpretation of history, 101, 116–17, 121, 128; and education, 102, 103, 107, 108–9, 118–19, 128, 132; and politics, 102, 104, 109–23, 127–28, 164; and economics, 102, 106, 107, 109, 118, 119, 120, 122, 132; and evangelicalism, 103–6, 109, 110, 111, 115, 122, 125; and righteous anger, 103; and social change, 103, 109–23; and Black Jeremiad tradition, 104–5; and public anger, 106–9, 123–28, 130; literary ambitions of, 108–9; and displacement of anger, 109; and gendered ideologies, 110–11, 123, 125–28, 131–32; and nation-

anger, 53; and expressions of anger, 53, 143, 154; and Fern, 145–46, 153; and slave narratives, 190

Wide, Wide World, The (Warner), 52–53, 182–83, 184, 185, 203 (n. 29)

Willis, Nathaniel Parker, 33, 137–38, 145, 213 (n. 28)

Willis, Sara Payson. *See* Fern, Fanny

Wilson, Harriet: and analysis of anger, 5; and expressions of anger, 16–17, 40, 66, 133, 171, 175, 190, 191; and anger at exclusion, 17, 24, 186, 189; and moral emotionalism, 24; and masking techniques, 39, 164, 165–72, 174, 188, 216 (n. 5); and depictions of white mistresses, 44–45, 201 (n. 11); and Fern, 162; and vengeance, 164, 165, 169, 174, 175, 176–78, 182, 184–85, 188, 189, 190; and slavery, 164, 167, 171, 180, 184, 189; and democracy, 164, 171, 174, 178, 188, 189; and credibility, 164–65, 168; and abolitionism, 166, 169–73, 176, 216 (n. 17); and economics, 166–67, 169, 174, 178, 179–80, 185, 189, 217 (n. 26); and gendered ideologies, 167, 169–70, 181–82; sources of public rage, 172–74;

and truth, 186–88, 190. See also *Our Nig* (Wilson)

Woman's Record (Hale), 23

Woman's rights movement: and expressions of anger, 17, 138–39, 142, 143; and democracy, 19; and black women's literature, 33; critics of, 65; and gender injustice, 66; and Child, 78; and white women, 105; and nation-building project, 132, 139; and abolitionism, 139, 144; and righteous anger, 162

Women's literature: analysis of anger in, 4–5; and expressions of anger, 5, 6, 25, 194; and anger paradigm, 5, 7, 10, 194; and anger at exclusion, 5, 7, 32, 40, 65, 67; and public anger, 5, 15–16; and anger metaphors, 7; and gendered ideologies, 8, 23, 65; and masking techniques, 16, 37–39, 65; role of writing, 20; and economics, 22, 23, 154, 214 (n. 39); and Wilson's testimonials, 167–68. *See also* Black women's literature; White women's literature

Yee, Shirley, 125, 170, 173, 211 (n. 30)

Young, Elizabeth, 22

GENDER AND AMERICAN CULTURE

*Women Against the Good War: Conscientious Objection and Gender on the American Home Front,
     1941–1947*, by Rachel Waltner Goossen (1997)

Toward an Intellectual History of Women: Essays by Linda K. Kerber (1997)

Gender and Jim Crow: Women and the Politics of White Supremacy in North Carolina, 1896–1920,
     by Glenda Elizabeth Gilmore (1996)

*Delinquent Daughters: Protecting and Policing Adolescent Female Sexuality in the United States, 1885–
     1920*, by Mary E. Odem (1995)

U.S. History as Women's History: New Feminist Essays, edited by Linda K. Kerber, Alice
     Kessler-Harris, and Kathryn Kish Sklar (1995)

*Common Sense and a Little Fire: Women and Working-Class Politics in the United States, 1900–
     1965*, by Annelise Orleck (1995)

How Am I to Be Heard?: Letters of Lillian Smith, edited by Margaret Rose Gladney (1993)

Entitled to Power: Farm Women and Technology, 1913–1963, by Katherine Jellison (1993)

Revising Life: Sylvia Plath's Ariel Poems, by Susan R. Van Dyne (1993)

Made From This Earth: American Women and Nature, by Vera Norwood (1993)

Unruly Women: The Politics of Social and Sexual Control in the Old South, by Victoria E. Bynum
     (1992)

The Work of Self-Representation: Lyric Poetry in Colonial New England, by Ivy Schweitzer (1991)

Labor and Desire: Women's Revolutionary Fiction in Depression America, by Paula Rabinowitz
     (1991)

*Community of Suffering and Struggle: Women, Men, and the Labor Movement in Minneapolis, 1915–
     1945*, by Elizabeth Faue (1991)

All That Hollywood Allows: Re-reading Gender in 1950s Melodrama, by Jackie Byars (1991)

Doing Literary Business: American Women Writers in the Nineteenth Century, by Susan Coultrap-
     McQuin (1990)

Ladies, Women, and Wenches: Choice and Constraint in Antebellum Charleston and Boston, by Jane
     H. Pease and William H. Pease (1990)

The Secret Eye: The Journal of Ella Gertrude Clanton Thomas, 1848–1889, edited by Virginia
     Ingraham Burr, with an introduction by Nell Irvin Painter (1990)

Second Stories: The Politics of Language, Form, and Gender in Early American Fictions, by Cynthia
     S. Jordan (1989)

Within the Plantation Household: Black and White Women of the Old South, by Elizabeth Fox-
     Genovese (1988)

The Limits of Sisterhood: The Beecher Sisters on Women's Rights and Woman's Sphere, by Jeanne
     Boydston, Mary Kelley, and Anne Margolis (1988)